G000094349

JOURNEY OF A BETRAYED HERO

VOLUME 1

Written by Brandon Varnell
Illustrations by Aisoretto

This book is a work of fiction. Names, characters, places, and incidents are the products of the author's imagination or are used fictitiously. Any resemblance to actual events, locales, or persons, living or dead, is coincidental.

Journey of a Betrayed Hero, Volume 1
Copyright © 2019 Brandon Varnell
Illustration Copyright © 2019 Aisoretto
All rights reserved.

Brandon Varnell and Kitsune Incorporated supports the right to free expression and the value of copyright. The purpose of copyright is to encourage writers and artists to produce creative works that enrich our culture.

The scanning, uploading, and distribution of this book without permission is a theft of the author's intellectual property. If you would like permission to use the material from the book (other than for review purposes), please contact the publisher. Thank you for your support of the author's rights.

To see Brandon Varnell's other works, or to ask for permission to use his works, visit him at www.varnell-brandon.com, facebook at www.facebook.com/AmericanKitsune, twitter at www.twitter.com/BrandonbVarnell, Patreon at www.Patreon.com/BrandonVarnell, and instagram at www.instagram.com/brandonbvarnell.

Want to know when my next book is out? Sign up for my mailing list at https://www.varnell-brandon.com/mailing-list.

ISBN-13: 978-0-9989942-1-5

CONTENT

PROLOGUE -A NOT SO HUMBLE BARKEEP

The Hero's Journey was a small bar located in the free city of Albany. The friendly atmosphere was complemented by warm woods and bright lights, thanks in no small part to the fairy lamps hanging from the ceiling, from which numerous tiny sprites danced around like incandescent balls. Despite its small size, *The Hero's Journey* was always crowded, especially at night.

"Hey, Barkeep! How about some booze over here?!"

"Barkeep! Barkeep! Get me another of them pork loins!"

"Barkeep!"

"Barkeep!"

"Hey, Barkeep!"

"Coming right up!" Jacob Stone, proprietor and barkeep, shouted.

Several trays were being balanced on his arms and head, each one carrying either a meal or drinks. He slid between seats, ignoring the pungent odor from the mixing of many different bodies. Without hesitating, he slid drinks onto tables and food in front of customers, all the while trading snipes with the people who spent their time drinking there.

It had been one year since he'd opened this bar. He'd never actually expected it to be so successful, but he supposed good cooking and good ale would bring anyone over. Perhaps it was a wise thing that he'd learned how to cook from Freya before they'd parted ways.

Shouts filled with bar, a constant stream of never-ending noise, and Jacob needed to holler over everyone to be heard.

"Here you are, one ale!"

"One pork loin!"

"Here's your ale, though I think you're about nearing your limit!"

Jacob worked alone at this bar. Sometimes people asked him why he didn't hire anyone. He would always force a smile, tell them that no one would want to work for a scruffy place like this, and keep working. These days, such conversations had practically become tradition. He tried not to let it bother him and continued on, business as usual.

As the evening wore on, many of the people—mostly men and women mercenaries—got up and left. A few were so drunk that their friends needed to drag them out. The only ones that remained as night fell were those who liked to stay late. Jacob would tell them to leave soon. He was almost ready to close the bar.

Creaking wood. A soft groan. Jacob heard the door open as he stood behind the counter, cleaning a glass.

Looking up with a frown, Jacob glanced at the people who'd entered his bar.

His frown deepened.

These weren't patrons who had come for a drink.

Decked out in gleaming silver armor, their joints clinked as they waltzed forward with an arrogance that befitted those who served the kingdom. They carried weapons at their sides. Finger joints clinked together as swords were fiercely gripped leather-covered hands. The air was cut as staves were lightly swung as though trying to intimidate everyone there. Claymores hung from backs. Maces were carried over shoulders. Jacob knew who these people were. Knights from Terrasole, the ruling kingdom of the continent.

It was the person in the center who had most of Jacob's attention. An iron wrought helm studded with gems and inlaid with gold. His armor, polished to a shine, had a crimson cape thrown over it. Crimson. The color of a vanguard captain.

While the remaining patrons eyed the knights warily, and some even reached for their weapons, Jacob remained calm.

"May I ask what the Knights of Terrasole are doing in my humble bar? If you've come to get a drink, then I'm afraid you've come to the wrong place. I'm getting ready to close up for the night."

"We're not here for a drink, Scum!" one of the knights snapped. "Tell us what you—"

"At ease, soldier," the captain said as he took off his helmet, revealing the chiseled features of an older gentleman with pepper hair and a goatee. "My apologies for my subordinate's poor behavior. We do not travel this far out very often, and I'm afraid that he's jittery."

Jacob eyed the knight who'd spoken out, then focused back on the captain. "There is no need for apologies. However, if you wish to state your business here, now would be the best time to do so."

The captain nodded. "We're looking for a young woman. Reports claim that she was last seen within this city."

"There are a lot of women in this city, captain," Jacob replied mildly. "If you would like me to state whether I've seen the one you're speaking of, then you'll need to be more specific."

"Insolent wretch!" the knight who'd originally mouthed off snarled and took a step forward. "I should—"

"I told you to shut up, knight!" the captain snapped.

"When my father—" the other knight started to say, only to snap his mouth shut when the captain turned around and glared.

"Your father placed you in this unit to teach you ethics and the meaning of hard work. He won't care what I say or do to you," the captain said. To that, the knight said nothing.

"Newbie?" asked Jacob.

The captain sighed. "He's the son of a noble. His father is a good man, though, and he asked that we teach him the meaning of right from wrong."

"Doesn't look like you're having much luck," Jacob said.

With a gallic shrug, the captain could only sigh as he said, "Give it time. He's only been with our unit for a month."

"If you say so. Now, about that woman…"

"The woman that we're looking for is young. Reports place her between the age of sixteen and eighteen. She has pink hair, pink eyes, and is said to be exceedingly beautiful."

Jacob raised an eyebrow. "Might I ask what such upstanding knights want with a girl like that?"

"She's a murderer!" the knight, who Jacob decided to call Douchenozzle Number One, said.

The captain's face turned red. "That's enough! As of right now, you are under official probation! I'll be reporting what transpired here to your father!"

Douchenozzle Number One turned pale. "Y-you can't!"

"I already did! And if you don't want to suffer even worse, then you'll do yourself a favor and keep your mouth shut from now on!"

Watching the proceedings with a keen eye, Jacob almost snorted. It didn't look like anything had changed since he left the capital of Terrasole. The nobles were still mostly pigheaded and foolish, the knights still screamed to get their point across, and the people were probably still underrepresented, just as they had always been.

It looks like Alice wasn't able to control her council, after all. It was a good thing I left when I did.

The captain looked back at him. "The woman we're after is wanted on charges of theft."

"Theft?" Jacob raised an eyebrow. "She must have stolen something mighty important if you chased her all the way out here."

"Unfortunately, I'm not allowed to disclose any information pertaining to what was stolen."

"Of course not." Sweeping a hand through his tousled, dirty blond hair, Jacob sighed. "And unfortunately for you, I have no information pertaining to the woman you're talking about. If she is in this town, she hasn't come to this tavern."

"Is that so?" the captain grunted, his eyes narrowed. Jacob met his gaze head on with his own placid expression. One second passed. Then two. Three. Finally, the captain sighed. "Very well, then. It seems we have no choice but to continue our search."

"So it seems."

The knights all looked ready to groan as the captain started to usher them outside. They must have been traveling for quite some time. Before they could actually leave, however, one of the men near the back glanced at him... and then froze.

His eyes widened to the size of dish plates.

Well, shit.

"I know you!" The knight pointed at him.

Jacob set his rag on the table. "I'm sorry, sir knight, but I'm afraid to say that you don't know me. You and I have never met before."

"No, I do know you! I know you! You're Jacob Stone! You're the slayer of the Dark Lord!"

Everyone who was in the bar, knight and patron alike, stopped and turned to stare at him. One by one, their eyes widened. One by one, their jaws slowly dropped.

Jacob scowled. He opened his mouth to speak, to deny this man's accusation—

"By Alaya! You are," the captain said, his tone of reverent awe rubbing Jacob in all the wrong ways. "It really is you. I only remember seeing you once before you went on your journey, but I'd never forget a face, even if it has matured a great deal. You're really him. Jacob. The hero who slayed the dark lord, Alucard Blackmore."

As he spoke, the captain had walked closer and closer, until he was standing right in front of the counter.

Jacob discreetly placed his right hand underneath the table. His finger wrapped around a cold leather hilt.

"So, this is where you've been all this time, Lord Jacob," the captain said. "We had all wondered where you'd gone off to, why you disappeared. What are you doing all the way out here?"

"Okay. Two things. First: Do not call me 'Lord.' Ever. I repudiated the knighthood granted to me two years ago. Second: Where I was, what I've been through, and how I came to be here is none of your business. I'd like to ask that you and your knights now leave."

"Hold on a moment." The captain placed his hands on the counter. Jacob twitched. "Please, Lord Jacob. I do not know what went wrong, or why you left, but I beg that you reconsider. Return to the capital with us. The people will be overjoyed to see you again."

The people.

Jacob almost scowled. As if they would be happy to see him. As if those who lived in the lap of luxury would be pleased if he returned. As if he would even want to return to those people, so slovenly, so decadent. The very thought made him want to puke.

"I am only going to say this one more time," Jacob said, and he thought he'd done an admirable job of keeping the coldness out of his tone. "Leave. Now."

"But Lord Jacob! You must return with us! You're a hero!"

"Correction, I was a hero. Now I'm a barkeep."

"Why won't you return with us?" the captain asked, finally losing his composure. "You were our hero! Our savior! Queen Alice would be so pleased if you came back, so why can't you—"

All words were sliced to ribbons when, without warning, Jacob pulled a knife and stabbed it into the counter directly between the captain's fore and middle fingers. The captain yelped. He would have stumbled backwards, but Jacob had grabbed the front of his cape and pulled him in until their noses were nearly touching.

"Let me tell you a little story, Captain, about a young boy who was summoned against his will to fight in a war that he had nothing to do with."

Though his voice was calm, Jacob could feel his emotions slipping. Anger bubbled beneath the surface of his skin. Rage crackled within his heart. The black taste of bitter betrayal was heavy on his tongue.

"There was once a young boy who lived with his family. However, one day, this boy was summoned to an unfamiliar world. The people who summoned him told him that he was the hero who'd been foretold in legends. They said that he had to fight to save them from the dark lord, who was terrorizing their lands. Despite the fact that the boy had no rapport with these people, no sense of duty to aid them, he did anyway."

The hand clutching the cape tightened as Jacob's arm shook.

"Despite how he had no love for these people, this boy journeyed out into an unfamiliar world. He faced dangers that would have killed adult men, fought against monsters and assassins that had slain people thrice his age. He fought and killed and bloodied his hands, all for the sake of a kingdom that was not his."

Jacob would've closed his eyes, but that would have done no good. If the visions that plagued his mind like an insidious disease could have been done away with so easily, he would have never become this bitter.

"That boy fought your war, he killed for your kingdom, he stained his hands in the blood of your enemies, and he slayed your dark lord."

Jacob smiled, but it was not a smile filled with jubilation. There was no happiness in his heart. All he felt was the cold bitterness that came from knowing he'd never be able to return home.

"And now, that boy wants you to get the hell out of his bar," Jacob finished, his smile gone.

Five years ago, there was a boy.

That boy, who was only twelve at the time, had fought for the sake of a people that were not his own.

He fought. He killed. He became a hero.

However, not all stories of princesses and heroes ended with a happily ever after.

Jacob knew this to be true. He had, after all, lived that life.

Once upon a time…

JOURNEY OF A BETRAYED HERO VOL. 1

CHAPTER 1 - A BEAUTIFUL STRANGER

All was quiet. Moonlight sprinkled in through the open window. Silent wind caressed the curtains, causing them to sway.

A freshly showered Jacob walked into his bedroom, a towel wrapped around his waist. The floorboards creaked underneath his feet. Jacob grimaced as he marched further into the room, grabbed the faded pants on his bed, and pulled them on.

This building was old. Faded walls were marked with stains not from abuse but from age. The ceiling had cracks running through it, and, though the foundation remained sturdy, the support pillars that kept the roof from falling were going to need to be replaced soon. Even now, he could hear them groan as if ghosts inhabited the grains.

He had bought it from an elderly woman who'd been on her deathbed. The price had been staying with her for the remaining six months that she'd lived. Afterward, he scattered the remains of her ashes on the wind, to keep them from being used in necromancy, and then he'd proceeded to turn what had once been a house into a bar.

Perhaps it's Granny Cho's ghost come back to haunt this place.

The thought amused him.

His bedroom was a simple affair, sparse, and with little to no decoration. It had a bed, a desk, a chest, and a nightstand. He needed nothing else.

"I heard the commotion downstairs, Partner."

Jacob clicked his tongue as he turned to the voice's source. Leaning against the desk was a sword sheathed in a crimson scabbard. Black lines ran along the sheath's surface, swirling designs like an ancient language telling tales of darkness and bloodshed, light and hope. The sword's hilt was wrapped in leather. The quillons did not look like most crossguards, shaped as it was to resemble a mouth. It was the mouth-shaped quillon that the voice had emerged from.

"What of it?" Jacob asked.

The sword's name was Durandal. It was a sentient blade that had been forged eons ago, supposedly by the man named Völundr. Jacob didn't know the truth on how this blade came to be, but he had discovered it in the ancient ruins of Alfheim, the long-forgotten city of the long extinct elven race.

"Nothing much," Durandal's mouth clacked as he spoke. "I was just wondering if it was a good idea to fly off the handle like that. From the sounds of it, those people were once your partners, Partner."

Jacob snorted. "If that's what you think, then the years must have been hard on you indeed. Those people were far from friends."

"Is that so?"

"It is so."

"Well, it's not like I care," Durandal said cheerfully before dismissing the whole matter for something more important. "By the way, did I ever tell you about the three little old ladies?"

Here we go again.

"No, you haven't."

"Kekeke. Well, three old crones were sitting on a park bench feeding the birds, when a man comes by and flashes them all. The first two little old ladies had a stroke, but the third couldn't quite reach."

A moment of silence passed in the room. Jacob waited, expecting to hear the *"badum tish!"* of a drum. When nothing happened, he shook his head.

"Those are the lamest dirty jokes I've ever heard in my life."

"Hey! Those jokes were my master's favorite! Don't diss them!"

"That old codger isn't your master anymore! I am! And I don't really like those jokes!"

"That's because you're still a virgin whose chastity hasn't allowed him to acquire the taste of a good dirty joke!"

Jacob was about to fire back with more sarcasm—when the atmosphere in the room suddenly shifted. The wind somehow felt tenser, not ominous, just tremulous. He could feel it. A new presence had entered the room.

Calmly walking over to Durandal, Jacob picked the blade up and glanced at the sheath, which now seemed to glow with a strange light.

"Durandal?"

"I feel them too, Partner."

Jacob nodded and gripped Durandal's hilt. The familiar feeling of leather on his fingers was comforting.

"I do not know who you are, but you have until the count of three to show yourself before I kill you. One—"

"There is no need for that," someone said, their voice soft, feminine. It was a woman's voice.

The pitch and timbre of the voice was young, probably around his age, Jacob guessed. Though they spoke with admirable calmness, the underlying strain that the tone carried denoted worry, or perhaps stress. He followed the voice to its source. Whoever this person was, they were above and slightly behind him.

Jacob turned around just as a light thumping alerted him to the person who'd spoken dropping from the ceiling. It was a figure clad in darkness, a cloak that hid almost everything. However, the way the cloak contoured to their body suggested this person was female. Pink strands stuck out of her hood at odd angles, and pale hands were pressed against the floor.

They knelt before him, their neck bared. Baring one's neck was often shown as either a sign of trust or a sign of non-aggression, the idea being that anyone who would offer such an opportune chance to slice their head off couldn't possibly mean harm.

"Who are you and what do you want?" Jacob asked. "Be aware that I'm not a patient man these days. You have five seconds to start talking."

"My name is Enyo. I have traveled many leagues to meet you, Jacob the Destroyer."

Jacob couldn't quite stop himself from sucking in a breath. Jacob the Destroyer was one of his nicknames, but it was not one known to the people of Terrasole. Only the dark clan, those who followed Alucard, knew of that nickname.

"Show me your face," Jacob demanded. "I refuse to speak with someone who hides beneath a hood."

"Of course. I meant no offense." Delicate hands left the ground and grabbed the hood. "I have been forced to hide my features, lest my pursuers find me. I guess it has simply become a habit to leave my hood up."

The hood soon pulled back, and Jacob stared into a face that was too beautiful to be human. Her unblemished skin was the color of porcelain. The hints of a blush covered cheeks more fair than even Alice Lannister D'arche herself. Ruby red lips, pink eyes, pointy ears, all of which was haloed by long pink hair that, no longer confined to her hood, descended like an evanescent waterfall.

A dark clansman.

The so-called Dark Clan of the Elūne. Dark clan members had an appearance that was almost human, save for the fact that all of them were inhumanly beautiful—an aesthetic meant to lure humans into a false sense of security. They were known for having pale skin and unusual eye colors. However, this was the first time he'd met a dark clan member with pink hair.

Durandal whistled. "Holy shit on a fucking stick! I've seen many hot women in my time, but this one takes the cake!"

The woman stared at the sword, her gawking face revealing her shock. She blinked. Then again. Then she looked at Jacob.

"Did that sword just talk?"

"No," Jacob said with a straight face.

"Of course I talked!" Durandal rebutted. "I'm Durandal! The greatest sword ever—doof!"

Durandal's words were cut off when Jacob slammed him into the desk.

"That sword just spoke," the woman said.

"Ignore the talking sword for now," Jacob rebutted, gripping Durandal's hilt more fiercely than before—both in preparation to unsheathe it, and to shut it up. "What does a dark clanswoman want with me?"

"I have come to ask for your help," she said.

"Sorry, but I don't offer help to random people anymore, especially not to thieves."

"I seek a way into Avant Heim."

"Good luck with that."

"I believe that you, the hero who slayed the Dark Lord, can get me inside."

"Are you even listening to me?"

"I can make it worth your while."

"That is what they all say."

Jacob's hand twitched as he resisted the impulse to run a hand through his hair.

Avant Heim was the castle belonging to Alice Lannister D'arche, the reigning queen of Terrasole. Not only was it located leagues away, but it was currently the most secure location in the entire world. Guarded by legions of paladins, protected by ancient magic, no one was stupid enough to try breaking into there unless they had a death wish or a lot of firepower.

"Please, you must help me," the woman said. "I... I don't have anyone else to turn to."

Jacob hesitated as she looked at him. He closed his eyes and reaffirmed his resolve.

I'll not allow myself to be fooled by a pretty face again.

"I'm not interested in helping you or anyone else."

"I'm not asking you to do this for free," the woman said. "I can give you something that you've always wanted, something you've been longing for."

Jacob's lips twitched. The hesitance vanished.

"Listen, lady, there is nothing that you or anyone else can give me that I would want. Riches? I turned those down two years ago along with my knighthood. Love? I stopped believing in that when I was betrayed by the woman I thought I loved. Happiness? That's a true fairy tale. Happiness doesn't exist in this world. You can't give me anything that hasn't already been offered and rejected. You're wasting your—"

"What about a way to return to your home?"

With ice filling his veins, Jacob froze. It couldn't be. He must have heard wrong. Yes, that was it. He must have gotten something crazy stuck in his ear.

"What did you say?"

"I know how you can return home. I can take you back to your world, the one you originally came from."

Jacob closed his eyes as emotions that he'd forgotten poured into him: longing, desire, a want so fervent that it physically hurt. To return home. For so long, he had wanted to return home. For two years after breaking his ties with Terrasole, he had tried to do just that before giving up. Now he spent his time idly his life away in this tavern.

"Do not lie to me," he whispered as rage coursed through his blood.

The woman's eyes widened. "I am not lying. I'm telling you the —"

"You're lying!" Jacob shouted her down. "You have to be lying! Do you think I've not searched for a way home?! Do you think I haven't already tried every half-crocked trick, followed every false lead, foolishly believed in every dumb legend, all so that I could return home? I spent two years trying to find a way back home! But it was all for nothing! There is no way back! If there was, I would have already found it!"

Breathing heavily from his emotional outburst, Jacob glared at the woman, whose eyes had gone wide and whose mouth had parted to form a pretty O shape. He clamped down on his guilt when pain flashed in her eyes. This woman was trying to play him for a fool. If he let himself get swept up in her appearance, he'd find himself lying dead in a ditch somewhere.

"I'm sorry," the woman said. "I did not mean to make you angry. However, please believe me when I say that I am neither lying nor trying to trick you. I can help you return home."

"That is what every liar and con artist says when they want you to believe them," Jacob said, calming down. He couldn't let his emotions slip like that again. He had to remain calm. "And I have been conned by many of those people. You're not the first one who's come to me with promises like that, though you are the first who I'm rejecting. Go back to whatever hole you crawled out of. I've no interest in being your bitch."

The woman flinched as if he'd struck a physical blow. Jacob tried not to let her hurt expression get to him. This woman was clearly a master at feigning emotions. If he let his guard down around her, then he'd surely suffer a knife to the back.

"I... maybe you would believe me if I told you who I am," the woman said.

Not likely.

Standing up, her lips twitching in a tremulous smile that belied her anxiety, she announced herself in a clear voice that rang throughout the bedroom. "My name full name is Enyo Valania Blackmore. I am the daughter of Alucard Blackmore, the Dark Lord whom was slain by your hand."

Jacob felt like someone had shoved a hot poker into his chest. At the same time, his blood froze over.

No way... there's just... no way...

"I have come to you in order to request your aid." Enyo placed a hand against her chest. Her imploring expression made Jacob's heartstrings quiver. "Please, help me and I promise to return you to your original world."

In the end, Jacob had turned Enyo down. Even though he wanted to return home, he had no reason to believe that this woman, who claimed to be the daughter of the Dark Lord, could do as she said. For one thing, he'd never heard of the Dark Lord even having a daughter.

The early morning sun slowly rose beyond the mountains, casting rays of light upon the land, illuminating the free city of Albany. Several shops were already open. The scent of freshly baked bread hung in the air, butchers were cleaning their shops to get them ready for the day, and vendors were outside by their booths, getting ready to set up shop. Men and women were returning to their stands. People were putting out their wares. It was going to be another busy day.

"Are you sure it was a good idea to let that girl leave?" Durandal asked as Jacob walked through the streets.

"I don't see why not. What she does now is no concern of mine," Jacob replied.

"If you say so," Durandal replied like it wasn't convinced.

Jacob always rose with the morning sun. Since he spent much of his time in the afternoon preparing meals for the people coming to his bar, he needed to get his shopping out of the way early.

"More importantly, we might need to leave this town soon," Jacob said after he finished paying for a bushel of apples.

"Because of the knights?" Durandal asked.

"Yes."

Walking down the street, Jacob visited many of the venders, buying all of the essentials he'd need. Since he was running low on eggs, he bought several dozen of those. They'd be used as appetizers. He'd also make his breakfast with those. Jacob also bought fresh bread and marmalade, honey, various types and cuts of meat, and flour to create pasta. Fortunately, he was still well-stocked on other ingredients, ones that lasted a long time and didn't need to be bought each day, so he didn't need to buy much.

As he made his way back home, Jacob continued his conversation with Durandal. "I have no doubt that the knight captain will tell Alice that I've been found. No doubt, once Alice learns of my location, she'll send more knights to bring me back."

"You really don't like Alice anymore, do ya?" Durandal's metal mouth clacked. "That's disappointing. I always liked her. She was hot."

"You like anything that's attractive and has two legs," Jacob rebutted.

"Not true. I only like certain gals."

"And what kind of women are those?"

"The ones that I've seen naked, of course!"

"Of course," Jacob sighed. Then he paused. "Wait. When did you see Alice naked?"

"..."

Jacob wished Durandal wasn't strapped to his back. His glare couldn't reach the blast sword.

"Durandal... were you spying on Alice and me?"

"I didn't mean to," Durandal said at last. "You two had just left me sitting against a wall while you got busy practicing procreation. What was I supposed to do?"

"How about not spy on us?" Jacob suggested.

"Out of the question. Asking me not to look at a free peep show when it's being blatantly displayed before my eyes is blasphemy of the highest order."

Carrying several bags of groceries in his left hand, Jacob used his free hand to rub his face. "Speaking with you like this is such a tiring affair."

"You know you love talking to me. We're partners, after all."

"If you say so."

On the way home, Jacob came across several people that he knew. The little old lady who owned a bookstore that he read books at was having problems getting the store clean, so he lent her a quick hand, sweeping the floor and making sure the books were lined up. She thanked him with a smile. A couple of old men were playing chess as he passed a bakery. One of them was losing badly, so Jacob gave him a tip. A few people that he knew from shopping greeted him with bellowing voices and great enthusiasm. He waved in return.

As he was passing by one of the buildings, a clothier called *Madame Price's Tailored Clothing*, he spotted a poster tacked to the wall. It was a wanted poster. The person depicted in the image was wearing a dark cloak with a hood that covered their head. Not much could be seen of their face, but Jacob didn't need to see their face to know who it was. This poster was obviously in regards to the girl who had come to him last night, Enyo.

"I guess the knights are still looking for her."

"I did see a few as we were walking the streets this morning," Durandal added. There was a slight delay in his next words. "Are you worried about her?"

"Of course not," Jacob said as he continued on his way.

There was a lot that he needed to do before noon rolled around. He had to prepare his own breakfast first. After which, he would clean the bar, then get started on preparing the ale for consumption, followed by getting the grill ready so that he could begin cooking once customers started coming in. It was a lot of work, more than Jacob had initially expected.

Whoever said that owning a bar was easy deserved to be smacked in the face.

As the day wore on, Jacob finished his tasks with ease of practice. Morning became noon, and noon became evening. Patrons started trickling in. Some came alone, others came in groups. Most of them were either mercenaries, miners, or farmers.

Albany was an independent city. That meant it wasn't a member of the Kingdom of Terrasole, which ruled over most of the continent. They passed their own laws, and they didn't pay taxes to Terrasole. While this normally would have been a problem, since Albany was far from the capital, Terrasole didn't bother trying to bring them to heel.

As a free city, there were any number of different peoples coming and going. Albany was mostly a mining town. About six klicks out were the Tuscany mines, a place that was abundant in rare minerals and gems. Most of the men living in Albany were miners because of this, though several people also owned farmlands. Mercenaries were another thing that was in abundance in Albany. Although the war may have ended when Jacob had killed the Dark Lord, that didn't mean there was no need for people skilled in combat. The mines were a dangerous place, filled with kobalts and other monsters, and the surrounding plains were home to kath hounds and various beasts.

Monsters were abundant in this world. During his travels across the continent, Jacob had faced more monsters than he had men. That was why mercenaries were still necessary, why they still had a job and hadn't stooped to become bandits, robbers, and highwaymen.

"Barkeep! Another ale over here!" a patron shouted over the din of multiple conversations.

"Coming right up!" Jacob shouted back as he filled a mug with ale and brought it over to the customer's table.

"Barkeep, I could use a pot roast if you have any!"

"It'll be ready in a few more minutes!"

As Jacob was traveling back to the counter, a conversation between two patrons a few yards away captured his attention. They were speaking in hushed tones, but Jacob, who knew the secrets to enhancing his body's physical limitations, picked it up easily enough.

"Did you hear? Those knights finally captured that girl."

"Aye. I saw that. Was there when it happened. It's a right shame they caught her. That lass was quite fetching."

"What do you reckon is going to happen?"

"They said she stole an important item that belonged to the Queen while it was being transported. I imagine they'll off her head."

"Now that's a real shame. She had quite the pretty head."

"Aye."

As the two men laughed, Jacob moved gracefully behind the counter. He did his best to keep up with his orders, to pretend that he hadn't heard the conversation between those two. However, no matter how hard he tried or how much he worked, the image of Enyo being placed on the chopping block wouldn't leave his mind.

Later that night, after Jacob had closed his bar, he lay on his bed, hands behind his head as he stared at the ceiling.

He hadn't been able to fall asleep. His mind kept replaying the conversation he'd eavesdropped on. Enyo had been captured. This shouldn't have bothered him, as he had already told the girl that he wanted nothing to do with her, but for some reason, he couldn't get her out of his mind. The image his mind presented him, a false vision of her downtrodden face as she was taken to the capital, seared his mind like a branding iron.

"Having trouble falling asleep, Partner?" Durandal said in a metallic voice.

"You could tell, huh? What gave me away? The fact that my eyes are open, or the fact that my breathing hasn't grown any lighter?"

"Sarcasm isn't your strong suit. You should go back to being an optimistic brat. It suits you more."

"Whatever."

A gentle silence ensued, broken only by the rustling curtain as it swayed in the breeze. Jacob used that time to think about the past. Like Durandal had said, he had been a naive and optimistic brat back in the day. He took what people said at face value, helped people even when there was nothing in it for him, and did his best to befriend everyone he met.

That was why it had been so easy for others to use him.

Jacob turned on his side. Thinking about the past made him remember how foolish he'd been to trust the words of others. People were greedy. They wanted what they couldn't have, desired what others had, and were willing to do whatever was necessary to acquire that which was not theirs. They used people like him in their mad schemes for power. Then, when they had no more use for someone, they tossed them aside like trash.

It sickened him.

"I'm sorry. I did not mean to make you angry. However, please believe me when I say that I am neither lying nor trying to trick you. I can get you back home."

Liar. She has to be lying. There is no way back home.

That woman had been the same, he was sure of it. She would've used him for her own purposes, and then, once she had what she wanted, Jacob would have found a dagger in his back. That was how this game was played.

"Are you thinking about that woman? Enyo?" asked Durandal.

"Absolutely not." Jacob scoffed. "Why would I bother thinking about that girl? I don't care about her. The only person who matters to me is me."

"I sense a liar," Durandal taunted. Jacob gritted his teeth. "Don't think you can fool me. We've been partners for way too long. I know you inside and out, so I can tell when you're not being honest with yourself."

"What do you know about me?"

"I know that you're a good person who used to never think about not helping someone when they were in trouble."

"People change," Jacob said softly.

"Aye, they do," Durandal agreed. "But you haven't. I watch you every day, Partner, and no matter how hard you try to pretend otherwise, I can tell that you still enjoy helping others."

Jacob twitched. "I don't know what you're talking about."

"Denial isn't going to help you here. Jacob, you've always been a heroic young man. When you journeyed into Alfheim to rescue those half-alf children, I saw your mettle. When you fought against Níðhöggr for the sake of a single soul, I acknowledged your strength and compassion. Whether you like it or not, you are, have been, and always will be, a hero. As such, it is in your nature to want to protect and save others. You can deny it, but I know that deep down, you know this is true."

Jacob rolled over again, trying to ignore Durandal's words to no avail. Much like Enyo's words the previous night, these words haunted him, taunting him with the truth that rang through them, the truth that he didn't want to acknowledge.

He would never be able to fall asleep like this.

"I am begging you. Please, grant me this one request, and I'll do whatever you ask of me."

The harsh memories of rejecting Enyo burned a vivid image into his mind. The dejection on her face as she left via the window wracked him with guilt. He'd done what he could to ignore his own feelings, but the longer and harder he tried to deny him, the stronger they became.

Alaya, damn it...

Jacob stood up. His bare feet padded across the creaky wooden boards, over to where his clothes were hanging. He grabbed his faded brown leather pants and put them on. Then he threw his long-sleeved off-white collared shirt on. Wandering over to the chest, he opened it. Inside was his armor, chainmail and an enchanted tunic.

"Partner?" Durandal asked as Jacob put on the chainmail, which glistened a vibrant silver in the moonlit night.

"Be quiet. You're the reason I'm putting this on."

The glossy tunic shone brightly in the light as he pulled it over the chainmail. When he turned, symbols revealed themselves as moonlight illuminated them, silvery letters to an arcane language that few people knew. Jacob then put on his gloves and strapped his vambraces to his forearms, followed by his socks and leather boots before, finally, he strapped Durandal's sheath to his bandoleer.

"I'm guessing you're planning to rescue the young lady?" the sword asked. "About damn time."

"Shut up." Jacob scowled. "This is all your fault. If you hadn't bugged me so much, I wouldn't be doing this."

Jacob looked at his reflection as he closed the window. His blond hair was darker than it used to be. It was also longer, reaching all the way down to his chin. Messy bangs hung over his ice blue eyes, which appeared more cynical than they had been so many years ago. Despite only being eighteen years old, Jacob felt like he looked much older. It must have been the haggard appearance of his face.

Durandal continued talking. "So you say, but I know you better than you seem to think I do. You would have rescued her anyway. I'm just pushing you along so it happens without delay."

"I think I've been too lenient on you. From now on, you're only getting sharpened and oiled once a month."

"If you did that, you wouldn't have an awesome sword to slay your enemies with."

"I'm sure I'll manage somehow."

Bickering with his sword as he left the bar, Jacob grabbed his cloak on his way out, stepped onto the mostly empty street, and swiftly moved through the town.

The moon hung over the free city, heedless of the events that were taking place down below.

***

The Knights of Terrasole did not have a base inside of Albany, a free city that did not belong to the kingdom controlling the continent. They couldn't afford to strong-arm the mayor into letting them stay, lest it ruin their image. That said, they did have a fortress several leagues outside of the city. It normally took around one day to reach.

Jacob was able to reach it in less than four hours.

"Man, that is some fast running," Durandal said. "I've never seen someone run as fast as you."

"The benefits of energy manipulations." Jacob shrugged.

A single tower jutted from the ground, standing several dozen meters over him. It was taller than the tallest building in Albany, which consisted of small single and two-story buildings. Jacob judged it to be at least four stories in height. The tower was surrounded by a wall, upon which several guards walked along, carrying bows and arrows. There was only one way in, a large archway that had no gate.

Well, only one way for regular people.

"So, how are we going to do this?" asked Durandal.

"You are not going to do anything," Jacob said. "I'm going to sneak in, grab Enyo, and sneak out. You just stay in your sheath and keep quiet."

"No fair."

"Life's not fair."

Jacob blinked several times as power flooded through his eyes. He'd heard it been called "ki" by some people, but that was back in his own world, and it was usually only in cartoons and stories. He didn't know if anyone had a name for it here.

He redistributed the power evenly, steadily enhancing his vision until he could see perfectly in the dark. Had there been a mirror or body of water near, he knew that if he looked at his reflection in it, his eyes would have been yellow.

There were six guards standing along the wall, two guarding the gate, and there were undoubtedly more inside. Knight squadrons were always grouped in units of twelve. That meant there were at least four inside. Two of them would be guarding Enyo. One of them was going to be at the entrance to the tower. The captain was probably sleeping.

Okay...

Under the cover of night, Jacob moved swiftly across the grassy plain. The rustling caused by his stealthy trot was masked by the blowing wind. He moved to the far side of the fortress, the back, where the guards were sparse.

Jacob eyed the guard standing on one of the lookout points. The wall was about... five meters tall. He calculated the amount of strength he'd need to jump that, judged it to be doable, and then channeled power into his legs and feet.

Strength engulfed his legs as he ran across the clearing, blood pumping to his muscles. Reaching the wall in record time, Jacob shot into the air, grabbed the wall's ledge, and flipped over it before landing in a crouch. He looked left and right. The guards still weren't paying him any mind.

He aimed to keep it that way.

Before the guards could look could in his direction, Jacob had already raced across the small walkway and dropped off the other side. His arm strained as he caught the ledge. Now hanging there, he observed the tower itself.

The tower was an ugly thing made from large stone bricks. Aging and weathered, the tower looked like something that had been abandoned centuries ago and had only recently been reoccupied. With his enhanced eyes, he could pick out the chips and cracks that lined the surface. They would make excellent hand and footholds.

It had been awhile since Jacob had used his abilities, but as he called on more power, the familiar sensation flooding his body felt like an old friend that he hadn't seen in decades. It touched him, suffused him. He could feel his muscles being strengthened. Care was needed when augmenting his muscles, however. If he used too much power, he'd end up busting straight through the wall... which would have been bad.

When he had what he judged to be enough power, Jacob shut the flow off and maintained it. He took a deep breath. He held it. Then, exhaling his breath one in go, Jacob launched himself off the wall and soared through the air. The wind whistled around him. It was only for a second, though, and then he slammed into the tower.

His strength enhanced, Jacob dug his fingers into the wall, gouging out tiny holes along the cracks and crevices. With his veins bulging, arms flexing, Jacob scaled the wall. He moved slowly. There was no need to attract attention by moving too fast and making noise. Several meters above, a window shone with the light of flickering candles. Five meters. Two meters. One. As he reached the window, Jacob lifted himself up and peered inside.

There were three people inside. Enyo was resting against a wall. She was in shackles. Her face was bruised, her left eye was swollen shut, and there was blood smeared across her mouth. The two guards were sitting at a table on the opposite side. One of them was the knight who'd spoken out when they had questioned him the night before.

"I still can't believe you let the wench get you like that," the other knight laughed.

Douchenozzle Number One's face turned red. "She just caught me by surprise! That's all! It won't happen again!"

Now that he was looking more closely, Jacob could see that the Douchenozzle had a large scar running along the left side of his face, throbbing an angry red. It hadn't been there before. He must have received it while they were apprehending Enyo.

"Well, you're not the only one she hurt. I imagine the captain is still keeled over in his bunk," the other knight said.

It sounds like Enyo put up quite the fight.

Jacob looked back at Enyo. Her clothing had been stripped away, leaving her in her underwear. This was standard procedure when interrogating someone. By stripping a person of their clothes, you strip away their dignity. It made getting information out of them easier. Judging from her labored breathing and the way her head bobbed, she must have gone through an interrogation already.

It was probably to get the location of whatever she stole out of her.

With his options limited, Jacob decided that the best method to rescue Enyo was to knock the two knights unconscious. With luck, no one would come in here for several more hours, and he would be able to sneak out unnoticed.

Timing was going to be essential.

Jacob lowered his head. The laughter from the uninjured guard penetrated his ears. He heard Douchenozzle scream back. Taking several deep breaths, Jacob counted down to three, and then he sprang into action.

Time seemed to slow as Jacob cleared the window. He could see Douchenozzle's eyes widening as he landed on the wooden floor. Jacob rolled across the floor, leapt to his feet, and thrust out his fist into the back of the other guard's neck. The man went stiff. Then his body went slack. Jacob caught him and gently lowered him onto the table before turning his attention to Douchenozzle, who had opened his mouth, presumably to scream.

Jacob wouldn't let him.

With his enhanced legs, he leapt over the table, catching the knight's face in a kick. Douchenozzle spun around. Jacob rotated in midair and kicked him in the face with his other leg.

Landing on the ground, he caught the knight before he could fall to the floor. Like the first one, he gently lowered Douchenozzle, whose wide eyes were rolled up into the back of his head, to the floor.

Time returned to normal. Jacob had a headache.

Standing up, Jacob made his way over to Enyo, who must have heard his footsteps. She looked up with eyes that were narrowed and fierce. The expression of defiance left, however, when she finally realized who was standing before her.

"J-Jacob?" she asked as if unable to believe her eyes.

"Enyo," Jacob said. "I'm here to get you out of here."

"W-why?"

Jacob looked away. "Because I've... I've decided to hear you out."

Enyo's eyes widened as Jacob grabbed her shackles and, with a bit of physical augmentation, ripped them apart like paper.

"Don't misunderstand me," Jacob continued as he held out his hand. "I haven't agreed to help you. I've merely decided to at least here what you have to say before coming to a decision."

Tentatively reaching out, Enyo placed her hand in his. Jacob marveled at how soft it was as he pulled her up. She had calluses from what he guessed were daggers, or maybe short swords, but they didn't detract from the silken feel of her skin.

"That is a prudent course of action, I think," Enyo said. "Once we are away from here, I will tell you everything."

"I'll hold you to that."

Enyo nodded and followed Jacob as he walked over to the window. He peered outside. The guards were still standing as they had been before. It appeared as if no one had heard the short fight between him and the two knights. Good.

"How are we going to escape?" asked Enyo.

"You're going to wrap your arms around my neck, and then I'm going to scale down the wall."

"But you don't have any climbing equipment."

"I don't need it."

Enyo accepted his words with a nod. Jacob climbed onto the windowsill, and then lowered himself down the other side. Enyo followed him. She stood on the sill, careful not to step on his fingers, and then climbed over him until she could wrap her arms around his neck.

There was a moment, just one, where Jacob remembered that Enyo wasn't wearing anything except her underwear. Her breasts pressed into his back. He took several deep breaths to keep his mind on the task at hand.

Her breathing hitched in his ear.

"Are you scared?" he asked.

"Not scared so much as nervous," she admitted. "But I trust you."

"That's an awful lot of trust to place on someone you just met. It sounds foolish to me."

"Then I guess I am a fool."

"Oh, I like this girl," Durandal said.

"Didn't I tell you to be quiet?"

Grunting, Jacob proceeded down the wall, digging his fingers into the stone. There were going to be a lot of holes in this wall, but he hoped no one would notice them until the next morning. As he scaled down, reinforcing his arms, neck, back, legs, and fingers, he tried to ignore Enyo's breath against his ear and her chest as it pressed into his back.

How distracting.

They reached the bottom without incident. Jacob thought about their next move. His body was beginning to feel the strain from being augmented, so he couldn't afford to do anymore climbing. That left traveling out through the front.

I'm out of shape.

"Can you fight?" Jacob asked.

Enyo nodded. "I'm versed in martial combat, though I work better with daggers than fists."

"We're going to knock out the guards at the front entrance. Don't kill anyone."

"I have no intention of killing."

"I'm not even gonna be used," Durandal mumbled, as if trying to one-up Enyo.

Jacob ignored the sword.

He and Enyo moved around the tower, traveling toward the front. There was one guard standing at the door to the tower, a bored looked etched upon the man's face.

Jacob turned to Enyo. "What is your magic aptitude?"

Enyo blinked in surprise, but she still answered. "My magic is... light based."

Now it was Jacob's turn to be surprised. "Light...?"

Light magic wasn't necessarily rare, though it was unheard of for a dark clansman to be capable of using it. Their nickname hadn't sprung out of nowhere. They were called "dark clansmen" because their magic was always darkness based. Poison. Mind control. Shadow manipulation. Alucard had been a master at using death magic. He had expected the man's daughter to have a similar power.

Enyo squirmed. "I-I can use light and darkness... but I'm better at using light magic."

She has two types of magic?!

Jacob pressed a hand to his head. "Woman, are you trying to give me a headache?"

"I-I'm sorry."

Dual magic was nearly unheard of. It was so rare that in his years of travel, the only indication that there may have been people capable of using two types of magic was through folktales and legends.

People in Terrasole were born with one type of magic. Most people were born with an elemental magic, though a few had more esoteric magics like Freya's mimic. However, even Freya only had one type of magic.

"It's... fine," Jacob struggled to return to the matter at hand. "Do you have a spell that can put that guard to sleep?"

Enyo's thoughtful expression was rather cute. She nodded once. "I do... it's a dark spell, though."

"That's fine. Use it to put that guard to sleep."

Nodding, Enyo took several deep breaths. She held her hands up, spread her feet shoulder width apart, and muttered in ancient tongues.

"Somnum. Dormitationem. Lethargis."

A ball of black energy formed in her hand, which compressed as she brought her hands together. When it was about the size of a coin, she opened her hands, fingers spreading like a blooming flower, and let the spell hit the man standing guard. Barely a second passed before the guard slumped to the ground. His staff and metal armor created a loud clattered.

"Hey, Ezio! What are you doing back there?!" one of the guards at the front shouted. "Ezio?"

When "Ezio" didn't respond, the two guards rushed through the arch and toward the unconscious guard. They knelt to check him. While they were preoccupied, Jacob grabbed Enyo's hand and swiftly darted for the archway.

Bursting into the open field, he and Enyo rushed into the grass. Shouting from behind alerted them that they had been spotted, but Jacob didn't stop. He tugged on Enyo, eliciting a yelp as he scooped her into his arms, and then augmented his legs.

"Hang on tight," he warned.

"What?" Enyo asked right before Jacob shot forward more quickly than a bolt fired from a crossbow.

Her screams echoed across the vast plain. Jacob hoped to the goddess Alaya that the knights wouldn't be able to track their location. That would suck.

***

Jacob didn't know how far he'd run, but he eventually stopped. His legs were getting tired. It had been so long since he'd used physical augmentation that his body couldn't handle it for too long.

The knights located at the fortress didn't have horses, from what he'd seen, so there was little chance that they would catch up to them before daybreak.

"Can you stand?" he asked.

"I-I think so," Enyo muttered. She still seemed shell-shocked by Jacob's running. Her pink hair was in disarray, though somehow, even with her hair a complete mess, it still looked enchanting.

Jacob set her down, but he was forced to catch her when Enyo stumbled. She fell into his chest. Her knees buckled.

"It seems your legs are shaky from being forced to travel at such high speeds. Sorry about that. I should have known this would happen. The same thing happened to me whenever I rode on the back of my dad's motorcycle."

"Motor...sickle?" Enyo tilted her head. "What is that? Some kind of weapon?"

"...Never mind," Jacob muttered.

"Don't mind him," Durandal said. "Partner is always saying weird things like—clack!"

"Can it," Jacob muttered as he shoved the sword back into its sheath.

After Enyo had regained the use of her legs, they traveled together through the plain, guided only by the moon's luminescence. Enyo held onto Jacob's left sleeve to keep from being accidentally separated. The grass was high, easily ascending over both of their heads. Durandal was mercifully silent.

"Where are we going?" Enyo asked after a time.

"We're going back to Albany," Jacob said.

"Isn't that dangerous? Won't Albany be the first place they look?"

"No." Shaking his head, Jacob extrapolated on his reasoning. "The knights will assume you went in the opposite direction because they captured you in Albany. The most obvious choice is always the least expected choice."

Enyo silently considered that before nodding. "I guess that makes sense."

"It helps that these knights are kind of stupid," Durandal added.

Jacob let loose with a grim chuckle. "Indeed."

They didn't make it to Albany that night, sadly. Jacob had misjudged how far it was. He could've gotten there in two hours if he'd augmented his legs, but his body was already strained from overusing of his powers. Walking to Albany like a normal person took an entire day. He had been up all night, Enyo was wounded, and the sun would be rising soon.

They found a small clearing that was devoid of grass, with a large rock jutting from the ground, acting as a shelter. It had probably been a den built by a monster that had abandoned it. Such primitive domiciles were not rare.

As Jacob started a fire by using two rocks as a makeshift flint and some grass, Enyo sat with her knees curled up to her chest. Her long hair was still a mess, and her bruise had become a dark black. The swelling of her eye was also turning purple. Despite this, she didn't complain once.

"Thank you for rescuing me."

Jacob looked up. The light from the newly flickering fire cast stark shadows against Enyo's pale skin, which flickered and changed as the flame danced. Thanks to her posture, she seemed quite small.

She was also still quite naked, clad as she was in just her undergarments.

Somehow containing the heat in his cheeks, Jacob unhooked his cloak and, moving over to her, he set the cloak on her shoulders. She looked up at him, her startled eyes wide.

"It's to cover up," he explained unnecessarily, as if he needed justification for his actions.

"Thank you," she said, accepting his gesture with a smile and wrapping the cloak around herself.

Jacob nodded as he moved back to the fire. Durandal, leaning against the rock, glistened with a crimson hue.

"I knew that you would come for me," Enyo said at last. "You turned me down before, but after I was captured, I knew that if you found out, you would rescue me."

Jacob didn't look up as he fed grass to the fire. He didn't want her to see him blush.

"Don't misjudge me. I only saved you because I was curious about what you said. I saved you for purely selfish reasons."

"I do not believe that," Enyo countered. "You may not know it, but I know a lot about you. My former maid told me the tales that our spies reported when tracking your movements. She said that you would save everyone from entire cities to individual people without asking for any form of compensation. She told me about how you braved fierce monsters, battled atrocious horrors, all so you could protect the people you came across. You're not the kind of person who would leave someone to their fate when you know you can save them."

"That was in the past. I'm different now."

"And yet you still saved me."

Jacob said nothing at first. He didn't like speaking about the past. He didn't even like remembering it. It reminded him of all his mistakes, of how naive he had been to trust others without question.

"Tell me… why would the daughter of Alucard request my help?" Jacob asked.

"Because what I seek is something that only you can give me."

"Revenge?"

Enyo shook his head. "I do not seek revenge. Revenge is something that people desire when they feel like taking justice into their own hands. You have done nothing that warrants my seeking justice."

"I killed your father," Jacob pointed out.

The weak smile on Enyo's face made him flinch. "I know. However, I did not know my father that well. I was hidden away after my birth, locked in a mansion far removed from even the darklands. I only saw him once or twice a year, and when the war started after I turned ten, I saw him no more."

Hugging her legs, Enyo stared into the fire, her eyes glassy as if remembering something that had happened long ago.

"Besides, my father was the Dark Lord. He knew that a hero would rise up one day and slay him. The last time I saw him, he told me this: 'One day, I shall be slain. A hero shall rise from the land of light, take up arms against me, and crush me utterly. When that happens, I want you to go with this hero, for he shall be the only one who can grant you salvation.'"

"Salvation, huh?"

The fire crackled and popped. Jacob's eyes drooped. The effects of physical augmentation were hitting him at long last.

"Even now, I don't know what he meant," Enyo admitted in a soft voice. "However, after hearing the stories of your heroism, I believe that my father was correct. That is why I have decided to place my trust in you."

Trust. It had been so long since Jacob had trusted anyone. The last time he had allowed himself to trust, it had ended with him being used, his reputation being smeared in the mud, and him being stabbed in the back. That was what trust got people.

Yet here was this girl who claimed to trust him, a person she had never met, the person who had killed her father no less. Was she being serious? Was she lying to make him drop his guard? He didn't know, and because he didn't know, he decided to be cautious.

"We should get some rest," he said at last. "The knights won't be able to send out a search party for some time, and even if they do, they're likely to travel in the opposite direction, toward the next city. But we can only rest for a few hours. I'll wake you when it's time to leave."

"Okay." Enyo didn't even put up a fuss. Wrapped up in his cloak, she laid on her side, shut her eyes, and slowly drifted off. "Good night."

With her eyes closed and her mouth parted as she breathed evenly, the girl looked like nothing more than an extremely beautiful young woman without a care in the world. She was so defenseless. If he had wanted to, he could have plunged Durandal through her throat, and she would have been none the wiser.

Watching the girl for a moment longer, he wondered how someone who had every reason to hate him could act so defenseless. Was this really a ploy to make him lower his guard?

"Durandal?"

"Yeah, Partner?"

"Keep an eye on things for me."

"I would, but I don't have eyes."

Jacob rolled his eyes as Durandal cackled. "Also, wake me up in four hours, will you?"

"Sure thing. Sleep tight."

Closing his eyes, Jacob entered a light sleep. He never sank deep into slumber anymore. Having been attacked by assassins more times than he could count, he'd learned to remain in a light state of alertness. If anything moved, if any sound was heard, he would wake right up.

He also didn't want to deal with the nightmares that came when he did fall fully asleep.

Four hours wasn't much time—certainly, it was nowhere near enough to get a good night's rest. Yet four hours passed, and Jacob and Enyo woke up to continue their journey. Durandal had tried to tell Enyo dirty jokes during the journey, but Jacob had shut him up after the first one, though he sadly hadn't been quick enough. He didn't think anyone's face had been capable of turning the shade of red that Enyo's had been.

Within two hours, Albany came into sight.

Cities were often divided into three classes based on their size: small, mid, and large. After small cities, there were villages, which were too small to be considered a city.

Albany was a mid-sized city. Sprawled out for over a dozen kilometers, its buildings followed a uniform style of architecture as they continued beyond one's line of sight in evenly spaced lines. Well-maintained cobblestone roads traversed through the city, intersecting with perfect geometry. There was an old legend about how the person who built this place, Albion, had been an architect who was obsessed with geometry.

It was midday by the time they arrived. Everyone was already awake, and the bustling crowd made it easy for them to blend in. Keeping a tight hold of Enyo's hand, Jacob merged with traffic. Together, they slipped through the gaps within the crowd.

Enyo was incredibly graceful, Jacob discovered as she followed his lead, never stumbling or being forced to stop. Like him, her feet appeared to glide along the ground. It was the kind of grace that could have only come from training.

She mentioned being trained in the use of daggers. I guess that's where it came from.

He hoped there wasn't a dagger waiting to slide into his back.

A few people greeted him on his way home. They called out and waved. Several of them noticed the cloaked girl, and a few catcalled or whistled.

"Where ya going with that pretty young thing?" they'd ask. Jacob did his best to shake off their mild teasing with a smile. Enyo just blushed beneath her hood.

They finally entered his bar, and Jacob locked the door behind them and led Enyo upstairs. Once there, he allowed her to sit on the bed. Meanwhile, he leaned Durandal against the desk, grabbed the chair, spun it around, and sat down. Resting his forearms against the headrest, he pinned Enyo with a stare.

"All right. Now that we have some privacy, why don't you tell me what it is you want from me." It was not a question.

Enyo nodded. "As I said before, I can send you back to your world."

Jacob continued to stare. "Yes, that is what you told me before, but that doesn't tell me what you want."

A moment of silence passed between them as Enyo, looking down at the hands on her lap, squirmed. She seemed reluctant—no, maybe embarrassed was a better word. Her cheeks were slightly red, and she was biting her lower lip as if she was preparing to ask something that she wanted badly, but she was ashamed of asking for it.

"I… want you to take me with you," she said at last.

"E-excuse me?"

"I want to go with you. When I help you get back to your world, I want you to take me with you."

Silence reigned for a time. Jacob sighed and ran a hand through his hair.

"Before we get into how such a thing would even be possible, could I know why you want to go with me?"

Looking away, Enyo nevertheless answered his question. "I'd like to start anew. If I remain in Terrasole, then all that will happen is a repetition of the cycle that has plagued this land for many, many centuries."

Known as the Vicious Cycle, it was a common fact that upon the death of the previous dark lord, a new dark lord was chosen. This dark lord would then start a new crusade against humanity. Humans would then summon another hero to fight for their cause, provided they did not already have a living hero ready to fight for them, and so the cycle repeated itself, over and over and over again.

From the books that he'd read in Avant Heim, Jacob was the twenty-third hero to have been summoned. He was the fourteenth to have defeated a dark lord. He was also the youngest to have ever been summoned in the entire history of human culture.

"If you remained here, then you would become the next dark lord," Jacob deduced.

Enyo shook her head. "I would birth the next dark lord, who would then be trained from a young age to do the bidding of the dark council."

"I think I vaguely remember hearing something about the dark council," Jacob frowned.

"I know of them," Durandal interrupted. "They're a bunch of old coots who like to stir up trouble. Back when I was forged, my first wielder fought against the dark council. I thought he had vanquished them, but I guess not."

"The dark council operates on a level of secrecy known only to the dark lord and his progeny," Enyo said. "As I understand it, all dark council members have gained a form of immortality. They're the ones who proclaim a new dark lord and raise that person to be their pawn in this never-ending struggle with humanity."

Pressing a hand to her chest, Enyo's eyes lost their luster as if recalling unpleasant memories.

"I don't know how many council members there are, but my father once warned me about them. He told me they were not to be underestimated, and that if possible, I should never get myself involved with them."

From the way she spoke, it sounded like Alucard had actually cared about her, but... that couldn't be true, could it? The Alucard that he had fought was the evilest man he'd ever met. He laughed at the thought of killing his own subjections, sneered as he threw people in front of Jacob to slay, and thought nothing sacrificing of entire villages of dark clansmen for the sake of his goal. His every action had caused only death and destruction. A man like that could never care for another...

...could he?

"Let's get back on our original topic." Jacob decided to think on this later. There were more important things to worry about. "You mentioned getting me home. How do you plan on doing that?"

Enyo brightened as if the subject they were talking about was one that made her much happier. "Within Avant Heim, there is a massive gate. It is said that this gate leads to a world beyond our own. Supposedly, all the heroes who are summoned to Terrasole pass through this gate."

Despite having been summoned to this world, Jacob had never heard of this gate before, nor could he remember passing through one. The first thing that he remembered upon coming to this world was standing in the middle of a circle of old men dressed in white robes.

Of course, at the time, he had been weak and delirious. He barely remembered what happened those first few days. He'd passed in and out of consciousness, until he'd one day fully awakened. According to the old men who made up the Council of Light, it was called transportation sickness.

"And this gate leads to my world?" Jacob asked.

"Yes." Enyo nodded. "It's a portal that connects your world to Terrasole. However, there is a catch."

Jacob would've groaned, but he'd already expected as much. There was always a catch.

"What's the catch?"

Enyo held up a finger. "First: A key is required to unlock the gate. Second: Only someone who is from your world may pass through the gate."

Another moment of silence passed. Jacob stared at Enyo, who didn't seem to realize what she had said.

"Question."

"What is it?"

"If only someone from my world can pass through the gate, then how, exactly, do you plan on traveling with me?"

Nodding at his perfectly valid question, Enyo, with a completely straight face, said, "I'm hoping that I can pass through the gate if I'm with you."

So that was it. She was banking the entirety of her favor on the off-chance that she might be able to slip through the gate with him. There was no proof that she could. In fact, there was nothing in the history books that even mentioned heroes returning to their previous world after they'd been summoned. However, she was willing to take this one in a million chance that it would work.

"What if you can't pass through the gate?" he had to ask.

Enyo's self-deprecating smile was not the kind that he wanted to see on anyone, much less someone who, up to this point, seemed to be quite kind.

"Then at least I'll have done a good thing by letting you return to the place you belong," she said.

To that, Jacob could say nothing. What could he say? She was essentially telling him that she would help him, and that there was a possibility that she would get nothing out of it.

During his time traveling across the land, Jacob had saved many people. He'd asked for nothing in return. As a hero, he had accepted that this was how it should be. Now he was having someone who may or may not get something out of helping him, but she was going to do it anyway. How was he supposed to feel?

"Jacob?"

"Hm? Yes?"

With her hands resting on her lap, Enyo squirmed underneath his cloak. "W-will you help me? Please?"

Jacob took a deep breath. "Yes, I will help you."

Enyo's eyes went wide. "You will?"

"Yes."

"That's great!" Enyo stood up and raised her hands in the air. She seemed to have forgotten that underneath the cloak, she wasn't wearing anything except a pair of panties. "Thank you so much, Jacob! I promise, no matter what happens, I'll make sure you return home."

Jacob looked away. "That's, um, nice and all, but maybe we should, ah, buy you some clothes first."

"Clothes?" Enyo didn't seem to understand, not for several seconds, at least.

She looked down. Then she looked back at Jacob. Then down again. Back at Jacob. Down once more. After doing this several times, Enyo finally seemed to have realized what he meant.

Her scream nearly burst Jacob's eardrums.

***

There were numerous clothing stores in Albany. However, Jacob only went to one store for anything clothing related.

Justine's Seams sold both men's and women's clothing, and the seamstress, Justine, was excellent at patch jobs. Jacob had been wearing the same leather pants for over a year now thanks to her.

As he and Enyo entered the store, a middle-aged woman with slightly graying hair and crow's feet around the eyes and mouth greeted them, her long brown skirt swishing as she spun to face the two.

"Welcome to—oh, Jacob. What are you doing here? Did you rip your clothes again?"

In the face of Justine's almost childish pout, Jacob could only raise his hands and smile. "No, no. Nothing like that. I'm actually here because she needs clothes." He hiked a thumb at Enyo, who was busy looking around, still dressed in his cloak. "Her last pair were… lost. Think you can help her?"

Justine took one look at Enyo, and then she looked back at Jacob. She squealed.

"I can't believe it! You've finally found a girlfriend after all this time!"

"Wha…?" Enyo and Jacob said at the same time.

"Oh, this is so great! I'm so happy for you!"

"Um," Jacob started, "I think you've got the wrong idea about us—"

"I was beginning to wonder if you would ever settle down. I'm glad to see that you're finally starting to take your life seriously."

Okay. Jacob was beginning to get annoyed now—and Enyo was blushing up a storm. It was time to put a stop to this.

"Hey! You've got the wrong idea about us!"

Justine stopped gushing and stared at him. "What?"

"Enyo and I aren't dating," he said, running a hand through his hair. Enyo nodded alongside him. Her face reminded him of a fire truck. "She's just an… acquaintance."

"An acquaintance?"

"That's right."

Justine looked at Enyo. "Is this true? You're really not his lover?"

With cheeks that could've outshone a crimson flame, Enyo nodded. "Y-yes. He and I only met two days ago, so there's no way we could be lovers."

For reasons that Jacob couldn't begin to understand, Justine's shoulders slumped as though she was mightily disappointed. "Way to get my hopes up. Thanks a lot."

"I'm sorry you have such an unhealthy interest in my love life," Jacob responded with the best sarcasm money could buy. "Now, if you could do me a favor and help Enyo find some clothes, I'd be much obliged."

"All right. Fine. Come here, Enyo. Let's find you something cute to wear." Justine grabbed Enyo by the hand and dragged her off. "We're going to find something so sexy, it'll knock that stick in the mud's socks off!"

"I think you mean knock the socks off that stick in the mud," Jacob muttered before he realized what she was saying. "And find something normal, please! Normal!"

"Yeah, yeah!"

As the two disappeared deeper into the store, Jacob found a wall to lean against and crossed his arms. There was nothing to do now but wait. He really hoped Justine wouldn't find something outrageous for Enyo to wear.

"I always liked that old woman, even though she's not hot," Durandal chimed.

"I swear, between you and that woman, my life has been nothing but misery."

"I think you like that we're so interested in your personal life," Durandal said.

"You mean my sex life," Jacob rebutted. "And I don't like it. I wish you'd both shut up."

"If ya really wanted us to shut up, ya could have made us done so easily enough. The fact that ya never actually make us be quiet is proof that ya like it." Durandal's hum contained a metallic quality. "I wonder if that makes you an M."

Jacob twitched.

Several minutes after he started waiting, shouts emerged from deeper within the store.

"H-hey! What are you doing?!"

"My, my, my. You have a lovely figure, Enyo."

"S-stop staring at me like that!"

"He he he, I've got just the thing for you! This outfit will be sure to knock that prude flat on his ass!"

"Wait? You want me to wear that?!"

"Yep! Now let's put it on!"

"No! I don't want to wear that! What are you—noooooo!!!"

Jacob strained to listen as Enyo's shouts were reduced to incoherent gargling before they disappeared altogether. He waited for several seconds on bated breath. Nothing happened. He then waited some more. Nothing happened. What was going on over there?

Seconds later, Enyo and Justine emerged from between several racks of clothes. Jacob could do nothing but gawk.

Enyo was wearing something that he wasn't entirely sure could be called clothing—unless the person saying it was being really polite. He wasn't even sure if it could be called underwear either. It was more like several straps of strategically placed leather. It covered her nipples, her crotch… and nothing else.

She was also wearing black garters.

A grinning Justin gestured grandly at Enyo, who did her best to cover herself. "Ta-da! What do you think? Sexy, isn't it? Doesn't it just make you want to ravish her?"

"I love it!" Durandal shouted. "Justine, you're a genius!"

"Aren't I?" Justine puffed up her chest in pride.

"I thought I said something normal!" Jacob shouted.

"This isn't what I wanted to wear! Now I'm wearing even less than when I had nothing but underwear on!" Enyo cried at the same time.

It took nearly fifteen minutes of arguing, Jacob chucking Durandal into the street, and he and Enyo ganging up on Justine to convince the woman that they wanted normal clothes. Finally, Justine had agreed. She'd been pouting the whole time.

What Enyo ended up with was an outfit that reminded him of a swashbuckler. Her brown pants were rather form-fitting and creaked as she moved. They flowed into a pair of knee high boots, which were held together with straps. Her off-white shirt stopped at the elbows, revealing her pale skin, and thrown over the shirt was a leather bodice several shades lighter than her pants. A belt went around the whole thing, though it seemed more for show than because she needed it.

"I'm glad we were finally able to get that woman to help you into some normal clothes," Jacob said as he picked up the complaining Durandal.

"What the hell's the big idea, Partner?! Ya think ya can just throw me on the street and expect me to—oof!"

"Shut up," Jacob said after slamming Durandal against a wall.

"I'm glad, too," Enyo said as she looked down at herself. "Though I'll admit that even these seem a bit too immodest. I feel somewhat exposed."

"You shouldn't feel embarrassed. Those look good on you."

"R-really?"

"Wouldn't have said it if I didn't mean it," Jacob replied to her embarrassed question with a shrug. "Let's keep shopping. We still need to get you a weapon."

Enyo had been trained to dual-wield daggers, and she was apparently quite good at it, according to her.

"I don't mean to brag, but my former maid trained me how to fight using daggers ever since I was a little girl. I'm quite formidable."

"You don't say."

Jacob had no clue if she was being honest or not, but he decided to let sleeping dogs lie. There wasn't much point in arguing. He would see her skills eventually in either case.

They went to the nearest blacksmith and picked out a pair of daggers. There was nothing special about the ones they bought. They were just a plain pair of daggers made from steel, but it wasn't like they could get anything better. Blacksmith around here usually carried weapons that were decidedly average. If someone wanted something stronger, they needed to either go to an enchanter, a master blacksmith, or find a legendary weapon in a dungeon.

There weren't that many master blacksmiths, and in fact, Jacob only knew of one. However, he was far from here. It was too far out for them to travel to, especially since he didn't know their first destination yet.

Jacob also bought her a pair of sheaths, which she strapped lower back so that the daggers hung off the small of her back. She said it would allow her to draw them more quickly and in secret. Having been attacked by more than one dagger-wielding assassin, Jacob knew this to be true. This also meant she really did have training, or at least theoretical knowledge.

After they returned home, he and Enyo took turns bathing. The bath was a simple thing. It was just a tub. Jacob fortunately had several water and fire fairies who helped him draw the bath. After they were done, the two adjourned to his bedroom.

"The key that you mentioned before," Jacob began as he searched through his chest, "wherever you hid it, that should be our first stop. There isn't much point traveling to Avant Heim if we can't even unlock the gate, right?"

"Right," Enyo agreed. She sat on the bed. Jacob could feel her eyes on him as he pulled out a large scroll and stood up. "I hid the key away inside of a cavern located near the edge of a deep ravine."

Jacob set the scroll on the desk and unfurled it. The scroll was old. The edges were frayed. However, the map detailed within the pages was impressive, showing everything in Terrasole with a high level of detail. "Do you know which ravine?"

Enyo stood up and shook her head. "No. I'm not familiar with the geography of Terrasole, but I do remember that the ravine had a strange feeling to it. I felt like there was always someone looking over my shoulder. It kind of creeped me out, to be honest, but that's why I hid the key there. I thought that feeling would keep other people away."

Nodding at her description, Jacob studied the map. Terrasole was shaped like a crescent. To the south was the Tenebrae Mountain range, which spanned one side of Terrasole to the other, essentially splitting the continent in half. It also separated this country from the darklands, home of the dark clan. The rest of Terrasole was surrounded by the sea. Avant Heim, the capital, was located at the furthest point of the crescent, right in the center.

"That sounds a lot like Kyöpelinvuori," he muttered.

"Is that the name of the ravine?" Enyo asked.

"Yes. Kyöpelinvuori is a ravine surrounded by thick forests. It's said to be home to damned spirits who were unable to cross over. Supposedly, the spirits all congregate there because there is a gate that leads to the underworld deep inside of the ravine."

From the way Enyo shivered as if she'd caught a sudden chill, she'd had no idea about Kyöpelinvuori's history and the rumors surrounding it. By the goddess Alaya, this girl really didn't know anything about Terrasole. It was a wonder she'd managed to find him.

"Kyöpelinvuori is about two weeks travel from here," Jacob continued. "There are several cities along the way, so at least we'll have a place to rest. We'll begin our journey tomorrow."

"Sounds good," Enyo said. She paused, and then, in a hesitant voice, said, "and Jacob?"

"Hm?"

Enyo gave him a smile that could have parted storm clouds. "Thank you for agreeing to travel with me. I promise, I won't let you down."

It took everything Jacob had not to smile back. He couldn't allow himself to smile. He couldn't allow himself to get close to her. There was still a chance that this was all a ploy to stab him in the back later on down the road.

"You're welcome. Now, I have to open my bar soon. Since the knights have been asking about you around town, I'd like you to remain here. I'll come up a little later with some dinner."

"Right!" Enyo nodded.

The last thing Jacob saw as he shut the door, was Enyo's smile, which remained as bright as the sun during midsummer.

INTERLUDE I - A QUEEN'S WOES

Alice Lannister D'arche was the reigning monarch of Terrasole, though she rarely felt like a ruler these days. Day in and day out her council undermined her authority, overturned her laws, and disregarded her words. Thanks to them, even her most loyal and cherished friend, the man whom she had loved, had abandoned the kingdom and left for lands unknown.

It was late afternoon. Rays of sunlight filtered through the windows of the hall that she strode down. Refractions caused the polished marble tiles to glitter. Her footsteps echoed along the hall, which was empty of life, save that of her own and her maid's. Within the numerous windows that she passed by, Alice could see her reflection.

Many people had often praised her as the most beautiful maiden in Terrasole. Compliments were heaped upon her golden locks, which sparkled with an effervescent sheen as it descended from her head in many drill-like curls. Her figure was considered the stuff of legends. Many a noble had proclaimed that her body was like that of a goddess, with elegant and womanly curves that sensualized the epitome of womanhood.

Looking at herself in the window's reflection, Alice could only wonder where people had come up with such farfetched flattery.

"My lady?"

Being mid-day, Alice had just finished eating a light lunch provided by her servants. That morning, like all mornings, she had allowed her people to come before her and speak their minds or make requests. As always, the only people who'd come were nobles.

Why is it that none of the commonwealth comes to speak with me anymore?

"My lady?"

There had been a time where commoners would travel to her doorstep, stand before her, and report on what was happening to her people, or express concern for something that was happening or not happening. Now the only people who came were nobles with complaints. It was a distressing state of affairs, to be sure.

"Queen Alice!"

Alice nearly jumped when a shout blasted in her ears. She looked around, seeking out the source, before realizing that the source was none other than her maid.

"Oh, Listy... you startled me."

"Considering I have been trying to get your attention for the past five minutes, you should not be so startled, My Queen."

Elizabeth Troule, or Listy for short, was a busty young woman with auburn hair that she always kept in an artful bun. Her elegant dress accentuated her figure, tight across the chest and waist before flaring out at the hips. While it was mostly white, the bodice that she wore was light blue. The dress was also sleeveless, so her slender arms were laid bare.

"I'm sorry," Alice apologized, feeling properly chastised. "My mind was... elsewhere."

"Clearly. What were you thinking about, I wonder?"

Alice turned away from the woman, whose intense gaze made her feel naked. "What were you saying?"

"I was trying to tell you your schedule." Sighing, Listy held a scroll in her left hand, her notes for that day. "Now that we've reached mid-day, there is much work that needs to be done. You have a meeting with Marquis Denivan of the White Council, and after that there are several reports that require your attention."

Alice wanted to cry. "That sounds like so much work."

"Yes, well, being a monarch is something that requires constant dedication. You know this as well as I, My Lady."

"Yeah... I know."

Listy's frown grew in prominence. "Is everything all right, My Lady?"

"Yes, everything is fine." Alice shook her head. "I am merely feeling a tad exhausted."

"You do look rather weary," Listy said in concern. "Maybe we should consider cancelling these events for today, so you can get some rest."

Alice shook her head as they walked past a set of large double doors. "No, it is fine. If I were to cancel a meeting with a member of the White Council, then the nobles would gain an even greater... foot... hold...?"

Their journey had taken them to a large room, one that could have passed for a library due to the number of bookshelves. Of course, this was not a library, but Alice's personal meeting chamber. Smaller than the great hall, it was still larger than most common houses. Tasteful columns were arrayed around the room, which had a vaulted ceiling that depicted the morning sky. A glittering wooden desk sat at the opposite end of the door, near a large window that overlooked Alysium, the city in which her castle, Avant Heim, resided.

Someone was already there.

He was a handsome man in his late forties. His graying hair was swept back and lent him a refined demeanor. The lines of his face were from a combination of age, battle scars, and stress. Despite this, his steel gray eyes were sharp.

His armor clinked as he turned around to face them, the polished surface of his platemail shining in the afternoon sun. Unlike most knights, this one carried a claymore on his back, a weapon nearly twice his size that was covered in magical runes. When she entered the room, the knight knelt in deference.

"Your Majesty," he murmured.

"Bayard," Alice greeted with a smile. "To what do I owe the honor of your visit today?"

Bayard von Heist was the captain of her castle's guard. A paladin of great power and much experience, Bayard had fought in several wars throughout his life, including the most recent one with the Dark Clan. He was also the person who'd trained Jacob in how to wield a sword. His skill in swordsmanship was such that even now, nearly a decade after passing his prime, he still whipped the younger knights like they were newborn pups.

In contrast to Alice's smile, Bayard's face was grave. "Your Majesty, I have some news that I believe you will want to hear."

Her smile leaving, Alice walked over to her desk, though she did not sit down. Several scrolls already sat upon it, waiting for her to peruse them, but she discarded those for now, focusing instead on the man before her.

"What is this news that you speak of? Judging from the grave expression you wear, I can only assume it is dire."

"Not dire, Your Majesty, but concerning nonetheless. A messenger bird arrived barely fifteen minutes ago. Apparently, one of the squadrons that we sent out to locate the thief who stole the gate key has discovered the whereabouts of Jacob Stone."

It felt a lot like being struck by lightning, hearing this news. Alice took a shuddering breath.

"S-so I see. Jacob… he is alive, then." She hesitated. "Is he… doing well?"

Bayard shook his head. "The reports did not confirm his health. It only states that Jacob Stone is living in the free city of Albany."

Albany was one of three independent cities within Terrasole. They were not a part of her kingdom, though many of her nobles had pushed her to take control of them. She'd not done so, however. Alice understood that not everyone enjoyed living under the rule of a kingdom, thus she had allowed the cities to remain free.

Thinking of Jacob made her chest ache. Six years ago, a twelve-year-old Jacob had been summoned to her world. During that time, she had befriended him, spending what time she was not in lessons with him, getting to know him better. He'd regaled her with tales of his home world. In turn, she told him everything that she knew about Terrasole. A year after he arrived, Jacob had left on his quest to defeat the Dark Lord.

He had succeeded, but it was not without cost.

Alice still remembered when Jacob had returned after slaying Alucard. News had already reached her by that point, and she had created an entourage to greet him as he entered Alysium. However, the Jacob that she had known and the Jacob who returned were not the same. Gone was the cheerful young man. In its place had been a quiet teen who brooded more often than not. Yet Jacob had not changed so much that he had neglected her after returning, and when they met again in front of the gates to the city, he had smiled at her. When she had welcomed him home, he had said, *"I'm home."*

At the time, she had believed that everything would be fine. Alucard was gone. Jacob had returned. Her people were safe. The war was over. Surely, things could only become better from there.

She had no idea how wrong she had been.

Her father, the King of Terrasole, had died shortly after the war ended. With her as his only heir, she'd become the reigning monarch, the queen. However, it was not without cost. The nobility had fought against the idea of her being queen, stating that a woman could not rule, for they lacked the strength to do what was needed. Thanks to Jacob and the many knights loyal to her, like Bayard, the nobles had been shot down, and she had become the queen two months after her father's passing.

Being queen was difficult, however. Alice had found her time consumed with meetings. Policies had to be created, deals had to be made. Alice had met with nobles and council members and commoners. With her life having been subsumed by the role of queen, she had no longer possessed the time to spend with Jacob. Perhaps if she had, then…

Alice shook her head.

Now is not the time to dwell on past mistakes.

"Bayard," she addressed the captain. "I would like you to send a detachment to Albany. Have them deliver a message to Jacob."

"You plan on asking him to return?" he asked.

"Yes."

"What if he refuses your summons?"

Alice's heart trembled. "I cannot force him to return, but I... I would at least like to give him the chance."

"I understand." Bayard bowed. "I will have the newest paladin seek out Jacob. I believe Caslain is eager to prove himself useful in either event."

"Thank you."

Bowing one more time, Bayard spun around and left the room. Alice turned and walked up to the window, placing her gloved hand upon the glass as she gazed out at the city, which appeared to be on fire thanks to the setting sun.

Jacob... I wonder what you are doing right now? Are you safe? Are you happy?

"Queen Alice," Listy started, "are you sure I should not cancel your meetings today?"

Alice debated the idea for a moment before shaking her head. She turned around, strolled toward the desk, and sat down. She sank into the red cushions.

"No, I cannot afford to be seen as weak before the nobles and White Council. They're still doing their best to prove that I'm not competent enough to rule. I'll not give them a reason to prove themselves right."

"Very well." Listy curtsied. "I shall have someone fetch the marquis for you."

"Thank you."

Sitting with the afternoon sun at her back, Alice prepared for another day of countless meetings with arrogant men who would continue to undermine her authority. She did her best to put Jacob out of her mind.

CHAPTER 2 - HEROES WANTED

Jacob and Enyo awoke early the next morning. They had packed all the essentials that they would need for their journey the night before, including food, money, whetting stones, and other necessities. As the sun rose above the mountains far off in the distance, the two quietly slipped out of Albany and began their journey.

Kyöpelinvuori was ten days travel from Albany. It was located in the south-eastern part of Terrasole. To reach it, one had to travel through several cities and towns, and then journey through the Phantasma Forest.

There were numerous dangers along the way. Terrasole was a land that had many monsters.

Thanks to the war's end four years ago, the knights no longer had to worry about Dark Clan members attacking them and could focus on protecting people from these monsters. Even so, many veteran knights had been lost during the war. Since knights didn't grow on trees and needed to be trained before they could become proper protectors of the people, most of the ones left over were inexperienced. This had led to an increase in monster activity.

Fortunately, Jacob knew the lay of the land quite well. Having traveled across the continent during his journey to defeat Alucard, he knew the hot spots where monster activity was at its greatest. With him leading the way, he and Enyo were able to reach the first town without incident.

Parvus was less of a town and more of a hamlet, with tiny wooden huts for buildings and unpaved roads. It was clear that this town was underdeveloped. What's more, as he and Enyo arrived, it was to see the entire hamlet surrounded by a massive wooden fence. Nearly ten meters in height and made from thick logs, the fence's appearance reminded Jacob of a bandit fortress.

"Halt!" a voice called from above. "Who goes there?!"

A man was standing atop the archway upon which a massive gate was embedded. Wielding a crossbow, which he pointed at the two, the man quivered as if fearing for his life.

"Just a pair of travelers!" Jacob called out as Enyo pulled the hood of her cloak up to further conceal her face.

Since the knights of Terrasole were looking for her, Jacob and Enyo had both agreed that it would be best if she hid her face from others. There was no telling who the knights had spoken with, or who they would speak with in the future. They wanted to avoid trouble. This was but one of several ideas they had come up with.

"Travelers?" the man questioned. "What are a pair of travelers doing in a town like this?"

"We're merely passing through," Jacob answered. "We were hoping to stay the night before continuing on our way."

"You'd best just keep going, stranger! There's danger afoot in these parts!"

"Danger, huh?" Jacob muttered, running a hand through his hair. It was already evening, so they couldn't afford to leave. Night was the most dangerous time to travel. "Would it be alright if we spoke to your chieftain? Perhaps we can help."

The man seemed stunned, though it was hard to tell from so far away. "Help, you say? Are you two traveling mercenaries or something?"

"Or something."

Jacob waited as the man appeared to deliberate. A second passed, then another before, finally, the gates opened.

"You may enter! The Chieftain's building is in the center of the village. You can't miss it!"

"Thank you!"

He and Enyo entered the hamlet, which truly was a tiny place. There were only about a dozen buildings in total, though they were less like buildings and more like huts, tiny constructs made of wood and straw.

It wasn't unusual for houses to be built like this. Small towns didn't have the architects that cities had, nor did they have the labor force required to build such large structures, so they made do with what they did have. That said, a strong storm would destroy these huts in an instant. It was fortunate that they lived in an arid place where storms were rare.

Slightly larger than the other buildings, the chieftain's hut was indeed in the center of the hamlet. Jacob and Enyo knocked on the door, which was less of a door, and more of a series of rickety sticks tied together with leather bands. They received a response almost immediately.

"Hold on!" an aging voice called out.

Loud thumping echoed behind the door. There was some banging, followed by a series of curses. Enyo's cheeks became visibly red beneath her hood. She must not have been used to such vulgar language.

The door opened, and an ancient-looking man who barely reached Enyo's chest stood in the doorway. He peered at them with small black eyes partially hidden by stringy gray hair.

"I don't recognize you two. Travelers?"

"That's right," Jacob said. Enyo remained silent, though she did shift away when the elder glanced in her direction. "We heard from the guard that there's trouble afoot in your village and wanted to offer our assistance in return for lodging for the night."

"You mercenaries or something?"

"Or something," Jacob answered with the same reply that he'd given the guard.

"Hmph! Come on in."

The elder moved away and opened the door, allowing him and Enyo to enter. The interior wasn't much to look at. The floor was made of dirt, there was only one room, and the decor was barren enough that even Jacob thought it was too bare.

They were led to an uncomfortable couch made of straw and threadbare fabric, thin and shabby. After setting their packs on the ground, he and Enyo sat down so as not to appear rude. The uncomfortable feeling of straw poking his butt was not enjoyable. Enyo squirmed beside him.

"The trouble we're having started about a month ago," the elder began. "A group of trolls made their home several leagues out near the base of a small mountain. We didn't think much of them at first. They weren't botherin' us or nothin', and we don't have the strength to fight them, but last month, they started coming down to our village at night. They'd come in, destroy our homes, kill our families, and then leave. This has been happening every night. Since then, we've built a wall, but it doesn't do a good job keeping them out. Have to repair the darned thing after every raid"

Trolls were notorious for three things: their incredible strength, their regenerative abilities, and their stupidity. They had ravenous appetites. They ate people, cows, basically anything that moved. Trolls also had furious tempers. Do something to agitate them, and they would fly into a berserker rage. Once that happened, the only way a troll would calm down was if someone killed it, or it killed everything in sight.

"Trolls, huh?" Durandal spoke up, startling the elder, whose eyes popped from his head. "It's been a long time since I've dealt with those. Hey, hey. Ya wanna know hear a joke? What did the male troll say to the female—doof!"

Durandal was cut off when Jacob slammed the sword back into its sheath.

"That sword just spoke," the elder mumbled.

"No, it didn't," Jacob said with a straight face.

"Yes, it did."

"You're imagining things."

"Do you know how many trolls there are?" Enyo asked, bringing their conversation back on track.

The elder glanced at her, causing her to look away. He narrowed his eyes, but answered her regardless. "We only ever see three."

"You mentioned that they're several leagues away, at the base of a mountain," Jacob said.

"Right." The elder nodded. "Longstand Mountain. It's a small mountain, more of a hill really."

If he ran there with physical augmentation, Jacob could probably reach the mountain in less than an hour. He'd be exhausted, though. It was also nearing nighttime. While the area around Albany was safe enough to travel at night, few other places were. Albany had many mercenaries coming through, and they often worked as monster hunters in exchange for cash at the local guild office.

They spoke with the elder a bit longer. In exchange for killing off the trolls, he and Enyo would be given a place to sleep. Since all their huts consisted of nothing but wooden walls and a poorly crafted ceiling, it wasn't going to be a comfortable sleep. That said, Jacob would take sleeping in an uncomfortable room over being outside where groups of undead could ambush them as they slept any day.

The hut they were given belonged to a family that had been killed by trolls during the last attack. He could tell from the different colored logs that it had been remade at least several times. There was no bed, which meant they were sleeping on the floor. Jacob was grateful that he'd had the foresight to pack two sleeping rolls.

Laying side by side, an uncomfortable silence settled over them. Jacob wondered if he should try to start a conversation. Sadly, he didn't know what they could talk about. Should he ask her about her past or hobbies? Wouldn't that bring up bad memories? The past evening, they had been able to avoid awkward silences by filling it with conversation about their journey. Now, however, with nothing left to discuss, an unsettling stillness blanketed them like a bad cold.

"Oh, for the love of—" Durandal grumbled into the stillness "—would ya two just hurry up and fuck already!"

"Shut up, you damn sword!" Jacob barked. He looked over at Enyo, who lay on her side, facing away from him. "I'm sorry about him. Durandal never could read the mood."

"I can read the mood just fine. You're the one who doesn't know how to read the mood."

"I said shut up!"

"It's fine," Enyo mumbled. She was still facing away from him. "I understand that Durandal is a really vulgar sword."

"I'm not vulgar."

"What about 'shut up' do you not understand?!"

"And I'm not... bothered by his words. Hearing them just makes me... self-conscious."

"That's what it means to be bothered." Jacob sighed. "Anyway, if he ever bothers you, just hit him with your dark magic. That will shut him right up."

"Don't be cruel!" Durandal cried.

"I'll be as cruel as I want," Jacob snapped.

Enyo giggled. "You two have an interesting relationship."

"I don't know if I'd call it interesting so much as annoying." Staring at the ceiling, Jacob thought of all the ways Durandal had humiliated him these past four years. "I sometimes regret picking him up thanks to that mouth of his."

Despite his harsh words, he was grateful to Durandal. Thanks to the sword's vulgar sniping, the tension seemed to have broken between him and Enyo, though he still didn't know what to talk about.

"What is your world like?" Enyo suddenly asked.

"My world?"

"Hm."

Rolling onto his side, Jacob faced Enyo, who must have heard him shifting because she rolled to face him seconds later. She was no longer wearing the hood. Her long pink hair visibly traveled down her back with strands sticking out all over the place from wearing a hood for so long.

"My world is... big, but it also feels really compact." Jacob's memories of his own world were fuzzy thanks to the war, but he still remembered enough. "The cities are all gigantic, bigger even than Alysium. The buildings tower over everyone. Some of them are even fifteen to twenty stories high."

"R-really?" Enyo's eyes were wide as she hung off his every word like they were the gospel truth.

Jacob nodded. "Really. We also have cars—erm, those are like carriages that don't require a horse to pull them. They move on their own."

"Like with magic?"

"Um, no..." Jacob trailed off as he tried to think of how best to describe them. "I... don't really know how they work, but they don't use magic."

"Oh."

"Anyway, it's a nice place, though it has its own problems."

"Like what?"

"Like the same kinds of problems that this world has: war, greedy people, politicians, crime... being in another world doesn't mean the problems caused by humanity will disappear. It just means there are different humans committing the same crimes."

Jacob had been young when he was summoned to this world. At twelve, he hadn't much cared for world affairs, so he knew very little about what went on in his own world. However, his father had often complained about world events when he was watching the news.

"Did you like it there?" Enyo asked.

"I don't know," Jacob admitted. "It's been so long since I've thought about my own world that I can barely remember how I felt when I was there." He paused. "But... I do want to go back. If nothing else, I would like to see my family again."

"I see. Family, huh?" Enyo's lips turned down, her eyes growing distant. "I can understand why you'd want to reunite with them. You were taken away from your family when the White Council summoned you here."

"Yeah, I was."

Another awkward silence settled over them. Fortunately, it was broken quickly. Unfortunately, what broke it was a violent roar from outside.

"Sounds like the trolls are here." Jacob leapt to his feet, put on his boots, and grabbed Durandal. Also standing up, Enyo put on her own boots and strapped her daggers to her back. He gave her a look. "You ready?"

"Yes." She nodded.

"Then let's go."

Together, he and Enyo rushed out of the hut to face down the creatures that had been terrorizing this hamlet.

***

Trolls were hideous creatures. Created centuries ago during one of the many wars against a dark lord, these creatures were bred solely for the sake of destruction. The dark lord had used them against humanity to great effect. The ones that confronted Jacob and Enyo were no different.

Towering over everyone there like massive trees, a trio of trolls lumbered forward on thick legs that were three times wider than Jacob. Their massive hands smashed into the wooden fence. Wood scattered everywhere and the people near that section were sent flying. Ugly maws filled with equally disgusting teeth opened to unleash fierce roars, which sent the men and women of the village scurrying. Green skin glimmered in the low light provided by the moon.

"Do you know how to kill a troll?" Jacob asked. Enyo shook her head. "There are several ways. Cut off their heads, light them on fire, or destroy them with black magic."

Black magic was the easiest way to kill a troll. One dark flame would incinerate such a creature. However, Jacob didn't want Enyo doing that. It would give her away as a dark clansman.

"Let's avoid using black magic, if possible," Jacob continued. "If you can distract one of the trolls, I can take out the first two."

"What if I kill the first troll before you?" Enyo challenged.

Jacob raised an eyebrow. "If you think you can, then be my guest."

Since they had met, Enyo had acted, not meek, but she hadn't been very competitive or fierce either. Gentle. That was the best word he could think of to describe how she had been acting. Now, with the moonlight casting a pale glow, and the roar of trolls blasting their ears like a war horn, Enyo's grin contained a fierceness that he hadn't seen before.

"I'll let you distract one of the trolls," she said before taking off.

Jacob felt his competitive spirit rise. "Not if I kill mine first!"

The three trolls varied in size, with two being about the size of a one-story building and the other standing a head above that. They were clumped together as they entered through the smashed fence—at first. Once they were inside, they branched off to cause more destruction.

Jacob went after the biggest one.

"You ready, Durandal?"

"Hell, yeah I'm ready! Let's do this!"

Durandal slid from its sheath with a hiss as Jacob grabbed the sword's handle and pulled. The sound of grinding steel was overpowered by the roaring of three trolls. His footsteps likewise went unheard.

Power flowed through Jacob's arms and into Durandal as he channeled his energy. His muscles became stronger, and Durandal, which was as much a part of him as his own limbs, became sharper as it was encased in a fiery blue glow.

The troll never noticed him until it was too late. Jacob swung Durandal as he ran past the troll, meeting only a slight resistance before the blade slid through flesh, muscle, and bone. The troll roared as its left leg was severed. Blood gushed from the stump, spurting out like paint being splashed onto a canvas.

As it fell, Jacob skidded to a stop, spun around, and then leapt onto the creature's back. Before the troll could regenerate, he sliced through its neck. Like a peeling apple, the troll's head slid off its shoulders. The now headless corpse then crashed into the ground with a thunderous clash as Jacob leapt off, landing several meters from the defeated monster.

He turned around to see how Enyo was doing.

He was shocked by what he saw.

Enyo had already killed one of the trolls. It lay on the ground, its body inert, its limbs sprawled out at awkward angles. Jacob couldn't see how it had been killed, but it was clearly dead.

Her cloak discarded, Enyo was fighting the last remaining troll, and she looked like she was enjoying herself, if the grin she wore was any indication. She wove between a hail of furious fists as the troll attempted to pound her into the ground like a butcher hammering meat. Yet no matter how many times the troll swung its fist, nothing could hit Enyo, who danced across the ground like a fleeting breeze.

Jacob was amazed. He considered himself rather fleet-footed, and indeed, judging by her current speed, he could actually move quicker than her. That said, he lacked her grace. She was elegance epitomized. The way she moved was beautiful, a deadly dance the likes of which he'd never witnessed.

With an earth-shattering roar, the troll lunged for Enyo, who moved into a series of back handsprings. On the last handspring, she crouched low. Enhancing his vision, Jacob could see the way her thigh muscles bunched. Then she leapt. Her jump took her high into the air, over the troll, whose shoulder she landed on. Without ceremony, she plunged her daggers into the creature's head.

There was no cry of agony, no roar of pain or anger. The troll's eyes rolled up into its head. It stumbled about in a drunken manner before it fell. Enyo flipped off its shoulder as it crashed into the ground, landing in a crouch as the troll twitched several times before going still.

Durandal whistled. "Damn. Wouldn't want to get on her bad side."

"You said it," Jacob agreed.

"Still, just imagine it. If she's that fierce on the battlefield, she must be a monster in the sack."

Jacob could feel heat rise to his cheeks. "Do you never shut up?"

"Course not."

"Tch."

Walking over to the discarded cloak, he picked it up and wandered up to Enyo. He glanced at her daggers. They were black and covered in cracks.

"That was impressive," he complimented.

Now that the battle was over, Enyo's smile regained its normal compassionate mien. "Thank you. I saw some of your battle as well. I had no idea you were strong enough to cut through a troll so easily. It looked like you were slicing through parchment."

He wasn't that strong. Most people assumed that his abilities came from pure brute strength, but that wasn't it at all.

"Thanks." Jacob glanced at the troll that Enyo had just killed. There were two perfectly circular holes in its head. "You used magic channeling to beat them, didn't you?"

Magic Channeling was the act of channeling magic through a weapon to enhance them. Depending on the type of magic a person had, they could do things like encase their weapon in fire, shoot out blades of wind, pierce any substance known to man, etc. Since Enyo was likely using darkness magic, her swords had annihilated the trolls' brains. Of course, since she had used darkness magic, there was a backlash.

"I did." Enyo seemed surprised. "How can you tell?"

"Well, for one, there's no way those blades could pierce through that hide. For another..." he glanced at her daggers. "... you may want to take a look at your weapons."

"Huh?"

Blinking several times, Enyo didn't seem to understand what he was talking about. She nevertheless brought up her blades and looked at them. Her eyes widened. Then, as if to mock her, the cracked and blackened blades suddenly shattered, leaving only two bladeless hilts behind.

"It looks like we're gonna have to buy you another pair of daggers," Jacob observed coolly.

Enyo's despairing wail echoed across the small hamlet.

INTERLUDE II - AN EAGER KNIGHT

Caslain Calahan was a young knight, the youngest to have ever earned the title of paladin. After he'd turned sixteen, which was the age of adulthood, he joined the knights and toiled for three years to prove himself. Through his blood, sweat, and tears, he eventually rose to the top, paladin, the highest rank someone could achieve without being a noble.

The person who had inspired him to become a knight was Jacob Stone.

Jacob Stone was a boy who, at the age of thirteen, slayed the Dark Lord Alucard and became a hero. Caslain could still remember the first time he'd ever seen the young hero. The newly minted Queen Alice had just announced that the war had ended, a parade was being held in honor of the hero who had made it possible, and Caslain, only fourteen at the time, had eagerly attended to catch a glimpse of this renowned hero.

He'd been shocked to discover that the hero was nothing but a boy—younger than him even! To think that there were people like Jacob who were already accomplishing heroic deeds at such an age! It had moved Caslain to tears. That was when he had decided to become a knight. He had dreamed of one day becoming a paladin, traveling to distant lands, and fighting alongside his hero.

Then Jacob had left. There had been no word, no warning, nothing. One day he'd been there, and the next he was gone.

Caslain had been torn.

Rather than let this get to him, he'd let it motivate him. If Jacob was gone, then Terrasole would need a new hero, and he was determined to be that hero. It was this motivation that led him to excelling past his peers, becoming a paladin in three short years.

And now, here he was, a paladin, and he was being asked to find Jacob, his hero.

It was like a dream come true.

Commander Bayard had personally requested his aid in this, and of course, there was no way he would turn such a task down. This wasn't just an important quest that he was being sent on. This was his dream.

Jacob's last known location was Albany, a free city located several leagues north west of Alyssium. It would take about a month to get there by foot, three weeks to get there by horseback. It took Caslain and his squadron three days.

Caslain was not just a paladin. He was a member of the Drakon Brigade. They were drake riders, an aerial unit that fought while riding drakes. What took a horse weeks to travel at a quick trot, it only took a drake a few days. They were just. That. Fast.

Wandering through the streets of Albany, Caslain, decked in resplendent silver armor, searched for a sign of his hero. Two of his men were with him. Their armor, like his, clanked as they walked. The rest were at the nearby fortress with their drakes. Apparently, the squadron that was stationed there were the ones who'd initially located Jacob while chasing after a criminal.

Fate must have brought that squadron to Jacob. Yes. It was fate, just like it was fate that Caslain would be the one to find Jacob and bring him back.

"Excuse me!" he boomed as he walked up to a pair of civilians. "Do any of you know of a man named—h-hey! Where are you going?!"

Caslain stared in shock as the two, an old couple, ran away screaming. What was their deal? Were they criminals? That must have been it. They were criminals who were on the run and became frightened when they saw him. Hmph! Those people were lucky that he had better things to do than catch petty crooks. He was on a mission from the queen herself!

It took Caslain nearly two hours of having people run away to find someone who was willing to answer his question.

"You lookin' fer Jacob, eh. I know him. Most people 'round here know him."

The man that spoke was gnarled, not old, but grizzly. Scars lined his face, pale white lines against dark brown skin. They mixed with stress wrinkles to create an odd network. His clothing was threadbare, though he did have some nice armor and a sword.

A mercenary.

"Where can I find him?" Caslain asked in a booming voice.

"If ye don't keep that voice of yers down, I won't tell ye!" Caslain closed his mouth. "Good. If ye lookin' fer Jacob, ye can find his tavern by going down this street, and then takin' a left. It's got a big sign of a man holdin' a mug o'er his head. Ye can't miss it."

A tavern? Did Jacob live in a tavern now? How appalling! A hero should not be in some tavern. They needed to live in a mansion, if not a castle!

"Thank you, good sir!"

"Ye won't be thanking me fer long." The man cackled. "Jacob ain't there no more. Couple o' his regulars busted inside when the tavern didn't open to find that he upped and vanished. He's gone. Ain't nobody knows where he is now."

For just a moment, Caslain felt like an ogre had punched a hole through his chest. Jacob? Gone? But they hadn't even met yet?! However, just before he could feel true despair, Caslain hardened his resolve. If the Jacob had left, then it merely meant that he needed to expand his search. He would return to his unit and have them spread out a net. If Jacob was traveling on foot, then it shouldn't take long to find him.

Come hell or high water, Caslain would return his hero to Alysium—even if it killed him!

CHAPTER 3 - THE GREAT EQUALIZER

Despite the trolls finally being slain, the village did not celebrate. No great party was held, no feast prepared. Most of their village had been wiped out before he and Enyo had even arrived, so it was understandable that they would feel no joy at the trolls' demise. Instead, the villagers had gathered their wounded and dead, and spent the rest of the night either burying their dead, tending to the wounded, or repairing the destroyed fence and houses.

He and Enyo had only stayed for the night. When the sun rose, the two packed their bags and left, traveling south east.

It took two days to reach the next city by foot, which meant that he and Enyo had been subjected to two undead attacks.

Undead were the reanimated corpses of people and creatures. Long ago, a powerful dark lord whose magic was necromancy had cursed the land of Terrasole, making it so that the dead would rise. Unless the remains were sanctified, and then cremated, anything that was killed would eventually come back. Fortunately, there had been no humans among those they faced. It was just animals.

They reached the next city within two days.

Unlike Parvus, which had been little more than a hamlet, Altus was massive—comparatively. It reminded him a lot of Albany. Large buildings were squashed together, made of brick and wood, with thatched roofs colored red, black, or tan. Between the buildings were cobblestone streets. There were many people traveling down these streets, and several carriages passed by as he and Enyo blended into the traffic.

"Are we going to find an inn?" asked Enyo. Because there were so many noisy people, she had to talk directly into his ear to be heard.

Jacob shook his head and turned to speak. "Not yet. The first thing we need to do is buy a detailed map of the Phantasma Forest. I've been there once before, but it was so long ago that I barely remember anything about it. Also, Phantasma Forest is huge. I never reached Kyöpelinvuori, so you had to have traveled through a different part of the forest than I did."

Enyo nodded as she wove past someone who nearly bumped into her shoulder. This place was so lively that if they weren't careful, they'd be run over.

"Where can we find a map like that?"

"There are several places," Jacob answered, pointing to a large sign hanging off a building. It was a very basic building made of bricks. The sign said *The General Store* in bold print. "General stores like this usually sell maps. We just have to find one that sells a map of the forest."

"Mmm mphm mm mm!" A loud clattering was heard even over the noisy din of several hundred people.

"Did you hear something?" Jacob asked innocently. He kept firm hand on Durandal's hilt.

Enyo's lips twitched. "No."

"Mmmph!"

"Me neither."

With a goal set, the two traveled to several general stores and asked their clerks if they had any maps of Phantasma Forest. They didn't. In fact, whenever Jacob asked about the forest, they would clam up and kick them out, and no amount of bartering made them change their minds.

Jacob had contemplated asking Enyo if she could butter the clerks up. She was gorgeous, jaw-dropping even. Having once nearly been assassinated by a woman who excelled in seduction, he knew well how a little sex appeal could go a long way. He decided not to go that route. Not only would it have been rude to ask that of Enyo, but she was wanted. There were already several posters with her face pinned onto quest boards and walls.

In the end, they couldn't find a store that sold a map of the Phantasma Forest.

"What should we do now?" asked Enyo.

It took him a moment, but he eventually decided on their next course of action. "We need to learn why everyone becomes frightened when we bring up the Phantasma Forest. Let's find a tavern that has an inn. We'll rent a room for the night, then spend some time in the tavern to gather information."

"Gather information in a tavern?"

The look on Enyo's face was perplexed, and her head was tilted ever so slightly, as though she were trying to figure out why they would gather information in a tavern, of all places.

"A lot of different people like to visit taverns during the evening and night to enjoy a cold beverage and good company. Alcohol is a great inebriator. People who are drunk are more willing to let slip secrets they might have otherwise kept."

Enyo nodded. "That makes sense. Okay, should we travel to a tavern now?"

"Let's walk around a bit first," he suggested. "Get a feel for the city. The tavern won't be crowded until later tonight, so there's no point in going there now."

Enyo agreed, and together, they set off. Holding hands to keep from getting separated, they moved through the crowd of pedestrians. Jacob imagined that anyone seeing them would just assume they were a young couple... although Enyo's fully cloaked figure might have made them wonder about her. Still, it was better than letting everyone see her face. They'd be more liable to recognize her should that happen.

While the town was quite lively, the longer Jacob walked, the more aware he became that something was wrong. Some of the shops were closed. A few of the houses were boarded up, as if the residents had moved out. Tension hung in the atmosphere, light, almost unnoticeable, but there nonetheless.

"Is it just me, or is everyone here afraid of something?" asked Enyo.

So, she sensed it too? I'm not surprised.

Dark Clansmen were much better at sensing the emotions of others, especially negative emotions. Rumor had it that negative feelings were their sustenance. This was just a rumor, of course, but the rumor had originally sprung from a kernel of truth.

"They are." Jacob glanced at the sky. The sun was beginning to set. "Come on. Let's find a tavern."

Jacob chose a tavern located far from the main road, a place called *The Brawling Bar*. He didn't know what sort of idiot would name a tavern that. Still, the atmosphere was decent, the food smelled all right, and best of all, there were already dozens of people getting merrily wasted.

Most of the seats were taken. Jacob wove through the tables, Enyo's hand in his, until he finally found a place to sit at the counter. There was just one problem.

There was only one seat.

He sighed.

"Enyo," he whispered in her ear. "Please follow my lead, okay?"

Looking more confused than ever, Enyo nodded regardless. "Of course. Isn't that what I've been doing?"

Jacob offered her a pained smile. "Yes, but this time, we're going to do something embarrassing."

Enyo didn't say anything to that, perhaps because she couldn't. Before she even had time to so much as blink, Jacob sat down, and then, without ceremony, pulled her onto his lap. Enyo squealed. Her reaction caused several men to cheer.

Pigs.

Pulling the hood from her ear, Jacob whispered, "Remember. Play along."

Her cheeks were still red. Enyo was clearly still embarrassed. If what she had told him about living in seclusion was true, then she probably wasn't used to someone acting so intimate with her. Despite this, she nodded and did her best to play along.

Jacob sucked in a breath when she squirmed on his lap, likely to get comfortable. He wrapped an arm around her waist, steadied himself, and then looked at the bartender, a bald man with a handlebar mustache and dark eyes.

"Barkeep, get me two ales."

The barkeep smirked. "Sure thing," he said, grabbing two mugs, which he filled with frothing ale and set in front of them.

Wrinkling his nose at the scent, Jacob gave Enyo one of the mugs and took the other for himself.

"Well," he said, clinking his mug against hers. "Cheers."

The bitter taste of ale assaulted his tongue, and the slow burn of alcohol poured down his throat. Jacob didn't like to drink. Most would think that strange since he owned a bar, but the bar had merely been something he had created to occupy his time. He never liked the scent or taste of alcohol.

Judging by the way she was coughing after a single sip, Enyo had never drunk alcohol before in her life.

"Too strong?" he asked.

"Too bitter," she replied.

"Yeah, ale doesn't taste very good, no matter where it comes from." Jacob took another swig. "I guess some people will drink anything to get shit-faced."

Jacob drained about a third of his mug before setting it down. Enyo set hers down sooner. His companion jolted as he placed a hand on her thigh and began rubbing it.

"W-what are you doing?"

"We're pretending to be a young couple who are getting ready for a night of fun by drinking the night away," Jacob said before tenderly nibbling on her ear, causing the girl to squeal. "No one will think twice about us if we play the part. Actually, once people start getting really drunk, I imagine a few will even come up to us... to ask if I'd like to share you."

"S-share?!"

"Don't worry. Nothing is going to happen to you. However, we need to draw in the dumb ones who are stupid enough to ask such a question. They're the ones who will be willing to part with important secrets, like why everyone is afraid of the Phantasma Forest."

"I-I see," Enyo murmured. "That's pretty crafty of you."

"I learned this from a good friend during my travels."

His words seemed to settle her down, or it could have been the alcohol, which she had grabbed and took a big swig of. Coughing and sputtering in surprise, she eventually settled down and began taking tentative sips.

Jacob would've chuckled at her. The fact that she couldn't drink was surprisingly cute. His attention was elsewhere, sadly.

He observed the room, watching as the patrons laughed, sang, danced, and flirted with the barmaids. Jacob wanted to measure them all. He wanted to know which ones would be the most likely to come up to them.

Several yards away was one brave patron. A man whose face was so red he looked ready to pass out. At another table, several fools had slung their arms around each other and were singing off-key bar songs. There were indeed plenty of potential idiots who he could glean the information they needed from.

An anomaly made itself known out of the corner of his eye. Across the room, sitting at a round table, were several Terrasole Knights. Made visible by their distinct armor, they sat around the table, hunched over as they drunk from their mugs and eyed the other patrons in disgust. All of them looked like they had something really large and painful shoved up their rectum.

It was the one in the middle who had most of his attention, and how could he not? That resplendent silver armor, the sleek shoulder pauldrons, and the curved helmet with horns that curled around to the back, it was the easily recognizable armor of a paladin in the Drakon

Brigade. Whoever this group was, they were much higher ranked than the fools who'd interrogated him the night he met Enyo.

A group of people finally came up to them. Jacob forced his attention away from the knights and onto the three who'd stumbled over. They were about as drunk as they came. He could smell the alcohol on their breath, and so could Enyo, apparently, as she wrinkled her nose when the three breathed on them. Then again, maybe she was merely put off by how ugly their stained teeth were.

"Looks like someone's gonna get lucky tonight!" the man in the middle crowed.

"Remember, play along," Jacob whispered. Enyo nodded and, in a louder voice, Jacob said, "Of course I am. The wife's away visiting family, I finally have some time off, and the lady here says she's been looking for someone who can show her a good time. I intend to fulfill that wish entirely."

Perhaps acting on his words, Enyo smiled at the trio of men as she took a sip from her mug. She almost coughed. However, she held it in this time and took another, larger sip.

The man hollered with laughter. "I wish you luck, boyo, but don't you think you're a wee young to please such an exquisite creature? Why not let someone with a bit more experience have a whirl?"

Barely keeping his disgust in check, Jacob smiled as he replied. "Not on your life, old man."

"Ha ha ha! Suit yourself brat! I still think she'd be better off with me!"

Jacob grinned, even though he felt like decking this man in the face. "Why don't you three pull up a seat? I'll buy you all drinks."

Grinning, the three men sat down in a couple of seats that had been emptied a while ago. "Now there's an offer we can't refuse!"

Grabbing the barkeep's attention, Jacob had him make three more mugs of ale for the men. He then chatted with the unruly trio. By using a combination of small talk, subtle flattery, and more alcohol, he was able to keep them talking. As the evening wore on, the trio became even more inebriated.

Enyo was also getting quite drunk. She must have been nervous, sitting on his lap and having these men talk about her. He almost wished she would've stood up and beat the crap out of these three. That would have ruined their purpose for being here, however. He had to respect the girl. She was a trooper to put up with this shit. If it had been him, he would've wailed on these three already. Actually, he wanted to do that right now—too bad it was Enyo's right and not his.

"You know, I don't think I've seen you in this bar before," the mouthpiece said before taking a swig of his drink.

"Course not," Jacob replied, matching the man gulp for gulp. "If I came here when the missus was home, she'd be furious."

"Ha ha ha! Yeah, women are always like that!"

The men all cheered. Jacob grimaced as he took yet another swig of his drink. Setting the mug down, he leaned over. Still sitting on his lap, Enyo wrapped her arms around his neck and giggled. The scent of alcohol was thick on her breath.

"But it sure has been weird around here, hasn't it?" Jacob smoothly changed the subject. "Everyone's been acting so scared."

The mouthpiece wiped his mouth with his hand and shrugged. "Considering what happened to poor Alfred and his family, I don't blame them. Mutilated beyond recognition they were, or so I hear."

Mutilated? Sounds like this family was murdered. Could monsters be the cause for this?

"I heard that monsters have been coming out of Phantasma Forest," Jacob pressed.

Nodding, the mouthpiece said, "So the rumor goes. Got a friend who used to work in a mill by that accursed forest. He says there's been strange growling at night—even claims to have seen hunched figures crawling out of the forest!"

Hunched figures?

That didn't tell him much. Any number of monsters had figures that matched this vague description: drawgers, kelpies, undead… off the top of his head, Jacob could list at least two dozen. Still, it did let him know one thing. Monsters of some kind were coming out of the forest. They only came at night, which narrowed down what kind they were. Only certain monsters acted during the nights. It didn't tell him what kind, but he would find out eventually once they traveled into the forest.

Now, I just need to find a map...

"W-woah!" Jacob nearly squawked when Enyo slumped against him. Her body sagged, forcing him to tighten his hold around her waist. He expected her to be unconscious because of how slack she was, limp like a soggy noodle, but then she gained her second wind and giggled as her hold around his neck tightened.

"Naughty boy, you," she slurred against his neck. "Touching my butt like that. Hic! You're so naughty."

Great... she's drunk. Maybe I should have kept her from drinking so much...

"Looks like your lass is ready for a night of fun," the mouthpiece said.

"Seems like it." Grunting, Jacob scooped Enyo into his arms, making her giggle again as she kicked her feet. He almost lost his composure when she sniffed his neck. He barely reigned it in when she began licking his neck. "If you gentlemen would excuse me, I've got a lady to please."

The men guffawed and waved him off. Jacob asked the bartender for the keys to a room, which he got after paying the man —which was a lot harder than it seemed since his hands were filled with a beautiful girl.

"Your room is on the second floor, fifth door on the left," the barkeep said.

"Got it."

Jacob wove through the tables, ignored the catcalls, and made it to the stairs.

"Where are... hic... where are we going, Jacob?" asked the drunk Enyo.

"To our room," Jacob grunted.

"Are we gonna have some fun?"

"Nope. We're going to rest, and you are going to sober up."

"Blegh! No fair. I wanna have fun." Grinning, Enyo leaned up and kissed his cheek. "I want to have fun with you."

"That's the alcohol talking."

"No, it isn't. I really do love—hic!"

The stairs creaked as he wandered up them, moving slowly because Enyo was kicking her legs back and forth. He almost lost his balance. When he reached the top, he went to the door that he'd been directed to and opened. He had to carry Enyo over his shoulder as he wandered inside. This made her squeal and giggle.

"Bad, Jaco—hic! You're supposed to carry me like a princess!"

"And you're not supposed to drink so much," Jacob said dryly as he walked inside, kicking the door closed behind him.

"Are we alone?" Durandal asked. "Yes! We're finally alone! Damn, son! Well done! I never thought you had it in you to get the lass drunk!"

"Shut up, Durandal!" Jacob snapped. "I didn't get her drunk! She got herself drunk!"

"Drunk! Drunk! Drunk!" Enyo cheered, giggling and hiccupping.

"You are getting some tonight, you mustang you!" Durandal crowed.

"Getting some!" Enyo parroted.

"Awww! Would you two shut up already?!" Jacob shouted, though it did little good.

It looked like that saying he'd heard from Freya really was true.

In order to acquire something, something of equal value must be given.

I really hate it when she's right, he silently lamented.

✳✳✳

Enyo woke up with a headache. It felt like someone had smashed her head in with a warhammer, and then a horde of ogres had trampled on it for good measure. The spot around her temples and the front of her head was pounding. There was pressure around her nose as though someone was squeezing it. She didn't know what to make of this strange phenomenon, but it wasn't a pleasant feeling.

Shifting around, Enyo realized that she was lying on a bed, and that someone had tucked her in. She was no longer wearing her boots. Wiggling her toes, Enyo luxuriating in the feeling of freedom. Back when she'd been living in her secluded mansion, she'd often gone barefoot. Her chest also felt lighter, which made her realize that her bodice had taken off as well, though she still had her shirt and pants on.

A groan escaped from her parted lips as she sat up. Her throat was parched, and her tongue felt thick and dry. She smacked her lips, but that did little to help.

"You're finally awake," Jacob said.

Startled, Enyo looked around before finally spotting her companion, lying on the ground, on his back, and staring at the ceiling. His hands were tucked underneath his head. He seemed to be using them as pillows.

"Jacob? Where are we?"

"We're in one of the rooms inside of the tavern," Jacob said. "I carried you up here after you ended up drinking too much."

Heat rose to Enyo's cheeks. She had gotten drunk? And in front of Jacob no less? That was just... she couldn't believe she'd done something so... so embarrassing! She couldn't believe she had let her own anxiety lead to her imbibing so much alcohol.

"I-I'm sorry about that," she murmured.

"It's okay." Jacob sat up. "You were nervous, right? I'm sorry for putting you in that position."

Enyo shook her head. "No, it's okay. I know that you were doing that because it's easier to get information that way. I don't mind. In fact, I'm glad I could be of help. It was just..."

"Embarrassing?" Jacob offered when she trailed off.

"Yes," Enyo admitted, and she could feel the blush rising to her cheeks.

"I understand. I was pretty embarrassed myself."

"You were?"

Jacob had acted so confidently when he was talking to those three men that she would have never guessed he was nervous. The way he'd spoken, how he'd stroked her thigh as if she were a lover, and the borderline arrogance in his words as he told the trio his made-up story, it made her believe that he thought nothing of what they'd been doing.

A self-deprecating smile appeared on Jacob's face, barely lit by the sparse trickle of moonlight coming in through the window. "It would be hard not to feel self-conscious in a situation like that."

"I guess."

His words made her relieved. It was good to know that she hadn't been the only one who was nervous. It also let her know that Jacob wasn't experienced with romance, just like her, which was also a relief in its own way.

Enyo's bladder made itself known, and Enyo, feeling her cheeks heat up once more, sought Jacob's attention. "Ah... you don't... know if there's a restroom here, do you?"

"There is," Jacob answered. "If you go out this door, take a left, and then travel down the hall, it'll be the last door on your right."

"Last door on the right. Got it."

Enyo stood up, her legs wobbling slightly. The alcohol might have left her body, but that didn't mean she was in perfect shape. Having never drunk anything until tonight, it was a wonder she got off as lightly as she did.

"Do you want me to stand guard?" Jacob asked.

Her face burning even more at the thought of him standing outside of the door while she did her business, Enyo shook her head. "No, that won't be necessary."

"Okay." Jacob's shoulders relaxed. He must have asked out of a sense of duty. Despite his previous disposition when they first met, he was clearly a young man with a high moral fiber.

Enyo exited the room and walked down the hallway, the floorboards creaking underneath her bare feet. The restroom was indeed where Jacob had told her. After locking the door, she quickly relieved herself before seeking to return to the bedroom that she and

Jacob were sharing. She opened the door leading back into the hall—only to be startled when someone else appeared right in front of her. It was a young man with brown hair and eyes. He was wearing a tunic that looked to have been made from velvet. Likewise, he wore expensive-looking pants, which had golden designs running along it surface. The man stared at her for several seconds, blinking, as if he wasn't sure what to make of her.

"Um," Enyo started, "could you please move out of the way?"

"Huh? Oh, right. My apologies. It seems I'm still half asleep." The man moved out of the way, allowing her to slip past him.

"Thank you," she mumbled as she began making her way down the hall. However, before she could make it even halfway to her room, the knight called out to her.

"Hold on!"

She froze. Footsteps echoed behind her, getting closer. It was the knight. What should she do? Should she run? Fight? Maybe she should play it cool like Jacob had done down in the bar. He might not even know who she was.

Those thoughts were dashed with his next two sentences. "I thought I recognized you. You're the woman from the wanted posters!"

Enyo acted swiftly. She spun around, surprising the man who stumbled back, and then took two steps forward, getting into his guard. He didn't even have time to raise his hands before she struck. The palm of her left hand slammed into the underside of his chin as she thrust it forward. His teeth clacked together as he stumbled back. She then grabbed onto his wrist, pulled him forward, and struck him in the gut with a hard knee.

She stepped back as the man held his arms around his stomach, stumbling around before falling to his knees. His face was green. He looked ready to vomit. Enyo didn't wait for him to recover. She rushed down the hall, entering hers and Jacob's room, slamming the door behind her in her haste.

Jacob jerked up with a start. He must have fallen back asleep.

"What's wrong?"

"Someone recognized me. We need to leave," she said quickly as she searched for her boots.

"Your boots are over there." Jacob pointed to the foot of the bed. Indeed, both her boots and her bodice was there. Her sheaths were too, but those were useless without a pair of daggers.

She didn't bother with the bodice as she pulled on her boots. She also didn't bother to strap on her sheaths. There was no point. Turning to Jacob, she saw that he was already dressed. He'd put on his boots, his chainmail, tunic, and Durandal rested against his back.

"Should we go out the front or use the window?" Jacob wondered out loud.

Shouting came from beyond the door.

"The thief is here! She went into this room!"

"Let's capture her!"

"This might not be our mission, but even so, we can't let her escape!"

She and Jacob looked at each other.

"The window it is," they said before rushing toward the small window.

Enyo reached it first, and she climbed onto the windowsill, judged the distance to the next building over, and then jumped. Cold wind rushed passed her face. Its chill brought tears to her eyes. Her clothes were buffeted from the biting wind. Closer and closer she got to the other building's roof, until she was there, bracing herself.

Her knees jolted with pain as she slammed feet first onto the roof. Enyo knew how to fall, however, and she bent her knees to absorb most of the impact, and then kicked into a forward roll. She was back on her feet soon enough. Turning, she watched as Jacob also leapt out of the window. He was just in time. The man from before appeared seconds after her companion leapt.

"She has a companion!"

"There are two criminals?!"

"Don't let them get away!"

Jacob sailed through the air before landing on the roof, bending his knees only a little before running toward her.

"Let's go!" he shouted.

"Right!" Enyo agreed.

She and Jacob quickly leapt from their current building to the next one. Because the buildings were all spaced closely together, it was easier to bridge the gap. There were a few buildings that were further away, like ones that were separated by a street, but when they ran into that problem, Jacob would scoop Enyo into his arms and leap across the street like it was nothing.

Enyo thought they must have lost their pursuers by now; that was her hope, at least. When the loud roar of a savage beast rent the air and the sound of flapping wings blasted into her ear, she knew that her hope had been crushed.

Three winged creatures were soaring through the sky. Their leather bodies were illuminated by the moon. Sleek muzzles were covered in scales. Horns jutted from either side of their heads and curled back, looking almost demonic. They had four legs, two smaller front legs, and two thick and muscular hind legs. Large pinions spanning nearly two meters kept them aloft, flapping every so often when they descended too far. They were drakes, a type of type of dragon, one of the only kinds that could be tamed.

One of the dragons came up alongside them as they ran, and the man riding it, the same one who'd recognized Enyo, shouted at them. "Halt, you two! Stop running away and face justice, criminals!"

Neither she nor Jacob stopped. Bad enough this idiot thought they actually would do as he said. They continued running, continued jumping from building to building, though she knew they wouldn't be able to keep running for long. The dragons were hot on their trail. The only reason she and Jacob weren't bathing in fire right then was because they were in a city.

"Enyo! Do you have a light spell that can be used to blind them?" Jacob asked.

"Y-yes," Enyo answered.

Already knowing what he wanted, Enyo concentrated on channeling magic into her right hand. She felt a tug on her navel.

Then there was a slight drain of her magic. Her fingers soon lit up in a light glow.

"Lux. Lumin. Luminous!"

Jumping into the air, Enyo twirled around and thrust out her index and middle finger. There was a flash of light. A small sphere shot from her fingertips. It struck the drake in the face and ignited. There was no fire, no blazing heat. What exploded in the drake's face was light, pure and unfiltered, like an exploding star.

A roar shook Enyo's eardrums. The drake jerked as if it had been physically struck. Blinded and enraged, it spiraled out of control, crashing into one of the other drakes and sending them both sailing for the ground.

"Let's get down from the roof!" Jacob shouted.

"I don't see any place to climb down!" Enyo responded.

"Don't worry! Just be sure to hold onto me!"

"Wha—eek!"

Jacob scooped Enyo into his arms and leapt off the building. Enyo felt her stomach rise into her throat as the air whipped around them. The ground got closer. Closer. Closer. Enyo thought they were going to splatter against the ground, but then they landed and Jacob took off without pause.

S-such incredible strength!

She had already witnessed his prowess on the battlefield when he killed that troll, but seeing it again struck his physical strength home. Enyo could now understand how this man had killed her father. His strength alone was impressive.

"Hold on tight!" Jacob told her. "We're going to be moving pretty fast!"

"Faster than we are now?!"

"Yep! Hold on!"

"W-wait! I'm not prepared yyeeeeeeeeaaaaaaahhhhhH!!!!"

The air around them seemed to explode as Jacob suddenly picked up the pace. Enyo felt her cheeks being peeled back as Jacob ran. Her eyes stung as wind slapped her in the face. Everything passed by in blurs and streaks of color. She could make out nothing, and her stomach was rebelling, and she was going to throw up if she kept watching the world pass her by.

Not wanting to see anymore, Enyo buried her face in the crook of Jacob's neck. Oddly enough, this helped a lot. The wind still howled in her ears, her body was chilled by the cool night air hitting her skin, but her eyes no longer stung, and she no longer felt sick, and it was easier to breathe. Jacob's scent also helped settle her nerves. It was an unusually soothing scent—masculine, but not overbearing.

The wind stopped howling. It was such an abrupt change that it took her a moment to realize that Jacob was speaking. His voice sounded like it was coming across from a vast distance—at first.

"I don't think anyone is following us. Can you stand?"

"Yes... I think so," Enyo said.

Jacob set her down. Her legs felt a little weak, but she recovered quickly and looked around. The place they were in now appeared to be at the edge of town. There was a river running through the area, and a sawmill stood several meters away, its large wheel slowly turning with a low groan. Most of the ground was not paved, and grass was growing all over the place. Far from the sawmill, thick trees with twisted branches marked the entrance to the Phantasma Forest.

"Doesn't look like there are any monsters," Jacob said.

"Monsters?" Enyo asked.

"You probably weren't paying attention, but the reason everyone is afraid is because monsters have been coming out of the Phantasma Forest."

Enyo tried not to let her shame show. Even if he was too kind to say it, the reason that she didn't remember anything was because she'd gotten drunk.

"Should we go in?" she asked.

Jacob bit his lip. "I had been hoping to get a map before we entered, but..."

"Hold it right there!" a voice bellowed.

She and Jacob looked up. A drake flew by overhead, and a man leapt from its back and landed gracefully on the ground. This man, clad only in what looked like a nightgown, gripped the broadsword in his left hand tightly enough that Enyo could hear the leather hilt creaking.

"I do not know who you are," he said to Jacob before glaring at Enyo. "But you... I know you, the thief who stole an important treasure that belongs to Queen Alice! I demand that you surrender yourself and return the object you stole!"

Enyo didn't know what to do. She didn't have her weapon, so she couldn't fight, though there was always magic. What's more, she didn't want to kill this person, or anyone really. Her only goal was to leave this world with Jacob. She had no intention of becoming a murderer.

Jacob stepped in front of her, the sound of Durandal leaving its sheath echoing across the mostly silent clearing.

"Sorry," he said in a mockingly apologetic tone. "But the girl and I have no intention of giving you anything, and I have no intention of letting you take her."

Jacob stood still, watching as the paladin shook with rage. The night was dark, but by channeling energy to his eyes, he could easily see the man's reddened face. Not that it was hard anyway. The guy's face could easily outshine the sun.

"You would stand in the way of justice?" the paladin asked as if appalled.

"Justice? There is no justice here," Jacob said. "If there is one thing I've learned from my years of traveling, it is that justice doesn't exist. There are just different people who all have their own idea of justice."

"Don't try to twist this situation with your poisonous words!" The paladin snarled. "That woman stole something important from Queen Alice herself! She committed a crime. Those who disobey the law are criminals who deserve condemnation, and the innocent victims who suffer because of criminals deserve to have their justice carried out."

"Whatever," Jacob muttered. "I'm not going to trade banter with a witless sycophant. If you want the girl, you'll have to go through me."

The paladin's expression hardened. "So be it."

There was no warning when the paladin launched himself into a surprisingly swift sprint, but Jacob didn't need one. He waited until the last second, when the air was whistling as it was cut by the paladin's sword. Then he moved.

Two steps backward. Three steps left. The air howled as it was cut, but Jacob was no longer there. Having sidestepped the attack, he took two more steps in, bringing him past the paladin's guard, where he lashed out with a strike of his own. The paladin was swift to recover, and his sword came up to block the attack, the sound of which echoed across the makeshift battlefield with a resounding *clang!*

Jacob didn't want to become deadlocked. He leapt backward, putting distance between him and the paladin—or trying to. The paladin stayed stuck to him like glue. Jacob deflected several swings of the paladin's blade with Durandal. Each swing was strong enough to jar his bones. This paladin's physical strength was beyond impressive.

Fine, then. Let's see how he does when I use physical augmentation.

Jacob channeled and distributed his energy evenly through his body, regulating its flow so that it constantly cycled through him. Strength enhanced his limbs. Energy empowered him. With his own power strengthening his body, he attacked the paladin with renewed vigor.

Clang!

His first attack slammed into the paladin's blade. The ground cracked underneath his feet, and the paladin was sent skidding across the ground. Jacob followed.

Clang clang clang!

He flowed through more attacks, spinning and striking from different directions. The paladin did his best to guard against each strike. It was for naught. Jacob could tell from the last few clashes. This man, enviously skilled and incredibly strong, had no real combat experience beyond his training. He was a rookie.

Dirt was kicked up as Jacob shuffled across the ground. He avoided several swings, which cut the air with a harsh whistling noise. All of them were fast but predictable. Move left. Swerve right. The paladin swung his blade horizontally, but Jacob raised Durandal and blocked the blow. This time, when their blades met, he was not shaken by the impact.

"Who are you?" the paladin asked with angrily gritted teeth. "Why are you helping that criminal?!"

"Who I am is of no concern to you," Jacob replied calmly. "The same goes for the reason I'm helping her. This is just what I've decided on."

"You bastard!"

The paladin tried to push him back. Jacob let him. He moved backward, pulled his blade away, and, as the paladin stumbled forward, he reinforced his fist with energy and struck the paladin in the chest. A sound akin to clapping thunder rung out. The paladin was lucky that Jacob had accounted for him not wearing armor. Instead of having his ribs cave in, the young man was only sent flying. He hit the ground, tumbled, and then came to a stop several meters away.

Jacob sighed. The battle was—

A glint of light flashed in his eyes. There was a man standing on a roof, clad in darkness, a bow in his hand. The glint came from the notched arrow, which Jacob realized was pointing at Enyo!

"Look out!"

He rushed toward Enyo, his reinforced muscles pushing him further faster. The arrow was let loose. Jacob moved in front of the shocked Enyo and grunted as the arrow pierced his back. He hadn't been given enough time to swat it aside with Durandal or reinforce his back to protect himself.

"Jacob!"

"I'm all right."

Grimacing, Jacob pulled the arrow out. He ignored the pain and the blood gushing from the open wound. That could be healed easily enough. Looking back at the roof revealed that their assailant was gone. They didn't have time to look for him. If they wanted to escape from the knights, they needed to leave before the paladin and his comrades recovered.

"Come on," he continued, tossing the arrow aside. "Let's head into the forest."

"What about the map?" Enyo asked.

He shook his head. "We can no longer afford the luxury of trying to get one. Let's hurry up before the paladin recovers."

Enyo looked unsure, but she didn't argue with him, and they ran into the forest together, racing past the first line of trees and traveling ever deeper. Soon the view of Altus disappeared. All that remained were trees, plants, and the occasional animal.

Sounds assailed them from all sights. Scents assaulted their noses. Jacob used Durandal to hack away at several vines that hung from the branches of trees. Roots jutted from the ground, twisted and gnarled, some decayed as if they'd been infected, poisoned. The smell of rotting bark pervaded the air, making him wrinkle his nose.

Jacob stumbled slightly as he misjudged a step and his foot struck a root. Fortunately, Enyo was there to catch him.

"Thank you," he said.

Enyo smiled. "You're welcome." Her smile turned into a frown. "How's your wound?"

"It'll be fine," he dismissed. "It wasn't very deep. I was reinforcing my body at the time, so it only made it past a few layers of skin."

"Reinforce?" Enyo blinked. "Is that your magic?"

Jacob shook his head. "I can't use magic."

There was a slight pause in their conversation. "… What?"

For the first time since they had met, Jacob grinned. "Surprised? I don't know how to use magic."

"B-but that's… there's no way! I saw you using magic when we fought the trolls!"

"That wasn't magic." Shaking his head, Jacob began to explain the basics of his power. "It's called Linked Energy Manipulation. What it does is allow me to manipulate the energy within my own body and the energy of others to various effects. For example, I can strengthen my body up to fifty times its normal strength, or I can boost my speed by enhancing the muscles in my legs. Those are basic examples of internal manipulation. I can also externalize my energy, such as when I used it to sharpen Durandal's blade."

"It makes me tingly every time he does that," Durandal added.

Jacob rolled his eyes. "So, yeah. What I did wasn't magic."

"That's incredible!" Enyo sounded genuinely impressed. "I was once told about Linked Energy Manipulation by my maid. She said that it was an ancient power thought to have been lost to the ages. She'd be really surprised to find out that there's someone alive who still knows it."

"I sort of stumbled upon it myself," Jacob admitted. "It was listed in one of the books that I read in Avant Heim. I had gone there after discovering that I had no aptitude for magic. The book didn't say much, so I had to work out how to use energy manipulation for myself. It was a lot of trial and error, but I'm pleased to say that I'm quite proud of my progress."

"Hm!" Enyo nodded. "It's really impressive!"

"Thank you!"

Jacob hadn't realized how good it felt to receive praise from someone else. He'd spent so much time alone, or with campions who preferred sniping at each other, that he'd never been praised by anyone but people who were looking to use him. It was so refreshing to have someone like Enyo complimenting him. It actually made him feel proud of himself.

They had traveled much deeper into the forest. Jacob didn't know how far they'd gone, but he could see nothing except trees in all directions. The air had become muggy. Sweat accumulated on his skin. He wiped it off, but more appeared along his forehead and neck. His clothes were beginning to stick to him.

"Why is it so hot?" he wondered out loud.

"But it isn't," Enyo said.

"What?"

"It's actually quite cold."

Jacob turned around. Now that he was looking at her, she did seem cold. Her skin had broken out into goosebumps, and she was shivering. She was cold. Why was she cold? It was stifling in this forest! It was...

"Oh..."

The world became blurred, a mass of coagulating colors that turned grainy and unfocused. Jacob stumbled forward. His foot caught another root. He tripped.

"Jacob!"

A pair of arms wrapped around his waist. A refreshingly cool body pressed against him, though the person grabbing him couldn't hold his weight and sagged underneath him. Enyo's scent, which reminded him of anima blossoms—a rare flower that only grew on Mount Vita—filled his nose.

"Jacob! Jacob, are you all right? Answer me!"

Jacob opened his mouth to answer her, but the words would not come, or rather, they could not come. His tongue had become too swollen for him to speak. Likewise, his mind was slowly slipping into darkness. It took him a moment, but he quickly realized why.

That arrow...

Yes, it had to be the arrow that had pierced his back. Surely, there couldn't have been any other reason. It was clear to him what had happened.

He had been poisoned.

✳✳✳

It took everything Enyo had not to panic. Jacob was unresponsive, seemingly unconscious, but she couldn't figure out from what. His labored breathing rasped in her ear. His clothing was so covered in sweat that her clothes were beginning to get wet. She didn't know what was happening. However, she knew that she needed to get him somewhere safe.

Having been trained in combat from a young age, Enyo was quite strong. Her leg muscles flexed as she half-carried, half-dragged Jacob through the forest. Whistles and hollers and howls of strange animals filled the air. She tried her best to ignore them. They weren't important. Getting Jacob somewhere safe, somewhere where she could check him for injuries, that was all that mattered.

"Hey!" Durandal cried out. "What's going on? What happened to my partner?!"

"I don't know!" Enyo said. "I have no idea!"

"Damn it, Partner! If you die on me, who am I going to tell my dirty jokes to?!"

Enyo had long since lost track of where she was going. Everything looked the same. The trees, the plants, the ground. Even though she'd been walking in a straight line, she reached a point that she could've sworn she had already past half an hour ago. It was like the forest was playing tricks on her.

A strange growl to her left made Enyo's head snap in that direction. Yellow eyes peered at her from between the trees. Multiple eyes.

A tongue darted out from within the corpse. Enyo yelped as she stumbled back, dropping Jacob, who grunted but didn't otherwise move. The tongue flew over her head, smacking into a tree before retracting.

"What... what is—"

"It's a toad demon!" Durandal said. "They use their tongues to snag their prey and eat them. They'll eat just about anything, too, including people. Careful. Their tongues secrete a powerful poison that paralyzes their victims!"

That was good to know.

Enyo scrambled to her feet, and then jumped to the left as another tongue shot out, striking the ground before pulling back in the blink of an eye. Another tongue came from another direction. Enyo swerved along the ground to avoid it. The air whistled past her ear. Then another came from behind her. It was another tongue, which struck the tree to her left.

There's more than one toad demon...

This wasn't good, not one bit. They must have surrounded her and Jacob, creating an encirclement from which she couldn't escape —not that she intended to. She wouldn't leave without Jacob.

What she wouldn't give for a weapon. Damn her lack of foresight. She should have known that channeling dark magic through plain daggers would be detrimental to the daggers. If she had something that she could fight with, then...

Durandal!

More tongues shot out from the darkness. Enyo ducked and rolled along the ground, right next to Durandal, which she picked up —tried to pick up. She dropped him as pain shot through her fingers. It was a burning sensation that made her feel like her hands had been dipped in acid.

"Sorry, Enyo, but only my partner can use me," Durandal explained. "That's what it means to be a sentient blade."

"I wish you would have told me that sooner!"

Enyo gritted her teeth as she jumped to her feet, shunting the pain aside as she focused on the matter at hand. More tongues shot at her from all directions. She could tell where her opponents were by the yellow of their eyes. It was troublesome, but she needed to use magic to deal with these monsters.

"Ustulo. Uro. Torro."

A dark flame gathered on the palm of her hand. It didn't burn, and she clenched her hand into a fist as she fed the flame with her magic. The flame burned brighter. It was a dichotomy. The flame was pure black, but she cared not for such things.

She dodged the tongues that shot at her from all directions. Left. Right. Back. Spin. She lashed out with a chopping motion at the tongue nearest her, slicing through it with ease. The two separated halves then caught fire, and that fire quickly raced up the fleshy appendage, incinerating everything until it struck the toad demon. Loud squealing erupted from the beast as it was lit on fire. It hopped in her general direction in a mad panic.

Enyo took a deep breath.

"Sepio. Preatego. Contego."

A barrier of pure white sprung up around her, repelling the frog as it crashed into the dome. It flopped over onto its back. Black flames were still consuming it, though it didn't last much longer. Seconds later, the toad demon disappeared, turning to ash and dust.

Enyo breathed heavily as she glared into the darkness. She waited for the other demons to attack, but it didn't happen; no attack was forthcoming. One by one, the yellow eyes disappeared, and she was eventually left alone, in a clearing, with an injured and passed out Jacob lying on the ground.

"Jacob!"

Remembering her companion, Enyo rushed over to Jacob. He was lying on his back. His eyes were closed and his breathing was still heavy, though he seemed a little better than before.

"Durandal, how is he?" she asked.

"No change."

"Do you know what's wrong with him?"

"I'm guessing he was poisoned by that arrow," Durandal surmised.

Poison...

Enyo rolled Jacob onto his back and searched for the arrow wound. She found it, though the wound was surprisingly small, no larger than a small nick on his skin. If an arrow had pierced him, it should have been larger.

Is it because of his Linked Energy Manipulation?

She'd heard from her maid that Linked Energy Manipulation could be used to harden the body, acting in a manner similar to armor. He'd probably been hardening his skin. However, Linked Energy Manipulation took a lot of concentration, and his had likely slipped when he saw the person fire an arrow at her.

The poison must still be in his body. I need to suck it out.

Sucking out poison was generally impossible because it would have already flowed through his bloodstream. However, Enyo had light magic, which specialized in healing and defense. She could use it to suck out the poison, though there was no cure for it unless she had a poison magic type.

Enyo leaned down and pressed her lips against his skin. The coppery and salty taste of sweat mixed with blood nearly made her gag, but she shoved aside her discomfort, channeled light magic through her mouth, and began sucking the poison out.

Blood filled her mouth. It tasted acrid. That must have been the poison. She quickly spat the blood out, and then leaned back down and sucked more of it out.

"H-hey," Jacob murmured. "T-that tickles…"

Enyo spit what she had out of her mouth and crawled over until she was by his head. "Jacob! You're awake!"

Staring up through half-lidded eyes, Jacob presented her with a sleepy smile. "I've been awake the whole time. I just couldn't talk because getting rid of the poison required all of my attention." The smile evaporated as he grimaced. "I'm so out of practice. Had this been three years ago, that poison would have been expelled from my body seconds before it could take effect. Hell, I wouldn't have even let myself be poisoned like that."

Enyo felt a relieved smile tug at her lips. She didn't know what should have done if Jacob died.

"If you can complain, then you must be fine."

"Mm. By the way, where are we?"

"In the Phantasma Forest."

Jacob glared. "Let me rephrase that. I meant: do you know where we are in the Phantasma Forest?"

"I barely even know where we're going."

"In other words, we're lost," Durandal added.

Jacob sighed. "That's great. It's going to take forever just to find out way out, never mind locating the gate key."

Enyo winced. "Sorry."

"It's not your fault. We didn't have a whole lot of options. I'm just frustrated." Jacob's brows furrowed. "I hate being this weak."

To strong people like Jacob, being in a weakened state must have been a terrible experience. The strong were not used to being weak. That feeling left them helpless. Enyo wasn't sure if she would call herself strong, but she understood where he was coming from.

"What should we do?" she asked.

"We should find shelter," Jacob said. "There's no telling when those toad demons will return. If we can find shelter, then we can at least limit the chances of an ambush. A cave would be best, but even if we just find an overhang created by the trees, we can make do. Can you help me walk? My legs are still a little weak."

"Yes, I'd be happy to help you."

"Thanks."

Enyo grabbed Jacob's arm and helped him stand. His legs shook something fierce, wobbling and buckling, so she was doing most of the work. However, it was much better than before. As they stood up, he leaned on her, and she wrapped an arm around his waist, holding him close so they could walk off together.

They only forgot about one thing.

"Hey! Hey!" Durandal shouted from his place on the ground. "Don't leave me behind! Come back!"

✳✳✳

Jacob and Enyo were able to find a solid place to rest for the night, a small cave that must have belonged to some monster long ago. It had been abandoned. The remains of egg shells lay scattered around.

That night had been cold. The chill of the forest had seeped into their bones, but they didn't have anything that they could use to keep warm—except for each other. It had been embarrassing, but Jacob and Enyo had snuggled together to keep warm. It had helped, though only a little. The coldness didn't seem to be one of a physical nature. It reminded Jacob of the coldness of the dead.

When morning came, Jacob caught them a pair of rabbits that they could cook, and Enyo found some edible herbs. They needed to be separated because some had been poisonous. However, afterward, Jacob cooked them breakfast before they set off.

"Is it just me, or is it getting colder?" asked Enyo, who'd crossed her arms as if doing so would help her keep warm. She shivered. Goosebumps were already breaking out on her skin.

"It's not just you." Jacob narrowed his eyes. He observed the goosebumps on his arms before regulating his energy to warm up his body. "It's definitely getting colder."

Enyo shivered again. "Why is it so cold? It's the middle of spring!"

"It's the Curse of the Dead," Durandal answered.

"I think I've heard of that somewhere before…"

"The Curse of the Dead is the reason that souls with strong emotional attachments can't cross over," Durandal explained. "When a soul feels intense negative emotions, like hatred and jealousy, for example, they become attached to this plane of existence. This turns them into ghouls, lost souls that attack the living."

"Ghouls are made of ectoplasm," Jacob continued where Durandal left off. "Ectoplasm is cold to the touch because spirits lack the warmth of flesh and blood. If enough ghouls gather in one place, I imagine it would be quite cold."

Enyo was sharp. She seemed to realize what this meant barely a second after his explanation. "Then does that mean we're near Kyöpelinvuori?"

"Yep." Jacob looked back to grin at her, though it was darker than his usual ones. "Welcome to Kyöpelinvuori, home of so many ghouls that it feels like a winter wonderland."

A thick mist had enveloped the forest. White vapor seemed to waft off the ground, making it impossible to see more than a few meters in any direction. The mist was cold, bone-chilling even. Enyo couldn't be positive, it may have been hallucinations, but she could've sworn that several hands were appearing from within the mist, attempting to grab them.

She grabbed Jacob's hand.

"Scared?"

"N-no..." she bluffed. Jacob could see the way her eyes shifted. Her pupils were also dilated. "I-it's not like I'm afraid of ghosts or anything. I just... don't like them."

Jacob couldn't figure out why, but seeing Enyo acting scared while trying to deny that she was, in fact, frightened, was somehow cute. Freya had been fearless. Not cute at all. Enyo was strong, maybe as strong as Freya, but she displayed a side that was... he didn't know how to describe it... vulnerable? Yes, that was probably it. She could be strong and amazing one minute, fighting off trolls like they were nothing with a grin on her face, and then the next moment she was vulnerable and open, gripping his hand because she was scared of ghosts.

It was strangely endearing.

The mist cleared slightly as they left the forest, or at least part of the forest. Kyöpelinvuori was a ravine located within the Phantasma Forest. It extended for miles on either side of the forest, cutting it in half. There were no bridges leading to the other side as no one had ever built them, or, if they had, the bridges had long since been destroyed.

"This is Kyöpelinvuori?" Enyo asked, staring at the massive chasm in shock.

"I guess so." Jacob wandered over to the edge and looked down. He couldn't see the bottom, which covered in a thick layer of mist. "I can't imagine this being anything else."

Enyo also came up to the ledge and looked down, but she couldn't seem to deal with the heights and backed up again. Her face was a little green.

"That's... really deep."

"You're telling me." Jacob looked away and wandered back over to Enyo.

"F-for some reason, I don't remember it being this deep," she mumbled, breathless as if she'd been running without rest.

"You might have been at one of the places where the ravine isn't as deep."

"Maybe..."

"Ya know, seeing this place... I think I remember coming here before," Durandal said.

Jacob and Enyo peered at the sword.

"Really?" asked Jacob.

"Really," Durandal said seriously. "It was a really long time ago with a previous partner. I can't remember that partner's name, though..."

Durandal was an old sword, having been created during what was considered the first century, the founding of Terrasole. The blacksmith who'd created him had been a legendary figure. He'd also been a dirty old man, according to the sword. The first century had been around 2,700 years ago. Being that old, it didn't surprise Jacob that Durandal couldn't remember all of its partners.

"Do you remember what happened to that partner?" asked a curious Enyo.

"Oh, he died!" Durandal replied cheerfully. "I think he was killed by ghouls."

Enyo paled while Jacob gave his sword a dry look. "Gee, thanks. I really wanted to know that."

"You're welcome. Oh! Hey! Speaking of the past, I just remembered a good joke."

"I don't want to hear it," Jacob murmured.

After he and Enyo consulted with each other for a bit, they decided to follow the ravine, to see if there might have been a place where it wasn't as deep. If they could find that place, Enyo said that she was confident about her chances of rediscovering where she'd hidden the gate key.

Unfortunately, no matter how far they traveled, the ravine didn't seem to become any shallower. It remained an unfathomably deep chasm. Even after walking for hours, even after the sun had set, Jacob still couldn't see the bottom.

"Let's stop for the day," Jacob said.

Enyo agreed. "I don't think we'll be able to do much more anyway. It's getting so dark out, we won't be able to see soon."

Jacob nodded. "We'd probably fall into the ravine or something."

They decided to find a place to sleep, and then they would gather some food. Moving away from the ravine, because they didn't want to chance accidentally rolling in or something while they slept, the two—plus one sword—traveled back into the thicker parts of the Phantasma Forest.

The mist became thicker. Jacob wondered why it was becoming heavier the further they wandered from Kyöpelinvuori. This mist clearly wasn't natural. It had a dark feel to it, emotions like hatred and envy clung to the mist like a plague, or maybe the mist merely enhanced the feelings of others. He couldn't tell. What he could tell was that this mist had magic infused into it.

"This mist is really strange," Enyo murmured as she gripped his hand. "I can feel the magic flowing through it, and I don't remember it being here when I passed through last time."

"Hmm…"

"Jacob?"

"Sorry, I was just thinking…"

"About?"

"Well…" Jacob needed a moment to put his thoughts into words. "I was wondering if this mist might have been the result of the gate key? Do you know if the key holds any kind of magic?"

Enyo shook her head. "Not that I know of. I just thought it opened the otherworld gate."

"If it can open a portal to my world, then it must have some kind of power," Jacob pressed. "Maybe that power is manifesting here, though I can't imagine why."

"It might have been a mistake for me to leave it here."

Jacob didn't want to say it, but he agreed with her about it being a mistake. Of course it had been a bad idea. He understood that she'd hidden it in the event of capture, but she could have at least chosen a location that was easier to find. Enyo couldn't even find it now, and she was the one who'd hidden it.

They eventually happened upon a small clearing surrounded by boulders, which jutted from the ground like stakes set to spear the sky. Jacob frowned. Those boulders were larger even than the trees. Their formation also struck him as odd. If he didn't know any better, he would have said that they had been purposefully placed there.

"I'll gather some wood for a fire and hunt for something to eat," Jacob said. "Think you could find some circular stones to build a fireplace?"

Enyo looked around at the pebbles littering the ground, all of which were about the size of her fist, and then she looked at him, her lips quirking slightly. "I think I can find some."

"Right."

Chuckling, Jacob headed further into the forest. He marked his path by slicing gouges into trees. He wanted to be able to find his way back, but unless he had a means of tracing his steps, he'd easily get lost within this vast forest.

Firewood was easy enough to find. There were twigs scattered everywhere, and the dry grass that crunched underneath his feet would make excellent kindling. Catching their dinner was something else altogether. Most of the animals within the Phantasma Forest were poisonous. Those that weren't often hid. It took almost half an hour of searching to find and kill a single rabbit.

"This isn't gonna be much of a dinner," Jacob complained.

"You could always find another rabbit," Durandal said.

"And how long is that going to take?"

"…"

"My point exactly."

He sighed and began making his way back to Enyo. As he was returning, a loud screamed filled the air. It was Enyo!

"Hurry up, Partner!"

Jacob didn't reply to Durandal. He was already racing through the trees. He passed the slashes that he had made, burst into the clearing, and found Enyo doing her best to dodge a horde of flying tongues.

She had been surrounded by toad demons—four of them.

They were hideous creatures with different colored skin; some had green skin, some blue, red, and even orange. Their skin was leathery and rough. Large webbed hands and feet made indents on the ground as they hopped around. The toad demons would open their mouths wide, revealing a gaping maw as they launched their tongues at Enyo, who was doing her best to dodge.

"Enyo! Give me a light!"

Jacob didn't know if she would know what he meant, but Enyo quickly muttered an incantation under her breath. Light emitted from her fingertips. She thrust her hand into the air, shooting a sphere above her head that ignited like a newborn star.

Having already closed his eyes, Jacob wasn't as affected by the light. He saw the flash behind his eyelids. Nothing more.

The toad demons croaked as they were blinded. Jacob raced forward, using his foreknowledge of the layout and the demons' pained cries to guide him. He reached the first one and slashed it as he passed. There was a moment's resistance as Durandal met hardened leather, and then he tore through it like cutting a leaf. The toad's death croak was followed by the meaty thud of it hitting the ground.

Opening his eyes, Jacob went after the next toad, which had no time to do anything before he was on it. He leapt over the creature. As he did, he rotated and flipped around. He lashed out with his blade, tearing through the demon's neck, severing its head from its shoulders in a gout of blood that sprayed the ground. Then he was on his feet and heading for the next one.

There were only two more, and it appeared they had decided to run. Jacob growled. Not on his watch!

"Get ready to fly, Durandal!"

"What?" Durandal asked seconds before Jacob threw the sword at the furthest toad. "You know I hate it when you throw meeeeee!!!!!"

Durandal's cry was overpowered by the agonized death croak of the toad demon, who the sword had blasted through like a cannonball. A massive gaping hole had been blown in the toad's back. Jacob could see trees on the other side.

The last toad was killed, not by Jacob, but by Enyo. Having recovered from her surprise of being ambushed, Enyo muttered a quick incantation underneath her breath.

"Ustulo. Uro. Torro."

Black flames leapt from her hand and struck the toad's back. The creature roared. It hopped around frantically as if seeking to put the fire out. But this fire couldn't be extinguished in such a manner, and soon the toad was flopping onto its back, twitching spastically as the flames consumed it until there was nothing left.

Jacob nodded. "That's some really impressive magic. I'm surprised you can use such a strong magic attack with only three words."

Spells required incantations to use; these incantations invoked the powers of a person's magic, essentially telling their magic what to do. It was different from Magic Channeling, which was simply a person channeling their magic through a weapon.

Smiling, Enyo said, "Don't forget that my father was the former Dark Lord. I might not seem like it, but I was born with incredibly strong magic."

"I'll bet."

Enyo's dark magic reminded him a little too much of Alucard's. Her power, her abilities. Yes, she could use light magic, and Alucard had been a pure dark magic user, but the strength of Enyo's dark magic was reminiscent to her father's.

Granted, Enyo had a *long* way to go before she could come close to matching her father. Alucard had been capable of demolishing entire buildings with a single-word incantation. He had annihilated his own castle with naught but a few words. The battle between him and Alucard had destroyed the entire city of Skoteiní Gi, turning the once massive capital into a smoking crater. Alucard's powers had been on an unimaginable scale. That said, Enyo might not have her father's power yet, but the power that she did have was frightening.

"Anyway, I wonder where these demon toads are coming from," Jacob said.

Enyo frowned. "Me too. They weren't here the last time I came by."

"This fog wasn't here either, right? Think the two might be related?"

"Maybe…"

"It's a strong possibility," Durandal added. "I don't know about you two, but I've been sensing a strong magic for a while now."

Jacob and Enyo stopped talking to stare at the sword.

"And you're just now telling us this?" Jacob asked.

"It never came up in conversation—owch!"

"I hate clichéd lines like that." Jacob placed Durandal back in its sheath after properly slamming the flat of the blade against a boulder. "In either event, we should see if there are any more toad demons out there. I don't want either of us to be ambushed like this again."

"Me neither," Enyo said.

The toad demons had left tracks of where they had come from. Their footprints, large and webbed, had created a series of indents on the ground that were easy to follow. Sometimes the tracks branched off, but they always congregated again. He and Enyo eventually reached the ravine. More than that, they reached what appeared to be a path leading into the ravine.

"Do you think we should go down there?" Enyo asked.

"I think… we might not have much of a choice," Jacob said.

"Why not?"

"Look behind us."

Enyo did as instructed, turning around and looking behind them. She paled quite rapidly. The reason was, of course, because of the several dozen toad demons croaking at their backs.

She looked at Jacob, who stared back at her.

"Run?" she asked.

"Run." Jacob nodded.

With nary a thought, she and Jacob raced down the path that led into the ravine, several dozen toad demons releasing shrill croaks as they gave chase.

***

Jacob and Enyo rushed down the path, a horde of demon toads croaking at their heels. The pathway was of a decent size, wide enough that at least four or five people could stand shoulder to shoulder, which explained why the demon toads could hop down. They were only about three people wide.

"What should do?" asked Enyo as they ran.

"Hold on. Let me think for a moment."

Jacob studied the layout of the path that they were running down. It looped a lot. They travel down in one direction, and then it would curve, turning a full 180 degrees before moving down again. This created a series of walls.

If I could start a rockslide, I might be able to... but then we wouldn't be able to climb back out, would we?

"Let's keep going down," he suggested. "There might be a place where we can funnel them in and take them one at a time."

There was no telling how long they ran, or how far they had run, for time and distance seemed meaningless. He and Enyo raced down the path. They skidded along the turns, ran some more, only to skid for those abrupt turns again. The horde of toad demons followed them. Their croaking rang in Jacob's ears.

"I'm really... beginning to... regret... leaving the gate key... here..." Enyo gasped, sweat pouring from her forehead as she breathed in heavily through her nose.

"So am I," Jacob said.

They reached the bottom sooner than Jacob had expected. He guessed the fog had skewed his sense of perception. Unlike the top, the bottom was not covered in forest, but in rocky outcroppings that were devoid of life. There didn't seem to be a single plant in sight.

Croaking behind him reminded Jacob that they still needed to deal with the toad demons, and unfortunately, there didn't seem to be anything here that they could use.

I guess that means I'll be using more power than I wanted to.

"Enyo," he said, getting the girl's attention. "I want you to cover me. When you see an opening, light those toad demons on fire with some dark magic."

Her expression hardening into one of determination, Enyo nodded, a fire lit behind her eyes. "You can count on me."

"Thanks."

Jacob turned toward the toad demons as he pulled Durandal from its sheath, his vision sharpening as he narrowed his eyes. Power flooded through his body. Using his unique talent for Linked Energy Manipulation, he allowed for an evenly distributed flow of energy, enhancing his muscles as much as he dared.

Had this been three years ago, I would have been able to enhance them more. I'm so out of shape.

Well, there was nothing for it. He'd just have to make do.

"You ready, Durandal?"

"Of course I am! What sort of sword do you take me for?"

"The dirty kind."

"How cruel, Partner!"

"Here we go!"

Jacob leapt at the first toad demon, attacking before his foes had a chance to attack first. Initiative would be the key to victory here.

His first attack, a powerful hacking motion, sliced straight through the toad, cutting it down the middle. The acrid scent of toad's blood filled the air as dark crimson sprayed out of the bisected creature. As the two halves fell apart, Jacob leapt back. The blood of toad demons was toxic. Smelling it caused lightheadedness, and letting it touch bare skin would cause flesh to blister and burn.

Behind him, Enyo chanted a spell.

"Umbra. Premo. Religo. Nox!"

Several magic circles appeared on the ground underneath the four toad demons closest to him. Ancient scripts written in an arcane language formed letters and words within the circles. As the circles began to glow with a dark purple light, thick bindings of the purest black shot out, wrapping around the toads and tying them to the ground.

The toad demons struggled to free themselves, but the bindings appeared to have been made from the same flames that Enyo had used to light the previous toad demons on fire. It wasn't long before they had turned into a pile of ash.

What a frightening spell. It's hard to believe such a kind girl knows it.

Then again, it was hard to believe that Enyo was the daughter of the previous Dark Lord.

Not one to be outdone, Jacob channeled his energy into Durandal, which began to glow a light blue. With a ferocious cry, he swung the blade forward and unleashed the energy. A massive crescent shot from the sword. It sliced into six toad demons, cutting their legs and severing their lower half from their upper half. Blood splattered along the ground, staining the craggy surface, which hissed and spat as the acidic properties of the toad blood ate into it.

Coughing as steam rose from the now burning ground, Jacob backed up. "Let's move further in. We can't afford to let those fumes affect us."

"Right." Enyo agreed. "I'll cover our retreat."

Enyo launched more dark flames at the toad demons that tried to chase them. However, they seem to have learned from past experience, or maybe these particular demons were just more cautious. They leapt out of the way, the flames moving past them to splash against the cliff face. Still, even if the magic didn't hit, it gave him and Enyo the time they needed to make a tactical withdrawal.

The ravine was a lot like a maze. Rather than just a single straightaway, there appeared to be naturally made walls that branched off into sections. He and Enyo went down one of these paths. Sadly, the path they had chosen led to a dead end.

"It looks like we have no choice but to fight," Enyo said. For some reason, Jacob thought she sounded a little too excited. The smile on her face wasn't helping change his opinion.

"I knew that we would. Still, I had been hoping to continue using guerilla tactics to wittle away at the toad demons. Now we'll have to defeat all of them at the same time if we want to survive."

They had killed a dozen of those toad demons, but there were still about two dozen more to go. Jacob had an attack that could have killed them all. The problem was that it was too powerful. If he used this attack here, he might end up destroying the ravine. Also, and though he was loathe to admit it, he didn't even know if he could pull the attack off anymore. He was too out of shape.

"Here they come!" Enyo warned him.

Jacob turned around to see that, indeed, the horde of toad demons was coming. They hopped toward him and Enyo. Bulging yellow eyes glared at them with a hungry leer, like they were apex predators and he and Enyo were the prey.

Sweat gathered on Jacob's forehead. The demon toads were coming closer. Beside him, Enyo looked nervous but oddly excited. Her eyes glimmered a phosphorescent glow, as if she was actually looking forward to the coming battle.

They almost upon him and Enyo now. Ten meters. Five. Jacob clutched Durandal tightly in his hand as he prepared to fight harder than he had in the past two years. Two meters. He crouched down, spreading his feet as he prepared to attack. One meter. Jacob—

"Ignis. Fulmen. Fulgur. Lámpsi. Astrapi!" a cry echoed through the ravine.

A bolt of lightning descended from the sky, striking the toad demon closest to him, lighting it up like a series of fireworks. As the toad demon was fried from the inside out, the lightning leapt to another demon, and then another, and another. Before long, all two dozen demons were being fried by a single bolt of lightning that linked to each demon like a chain. They twitched and spasmed. Their eyes exploded as if they'd overheated. The scent of charred flesh pervaded the air, filling Jacob's nostrils and making him gag. Then the toad demons all died, dropping one at a time as their insides were destroyed.

"What the...?" Enyo looked as shocked as he felt. Neither of them had cast that spell.

"Are you two alright?" a voice asked from above them.

Looking up, he and Enyo spotted an old woman wearing a black cloak. Graying hair stuck out in all directions as if she'd been hit by a static shock. Her face, lined with age, had a wizened appearance. Crows' feet around her eyes and lines along her mouth made him think that she spent an awful lot of time smiling.

"We're fine!" Jacob called back. "Are you the one who saved us?"

"I am glad to hear that," the woman said. "Why don't you two follow me? If you linger here, more toad demons will come."

She ignored my question...

"I guess... it would probably be a good idea to follow her," Jacob murmured. "What do you think, Enyo...?" He trailed off when he got a look at the pout on his companion's face. "Is something wrong?"

"No, nothing's wrong." Enyo huffed. "Come on. Let's follow that woman and see what she wants."

Is she upset that she didn't get to fight those toad demons?

Jacob followed Enyo, who followed the woman, who had hopped down to their level and was walking several meters ahead. She walked with a cane, and she was slow. He and Enyo caught up to her in no time and walked alongside her.

"I was quite surprised to find two people wandering around in my ravine," the woman said in a light-hearted tone. "Even more so when I realized you were being chased by a bunch of toad demons. What did you two do to make them so angry?"

"I couldn't tell you." Jacob shrugged. "Far as I'm aware, they attacked first."

"Is that so?" The woman hummed. "Toad demons are quite cowardly. They don't often attack unless given no other choice. Maybe something else spooked them."

"Maybe…"

"Do you mind if I ask for your name?" Enyo interrupted.

"My name?" The woman looked at her askance. "It has been ages since I've gone by a name, so long even that I cannot remember what my original name was. If you have to call me something, then I guess Agatha will do for now."

"Agatha…" Enyo frowned. Jacob would have wondered what that was about, but they soon came upon the mouth of a massive cave.

"Come along, you two." Agatha gestured for them to follow her. "Let's keep going before more toad demons show up."

They followed Agatha into the cave, blinking as darkness engulfed them. No light seemed to reach this place. They couldn't even see their own hands. Fortunately, Agatha produced a light from the tip of her cane, which pushed the darkness back.

The cave was larger than Jacob expected it to be. He couldn't determine its size, but there were numerous stalagmites jutting from the floor, and there were stalactites hanging from the ceiling, some of which were nearly twice his size.

Agatha walked ahead again, guiding their path with her light, which Jacob realized was a ball of compressed lightning. She must have been a lightning type magic user. They eventually reached a dirty wooden door that was barely attached to a set of hinges. Agatha walked through the door. He and Enyo followed.

It was a small room, though that may have had something to do with the clutter. A lot of knick-knacks lay scattered around. Books were strewn across the ground, several stools lay on their side, there was a rickety old desk with parchment and quills on it, a bookshelf sat against one wall, and an ancient bead with a threadbare blanket rested in a corner. There was a door on the opposite side that they had entered.

"I apologize for the mess," Agatha said. "I don't usually clean it anymore since I'm the only one who lives here."

"It's fine," Jacob said. "Enyo and I aren't bothered by a little mess. Right, Enyo?"

"I guess," Enyo mumbled.

"I don't care about messes either," Durandal burst out.

Agatha blinked. "Did that sword just talk?"

Sighing, Jacob smacked Durandal's hilt, eliciting a yelp. "Please ignore the talking sword. Acknowledging its existence only empowers it."

"That's a rude thing to say to the weapon who's always saving your ass," Durandal rebutted.

"You say rude things all the time. We're even."

Taking a seat on a chair near the desk, Agatha smiled as she observed him and Durandal. "Talking swords are quite rare. I've only ever heard of them in legends. I never expected to see a sword that had gained the Sentience of Steel."

Sentience of Steel was the term used for a sword that had gained awareness. There were legends of other swords aside from Durandal that had become sentient: the legend of Ascalon, the tale of Caliburn, and the story of the Kusanagi-no-Tsurugi. Jacob had never come across those swords during his journey, but he'd certainly heard numerous stories surrounding them.

"They're rare because I'm one of a kind," Durandal boasted.

Agatha seemed amused by the sword's arrogant posturing. "Is that so?"

"Oh, yes. You won't find another blade like me. My creator poured his heart and soul into my creation. I was sentient the moment I was created. Even if other swords have gained the Sentience of Steel, they wouldn't be half as amazing as I am."

It was always amusing to see how arrogant Durandal could be. The sword had no proof of its claims, no evidence to suggest that it was right, but it still spoke with the utmost confidence.

"Oh, my," Agatha said. "You must be quite special, then."

"Damn right I am!"

"What are you doing living in a place like this?" Enyo asked suddenly.

"I guess it's because the dead gather here," Agatha admitted.

"Fweh?" Jacob was dumbstruck. "Then there really are ghouls in this ravine?"

"Oh, yes, though they are only deep within the caverns beneath the ravine. They don't come up to the surface often." Agatha hummed to herself. "I lost my husband many decades ago. With nothing left to tie me down, I did a lot of traveling. During that time, I heard rumors of a ravine located deep within a forest, which was said to be a place where the dead gathered. I wanted to be closer to my husband, so I traveled here in the hopes of finding his spirit."

"Oh…" Enyo looked away. Her left hand came up and grabbed the elbow of her right arm in a self-conscious gesture. "I'm sorry."

Agatha's smile reminded Jacob of a doting grandmother. "It is fine, dear. There's nothing wrong with being curious. Truth be told, I am quite pleased to be able to speak with the living once more."

It was getting late, and neither he nor Enyo had eaten anything. Agatha, fortunately, recognized the sound of their stomach growling for what it was. She made them dinner, a basic soup with some bread, before they all laid down to get some sleep.

Lying on his back, Jacob noticed Enyo out of the corner of his eye. Like him, she was still awake. She lay on her side, the sensual curvature of her hips drawing his gaze along the seductive lines of her figure. He frowned. Then he shook the thought off.

"Hey, Enyo? Are you bothered by how Agatha killed those toad demons before you could?" he asked in a whisper so as not to wake Agatha.

Enyo jolted as if she'd been shocked. "W-what makes you say that?"

"It's just… when we were trapped and preparing to fight to the death, you were smiling." Enyo said nothing, leading Jacob to continue. "Was it… battle lust?"

One of the reasons dark clansmen were reviled was due to their battle lust--the excitement and pleasure that they derived from mortal combat. Jacob didn't know if it was something intrinsically tied into their psyche. However, he had yet to meet a member of the Dark Clan who didn't become riled up when they were fighting.

"I-I'm sorry," Enyo murmured. "I try not to let it control me, but sometimes…"

"It's hard to fight against natural instincts," he finished. "I understand."

"I don't like that side of me," Enyo admitted. "However, when I'm in danger and the odds are stacked against me, I get really excited. Whenever there's a possibility of me dying, my heart races, my blood won't stop boiling, and I can't help but smile. I guess… that's the curse of being born to the Dark Clan."

Jacob remained silent for a time. He thought carefully about his words, about what he should say to make her feel better.

"You know, I remember someone else calling the Dark Clan's battle lust a curse, too," he started. "It was during my journey through the darklands. I had been injured and was found by a group of Dark Clan members who'd forsaken Alucard's rule. They had decided that they didn't want to fight in a war they didn't believe in. Their chieftain had said that their dream was to peacefully coexist with humans."

Memories came to him, appearing before his eyes like zephyrs floating on a breeze.

"The village they lived in was mixed with humans and dark clansmen. Seeing that place, speaking with its chieftain, it made me realize something important."

"What's that?" asked Enyo.

Turning on his side, Jacob smiled at his companion. "That humans and dark clansmen aren't as different as some people might try to make us believe."

Enyo stared at him in stunned silence, her eyes wide, though it only lasted for a second before her face lit up in a smile. Her cheeks also turned a surprising shade of pink. The glimmer of her pink eyes, visible even in the darkness, sucked him in and refused to let go.

"Thank you," she said. "Hearing you say that makes me feel like one day, my own dream can come true."

"What's your dream?" asked a curious Jacob.

Enyo's cheeks went from pink to red as she turned around, presenting her back to him. "I-i-it's nothing big… just a small dream. Um, anyway, good night!"

Frowning at Enyo's back, Jacob eventually turned to lie on his back again, staring at the cracked ceiling of the cavern.

What was that about?

Women were such a mystery.

✳✳✳

Enyo woke up with a start. She looked around in an attempt to locate whatever had woken her up. Jacob was asleep, resting on his back. His closed eyes and his parted mouth almost drew her in, but she shook her head and pulled back.

Now isn't the time for that!

It took her a moment, but she soon realized that there was something different from when she'd gone to sleep and now. Agatha's bed was empty. A strange creaking made her look in the direction of the door that was on the opposite side of the one they entered through. It wasn't open, but a soft breeze made it rattle.

Did Agatha go through there?

Standing up, Enyo made her way to the door. She gripped the handle and slowly opened it, wincing as a loud creaking hit her eardrums. That noise was so loud it could have awakened the dead.

She slipped inside. Darkness engulfed her, but Enyo muttered a quick spell that caused light to appear on her fingertips. She was in another hallway, one that noticeably sloped downward, leading deeper beneath the ravine. Enyo was reminded of a mine. Her footsteps echoed loudly as she walked, bouncing along the walls and making her wish that light and dark magic had spells that could silence one's feet, or at least muffle their footsteps.

There was light at the end of the passage, flickering like candles, albeit, a lot eerier. Enyo crept slowly, cautiously, before eventually passing through the cavernous tunnel, which opened into a massive room. It was so large that Enyo couldn't see the top.

However, a light from below allowed her to see the bottom as she peered around a stalagmite.

What she saw almost made her gasp.

Agatha stood before a stone altar, upon which sat a familiar object. It had a long handle with a gem on one end. The other end was like a blade, but flat and with grooved ridges. Archaic writings and symbols glowed along its surface.

That's the gate key!

Ghouls surrounded Agatha and the key. They were everywhere, swirling creatures with ghastly shapes that vaguely resembled humans. Their bodies were white and semi-translucent. Their faces were shaped sort of like people, but only in the sense that she could make out where their eyes and noses were supposed to be. They did have a mouth, but their mouths were more like gaping maws that yawed wide, stretching their faces in an obscene manner.

"Do not worry, my preciouses," Agatha said. "With this key, I'll be able to open a gate to the underworld. Then, all of us will be free. Yes, all we need is a proper sacrifice, and fortunately for us, one has stumbled right into our laps."

This time, Enyo couldn't contain her gasp. Agatha's head snapped up, and the woman's face turned into a snarl as she spotted her.

"Get that girl!"

A loud howling filled Enyo's ears as the ghouls turned to her, their mouths opening wide as if to suck her in. They flew up. No doubt they were getting ready to attack.

Blood pumped erratically through her body.

Unbidden, a smile appeared on her face.

"Lux. Lamina. Lunatis."

There was a tug on her navel as she announced her spell. The noticeable pull, which was her magic being drained, only lasted for a second. Enyo swiped her left hand through the air, producing a crescent blade of light that cut through several ghouls. The ghastly horrors shrieked as their bodies burst into a fine powder.

Agatha howled. "How dare you! You hurt my preciouses! You hurt them!!!!"

Lightning burst from the woman's staff. Enyo ducked seconds before it reached her, but even so, she could feel it pass overhead. The hairs on her neck were standing on end. Jolts like electric remnants made her grit her teeth. It hurt, but it could have been a lot worse.

The lightning bolt crashed against a wall, exploding with the force of a thunderstorm. Rock fragments scattered everywhere. Blue arcs of energy expanded outward like a wave, forcing Enyo to put up a barrier, lest she be shocked or rendered unconscious by a rock to the head.

More ghouls appeared.

Enyo's heart pounded in her chest and a fierce grin crossed her face as she found herself surrounded. The ghouls were closing in on her. They swooped down, slamming against her shield. Several cried out as they burst into flames. Her shield was made of light magic, the antithesis of anything dead. Ghouls would not be able to breach it.

However, as more ghouls crashed into her shield, cracks appeared along its surface. The cracks widened. Enyo gnashed her teeth together and strained to repair the shield. It didn't do much good. Repairing a shield required more effort than making a shield, and she didn't have enough control to fill the cracks with her magic while leaving the rest of the shield untouched.

The cracks continued to spread across her shield. Then, with a sound akin to shattering glass, it broke apart.

The ghouls closed in.

"Durandal! Cut!" a voice shouted.

A blue crescent wave burst across the cavern. Hellish shrieks resounded all around Enyo as the ghouls were sliced in half. They exploded, bursting into ectoplasm.

"NNOOO!!!!" Agatha's enraged howls echoed along the walls.

Jacob rushed into the cavern with Durandal in hand, racing toward her at speeds she could scarcely comprehend. He swung Durandal and blue light burst from the sword. It took the shape of a crescent wave and slashed apart multiple ghouls. Agatha's anguished and hate-filled screams rent the air.

"Enyo!" Jacob called. "What's going on?!"

"Jacob! She has the gate key!"

"What?!"

"We need to get it from her!"

Her companion seemed quite shocked, but he was nothing if not adaptable. He nodded once. His expression hardened as he gripped Durandal in both hands, hacking and spinning and slashing apart ghouls like a scythe cutting through wheat.

Enyo's darker half, that of the Dark Clan, couldn't help but admire his prowess. The way his arms flexed as he swung, the strength of his swings, and the fierce gleam in his eyes. She didn't want to admit it. Jacob would surely think ill of her if she did. However, the sight of him fighting made her aroused, for lack of a better word.

"I'll deal with these ghouls," Jacob said, snapping Enyo out of her daze. "I'll leave Agatha to you."

Enyo's eyes widened, but she nodded and tried to not let him see how happy his display of trust made her. "Leave her to me!"

As Jacob began hacking apart more ghouls, Enyo raced down to the bottom of the cavern. Agatha was waiting for her, biting and snarling and spitting. She looked like a rabid animal.

"I'm going to kill you!" Agatha screeched. "You're going to be the sacrifice to open the gate! Yes, you will!"

"That's not happening!" Enyo refuted.

Agatha's already angry face burned red. "Die! Fulmen! Percutio! Astrapí! Thráka! Péfko! Evito!"

"Finis. Sepio. Opsideo."

Agatha's lightning met Enyo's light shield. It slammed into her barrier, attempting to pierce it. Enyo's legs and arms shook from the strain of blocking the deadly lightning, which was more powerful than most magic she'd come across. Cracks appeared, lines of light that spread across the dome of light. Her shield was going to break.

It did.

However, Enyo was no longer there.

Ducking low, Enyo let the lightning travel over her head. She could feel the attack as it passed, static bursts of energy that made her body feel skittish. Ignoring the feeling, as well as how her hair felt like it was beginning to stand on end, she rushed forward, chanting a much longer spell than her usual ones.

"Mortem. Mors. Malevolentia. Displodo. Conflo. Fulgo."

Dark flames exploded to life on her left hand. Enyo appeared before Agatha, whose eyes had widened, bulging like the egg sacks of a spider. The woman didn't even have time to scream before Enyo slammed her hand into Agatha's chest.

A massive explosion of dark energy erupted from the point of impact, engulfing the wizened witch in dark flames, along with everything behind her. The flames continued forward, a cone of pure destruction. They rushed across the ground and slammed into the wall, detonating with an angry roar.

When the flames died down, there was nothing left of Agatha, not even ashes. She was gone.

The ghouls, as if sensing Agatha's death, all shrieked and scattered, disappearing through walls or just vanishing altogether.

Enyo sighed and wiped the sweat from her brow. How long had it been since she'd used a spell of that caliber? Not since her training with her former maid had she used such a powerful spell. She'd forgotten how exhausting it was.

A glint in her peripheral vision snagged her attention. It was the gate key. It sat on the pedestal, no longer glowing.

Reaching out, Enyo picked up the gate key, holding the shimmering object in her hand. As she turned it within her palm, the key coruscated as light bounced off its surface. If she didn't know any better, she would have said that the key was constantly changing colors.

Footsteps approached her from behind. "So, that's the gate key?"

"Yes."

Turning around, Enyo presented it to Jacob, who studied the key for a moment before reaching out. Rather than take the key, he closed her fingers around it. She gave him a confused look, to which he just smiled.

"I think you should keep it."

"Um, okay."

Enyo didn't have any pockets, so she placed the key inside of her cleavage... or she was going to.

"On second thought, maybe I should carry it for now," Jacob finished. His cheeks had been stained a mild red, and he wasn't looking in her direction, though his hand was outstretched.

"All right," Enyo agreed, placing the key in his hand. Jacob's fingers curled around the key before he placed it in a pouch that was strapped to his left thigh.

"I don't know about you," Jacob started, smoothly changing the subject, "but I think we've overstayed our welcome."

"I couldn't agree more," Enyo said with an emphatic nod.

INTERLUDE III - DARK TIDINGS

She knelt before the Dark Council, her head bowed low. She didn't look up, for to gaze upon the faces of those who were feared by the darkness itself was to invite death. While she didn't fear death, she also didn't seek it out.

"I have discovered the whereabouts of our runaway princess," she announced. "Enyo is currently traveling in the company of the hero, Jacob the Destroyer, though I have yet to ascertain the purpose."

Perhaps it had been a mistake to tell Enyo stories of the hero's adventures. She remembered the way a 12-year old Enyo's face would light up when she told her about how the hero had rescued such and such village from monsters, or how he had saved so and so individual from death. Personally, she blamed the girl's father for putting such outrageous ideas in her head, but there could be no denying that she was also part of the problem.

I suppose this is what I get for wanting to give Enyo a better life.

"This is a troubling situation," a voice said to her left.

"Indeed," another added to her right.

"Such an instance has never occurred before," a person directly in front of her said.

"The hero and the dark lady are supposed to never meet," said another voice. "That is how it was and always has been. Now that these two have met, all of our carefully crafted plans could be unraveled."

She said nothing. It was not her place to speak while the Dark Council was holding a conversation. These people were the seven most powerful members of the Dark Clan to have ever been born. Centuries old, they held powers that not even Alucard had wielded.

"I do not think we have anything to worry about," said a female voice, seductive and deadly.

"Do not be so sure, Lust," a wizened voice said. "We do not know why the dark lady has sought out the hero, or what her plans are."

"She probably just wants to get revenge for the hero killing dear old dad," Lust said.

"All the more reason we should reclaim her," someone said. "If the hero catches wind of what she plans on doing, he will kill her. The dark lady is powerful, but she is not her father. We cannot afford to let her die."

She wanted to say that they wouldn't have to worry about that. The chances that Enyo was planning on—or indeed, even wanted to —kill the hero was slim to none. That girl had been enamored with the hero from the very first story that she had been told. She said nothing, however. It was not her place to speak, and in truth, she wasn't that fond of the Dark Council. In fact, she had no plans on aiding this group of misbegotten old fools.

"There are other ways to kill the hero aside from combat," Lust mocked. "You should know that, Pride. Wasn't your father killed by me despite being stronger?"

"Hold your tongue, wench!" Pride snarled. "Be silent, lest I rip that vile appendage from your mouth!"

"Oh, my. Threats, is it? Do you really think you can take me on? I've grown in power since killing your old man. You wouldn't stand a chance against me now."

"Both of you should be silent," the voice in the middle said again. "Now is not the time for your quarreling. We must decide on what to do now that we know the dark lady's whereabouts."

Part of her wished she had never told the Dark Council about where Enyo was. Her wish had been for the Dark Council to never lay their hands on the girl, but she could not go against their wishes. If she did, then she'd never get the chance to save Enyo from whatever fate awaited her.

"It is obvious that we should have someone go and fetch her."

"But she's in the presence of the hero. Anyone we send would surely be destroyed."

"Then do you propose that we go ourselves? Preposterous!"

She listened to the Dark Council members argue, withholding a sigh as she realized that it was unlikely they would come to a decision. None of the Dark Council members had ever gotten along. Every time she made a report, they would bicker, argue, and issue death threats. None of them could agree on anything. However, they were the ruling council of the Dark Clan.

She didn't understand how that worked.

"It seems we are at an impasse," Lust said. "Since we cannot agree on what to do, how about each of us selects a champion to carry out the task of recovering the dark lady?"

A murmur spread through the Dark Council, who all seemed agreeable to the idea. One by one, each member seemed to come around to it. She could not see them because her head was still bowed. However, she could imagine the way their heads nodded along with Lust's suggestion.

"Very well," the middle voice said again. "Each of us will choose a champion, an avatar, who will do our bidding. They will go forth and reclaim the dark lady."

"What of the hero?" asked Pride. "Shall we dispose of him?"

There was a moment of silence. She almost smiled at the tension that settled around them. Jacob the Destroyer was an unprecedented hero, a boy who destroyed Alucard at the age of 13.

Who knew how strong the child was now, five years after the events had happened.

"There is no need to bother with him," the middle voice said at last. "He is of no concern. However, should he get in the way, then I see no reason why we can't kill him. After all, the hero has already served his purpose. His role in this world... has ended."

The other council members murmured in agreement. She sighed. It looked like the hero was going to be disposed of. She hoped he would prove up to the task of slaying the Dark Council's champions.

For Enyo's sake, if nothing else.

***

Alice had spent much of the day sitting on the dais greeting hall, listening to the nobles as they gave her reports on what was happening in their lands, or made requests of her, or even criticized some of her policies.

Those who were critical received a harsh tongue lashing. They were only upset because the policies that she had set in place kept them from lining their pockets with more wealth. She would not allow them to steal from her people, however. Their kingdom had been founded on justice and equality, and she would be damned if she allowed the corruption that had spread plague her kingdom anymore.

It was nearing noon when Bayard entered the greeting hall with a young knight in tow. Alice vaguely recognized the person. He had dark hair and eyes, a chiseled face, and broad shoulders. He walked with confidence, though he seemed a tad agitated. The silver armor of a paladin adorned his frame.

"Your majesty," Bayard said, bowing. The other paladin bowed as well. "This is Caslain, the paladin who I sent on the mission to locate and bring back Jacob."

Alice tried not to let Bayard know how much his words affected her. She had been impatiently waiting for any word on whether or not Jacob would be returning. She longed to see him returned to her side.

"And? How was the mission? Has he agreed to return?"

Bayard sent her a reproachful look. Even Listy was staring at her! Alice realized that it was because she'd lost her composure, leaning forward like some giggling lady-in-waiting who was looking for something to gossip about, and so she quickly tried to regain the demeanor befitting a monarch.

"My Queen, I regret to inform you that the mission was not successful," Caslain informed her in a regretful tone.

Alice couldn't contain her disappointment. "I-I see."

"Perhaps you should hear the reason that he failed to find Jacob," Bayard suggested.

"You are correct. Caslain?"

"The reason I failed is because I ran into the Dark Clan member who's wanted for stealing an important item from you, Your Majesty."

Alice would have rubbed her forehead if doing so wouldn't have been considered un-queenly. Caslain had run into the woman who'd stolen the gate key to the otherworld gate while he was searching for Jacob? Was this just a coincidence?

"It appears that the thief had been initially captured in the same city that the Morin Garrison said Jacob was located in. Someone then helped her break out after she was captured, and then both she and Jacob disappeared," Bayard continued. "Furthermore, when Caslain tried to apprehend the thief after happening upon her by chance, he and his squadron were attacked by a man wielding a longsword."

Narrowing her eyes, Alice sent Bayard a piercing look. "What are you trying to say, General?"

"I am saying that the time these two events took place, the thief being broken out of jail and Jacob disappearing from Albany, happened far too closely to be coincidental. I believe that Jacob is the one traveling with the thief."

Alice felt like someone had shoved a branding iron in her gut. It was a good thing she was sitting, because she lost all the strength in her legs. She couldn't believe what Bayard was saying.

"There's no way that could be true!" Caslain, surprisingly, was the one who came to Jacob's defense. "There is no way a hero like Jacob would ever ally himself with a thief!"

"I am surprised you can say that, having already fought him," Bayard replied mildly. "Did you not recognize your hero?"

Caslain's cheeks turned red. "I... it was dark, so I couldn't see very well. However, I stand by what I said. Jacob is a hero. Even if he left the kingdom, that doesn't make him any less of a hero, and a hero would never protect a thief like that woman."

"Caslain makes a good point, General," Alice said. "And that is a very strong accusation to make. What proof do you have that Jacob is the one traveling with the thief?"

"The mere fact that the one traveling with the thief defeated a paladin is proof enough that he's no ordinary man." Bayard spread his hands wide. "However, if you require more proof, then let us look at the facts. We know that Jacob's last known location was Albany. We also know that the thief was last seen in Albany before she was captured. She was then rescued by some unknown person and disappeared. Several days later, Caslain travels to Albany, finds out that Jacob has disappeared, and then runs into the thief and a man who can fight on par with a paladin in another city. Doesn't all that seem a little too suspicious to be mere coincidence?"

Looking at it like that, she could see why Bayard suspected Jacob. It really was suspicious. However...

"While your points are good, I would still like to give Jacob the benefit of the doubt," Alice said.

Bayard nodded. "As would we all. I merely wanted to convey the possibility that Jacob might have been coerced into helping the thief somehow."

"Your point is noted," Alice said. "In that case, since we cannot find Jacob, and since we don't know about the thief's companion, let us focus on the thief. Caslain, I would like you and your knights to track her down. You said that she and her companion were last seen heading into the Phantasma Forest, so start your search there."

Caslain brought his left fist up to his chest in a salute. "Yes, Your Majesty. It shall be done."

As Caslain turned and left the greeting hall, Alice looked up at the ceiling, feeling the exhaustion that came from bearing the crown seeping into her bones.

I wonder what you're doing right now, Jacob...

CHAPTER 4 - A QUEST GONE AWRY

It took two weeks to leave the Phantasma Forest. The problem was several fold; they didn't have a map, neither of them had spent any amount of time in the forest until then, and they had lost their way after all of the fighting with the toad demons, not to mention the incident with Agatha. In the end, they had simply picked a random direction and traveled in a straight line until they were out.

Unfortunately, they had been traveling north, which was the opposite direction that they needed to travel. Instead of ending up in Polavo, which would have been their next destination, or even Altsu, they found themselves in Deterion.

Deterion was a mining town. Built around the base of a mountain, all the structures were of a sturdier design than most. Made from steel and brick, there were no wooden structures to be found there. Since the mountain was actually an active volcano, the buildings had all been built specifically to withstand heat.

He and Enyo walked into the town, glancing around at the large buildings that towered over them. Numerous walkways could be seen beneath their feet. Much of the city was located underground. Paths branched out to reach doorways, and there were spiraling ramps that led deeper into the city.

The people walking around were a mixed lot. Lizafals and Alicants seemed to make up most of the population. They were bipeds, but they didn't look human. Lizafals possessed leather skin, had a reptilian muzzle, no ears, and a long tail jutting from their clothing. Alicants were furry. There were several different races of Alicant, which left small variations in appearance. Some looked like foxes, while others resembled cats, dogs, and rabbits. One thing about them remained the same. Their entire bodies were covered in fur, they had large ears, and tails protruding from their pants.

Enyo stared in awe at the place. Her eyes were like those of a child as she twisted her neck around, as if doing so would let her see more. Jacob chuckled, causing her to look his way.

"What is it?"

"I'm guessing you've never been here before?"

"No, I haven't. This is my first time seeing such a place."

Jacob had expected as much. "Deterion is known for two things: it's mining operations and its blacksmithing. Many of the residents go deep into the mountain and mine rare gems and metal. I hear this place has a lot of ore deposits because the volcano is still active. And, since they have such a large amount of ore readily available, blacksmiths have traveled from all over to set up shop."

Watching the way Enyo's face shifted was amusing. The first thing she did was gaze at him with an impressed look, then her face scrunched up as if she was confused, and then her eyes widened as she realized something.

"Are we going to buy a new set of daggers?" she asked.

Jacob shrugged. "I figured you could use another pair since you destroyed your old ones, and since we're already here…"

"Thank you!"

Durandal groaned. "We only got here, and I can already tell this trip is going to suck."

Enyo blinked. "What's wrong with Durandal?"

"Nothing," Jacob said. "Just ignore the sword."

"Oh, yes. Just ignore me. I don't have any positive input to add. No sirey."

"He seems awfully angry."

"Durandal is a very belligerent sword. You know that."

"True."

The key to getting a good pair of weapons was to find a good blacksmith. Fortunately, some of the best blacksmiths in Terrasole resided in Deterion. Even more fortunately, Jacob happened to know a good blacksmith who could help them out.

The shop was called *Dolton's*, and while the name was uninspiring, the weapons produced by Dolton, the owner, were top notch.

Sweat accumulated on Jacob's head the moment he entered the shop. The forge must have been burning in the back, which meant Dolton was working on something. His and Enyo's footsteps thudded against the wooden floor. While Enyo glanced around, surveying the store as a whole, he studied the many different weapons that were lined up along the walls. Swords. Axes. Polearms. He even saw a naginata. However, it didn't look like there were any daggers.

Loud stomping made him and Enyo snapped their heads toward the doorway behind the counter, which swung open seconds later. Enyo gasped as a dark-skinned mountain of muscle entered the room. With sweat clinging to his shirtless frame, revealing his thick chest and broad shoulders, he was less of a man and more of a monster.

Despite towering over them both, the man offered them a friendly smile.

"Welcome to Dolton's," he spoke with a thick northern accent. "What can I interest you... eh? Hm?" The man narrowed his eyes when they landed on Jacob.

"It's been awhile, Dolton." Jacob raised a hand in greeting.

"Well, I'll be! Ha! Jacob! It's been ages since you've come into my shop! You haven't come since you got that blasted talking sword of yours."

"That blasted talking sword is still here," Durandal growled.

"So you are," Dolton grunted. "You know my policy, Jacob. You and I can do business, but the talking sword needs to leave."

"What am I going to do? Walk out on my own two legs? News flash! I don't have legs!" Durandal paused as Jacob unstrapped the sheath from around his back. "H-hey, Partner? You're not actually going to listen to this guy, are you?"

"Sorry," Jacob said in a completely unapologetic tone. "But Enyo needs daggers, so you've gotta go."

"What?! You mean that you're abandoning me for the girl!"

"Only temporarily."

"Whatever happened to bros before hoes?!"

"I have no idea what that means, but I'm sure you'll be fine for a few hours."

"This is blasphemy! What kind of partner are you?!"

"The best kind."

Despite Durandal's protests, Jacob stabbed the sword into the ground outside of the shop, where it remained, its muffled complaints barely heard behind the closed door. Clapping his hands, Jacob walked further in. He stopped at the giggles coming from Enyo.

"You two really do have an interesting relationship," Enyo said when he raised an eyebrow.

"Ah, yeah. I guess we do. Then again, it's not every day you see a talking sword, so that's only natural."

"So true."

"I'd appreciate it if we could stop talking about the sword and get down to business." Dolton crossed his thick arms over his chest. "You mentioned something about daggers for the lady…"

At the invite, Jacob gestured to Enyo, who realized what he wanted and hurriedly described what she was looking for. "I'd like two blades. They need to be longer than the average dagger, about fifteen centimeters, and the blades need to be one-sided and curved with a jagged edge in the back. If possible, I'd like them to be made from obsidian, but mythril will do as well. I also want them to have runes inscribed upon the surface, and for the hilt, please use the hide of a manticore or griffin."

Jacob winced the more he listened. Enyo clearly didn't realize how expensive this was going to be.

"I can certainly make that order, though I'll need to buy some more materials," Dolton said at last. He turned to Jacob. "You got the money on hand?"

Jacob winced. "Not for something that extravagant."

"I guess we'll do this the usual way then," Dolton murmured. "Once you get the money, come see me again. I'll have the daggers ready."

"Thanks, Dolton."

"Anything for a friend."

Jacob and Enyo left the shop, the door closing behind them. He could hear the lumbering of Dolton's heavy footsteps recede. Knowing that man, he was probably going to get started on making those daggers soon. That meant he would need to scrounge up the money.

"Um, Jacob? I was wondering..."

"About?"

Enyo nodded as Jacob grabbed the silent Durandal, sheath and all, and strapped the sword to his back. "Yes. I mean, I just realized that we don't have much money."

"And you were wondering how I planned on getting some, right?"

Nodding as the Durandal slid into the sheath with a soft *click*, Enyo said, "Well, yes."

"That's simple." Jacob grinned at his confused companion. "We are going on a quest."

✳✳✳

Quests were basically jobs that people could take in order to make money. Every town had a quest board, usually in front of a tavern or inn, where wandering mercenaries or missionaries could grab them. These quests varied a lot in what was required for their completion. Some asked for the destruction of a bandit hideout, while others could be a monster extermination, and more still might be a quest to protect caravans on their journeys.

It had been a long time since Jacob had taken a quest, three years, in fact; he'd not gone on a quest since his journey across Terrasole.

Back then, Jacob had always been in need of cash. Traveling cost money. Paying for an inn, buying food and supplies... everything cost money. So, whenever he needed cash for whatever reason, he would take a quest or two in the nearest city.

The quest that he and Enyo were taking was a monster extermination quest. There were apparently several cockatrices that had been attacking travelers on the road west of Deterion. Several caravans that were supposed to have delivered ore and precious gems to Alysium had been attacked and their cargo lost.

Since Enyo couldn't fight up close until her daggers were finished, Jacob had her playing support. She was a strong magic user. With her light and dark magic, she could act as both a healer and a long-range attacker, both of which were important roles when traveling in a party.

Jacob ducked and wove around the cockatrices beak. Right. Left. Right. Right. Spin. The beak slammed into the ground, kicking up dirt. Jacob would have used that moment to attack, but the cockatrice was quick to recover. Its large, leather wings tried to swat at him, but he avoided them, moving only enough to not get hit. He could feel the attacks rustling his clothing.

He leapt back. The cockatrice roared. As it charged at him, its tri-tipped feet digging into the ground, Jacob swung Durandal, hitting the creature's beak. Rather than slice right through it, there was a loud *clang!* as the sword glanced off the beak.

"What the hell, Durandal? What are you doing?"

"Oh, I'm sorry. Are we fighting? I thought you didn't need me anymore."

"Are you still upset about what happened at Dolton's?"

"Of course not. Oh, no. I'm not upset. Certainly not. I mean, it's not like my partner decided to neglect me in favor of letting some chick get a pair of daggers to fondle."

The cockatrice's screech rattled Jacob's teeth, but by channeling energy into his ears, he blocked out the worst of it. It came at him again. Its headlong charge was halted when he slammed into it with a fist. As the cockatrice sailed backward, two more of them ganged up on either side in a pincer attack.

"Enyo! Light up the one on the left!"

"Got it!"

Several yards behind him, Enyo chanted a spell.

"Ustulo. Uro. Torro."

Black flames gathered in the palm of her hand, and, as she clenched her hand into a fist, the flames burst and became all the brighter. She sliced her hand through the air. The flames shot forth like a wave. They slammed into the cockatrice and overtook it, igniting its feathers and turning the large fire-breathing chicken into a flambé. The monster's death screech died seconds later as it turned to dust.

Jacob, meanwhile, dealt with the other one. Since Durandal was being stubborn, he sheathed his sword and engaged in the creature with hand to hand combat. This was normally a dumb thing to do. Cockatrices had the ability to petrify humans with a mere touch. Jacob counteracted this by coating his hands in energy.

His first punch caused cracks to appear along the creature's beak, and then his second punch shattered it. The cockatrice reared back and screeched in agony. Jacob silenced its screeching by unclenching his hand, straightening it until it was pointed like a knife, and then jamming his now knife-shaped hand through its chest. As he pulled his hand out, blood spurted from the wound. The cockatrice crowed once, then fell onto its back.

The last cockatrice shrieked as if enraged by the death of its comrades. Its wings flapped as it charged at Jacob, who bent his knees, channeled energy to the bottom of his feet, and shot forward like a lightning bolt. He walloped the cockatrice with a reinforced kick to the head. It wasn't until the head exploded that he realized he'd put too much power into his attack.

"Ugh…" He grimaced as he stared at his pant leg. It was covered in gore, and it was sticking to his leg, which didn't feel very pleasant. "This is gonna take forever to get out…"

"Jacob!" Enyo came running up to him. "Are you—ew…" She stopped running and plugged her nose. "You stink of blood."

"Thanks for letting me know that." Jacob sighed. "I hadn't realized it until you said something."

"S-sorry," Enyo apologized.

"It's fine." Jacob ran a hand through his hair. It felt sticky. "Would you mind if we find a stream or pond where I can wash myself off before heading back?"

"I think that's fine. I remember seeing one a little way out."

"I also think I should let Durandal soak in a nice pond as well."

"Do ya want me to rust?!"

"Yes," Jacob answered as he and Enyo headed off the road and into the surrounding groves.

The area around Deterion consisted of mostly open plains and rocky deserts. However, the area that he and Enyo had traveled to had a small patch of forest. Jacob was hoping to find a stream or something running through it that he could use to wash his pants and leg off in.

"How cruel! Partner, you are too cruel!"

"Who's the one that wouldn't fight with me while I was battling the cockatrice?"

"That's only because ya had me wait outside while ya spoke with that unappreciative idiot."

"That man may not appreciate you because a sentient sword is bad for business, but I need him to make some daggers for Enyo, or would you rather she not have weapons to protect herself with?"

Durandal made a sound akin to a *tsk.* "All right. Fine. I understand. She needs a weapon. I'll forgive ya this once."

"Thank you."

Jacob and Enyo shared a smile. Durandal did this every time Jacob did something to upset it. They would argue, Durandal would call him a bad partner, and then the sword would get over and life continued on. It had happened so much already that even Enyo seemed to have become a keeper of the inside joke.

It took longer than anticipated to reach a stream, but they eventually found one several kilometers from where they had slain the cockatrice. They wouldn't need to worry about anyone trying to claim the mission while they took a detour. All people who accepted a mission spoke with the bartender/innkeeper and were logged into a Quest Book, which stated that they had accepted the mission and only they could be paid. It was an efficient method of keeping thieves from trying to swindle people out of their rightful pay.

While Enyo stood several meters away, behind a series of trees, Jacob stripped off his pants and, after a moment's thought, decided to take off all his clothes. Since he was there, he might as well clean himself more fully. Durandal rested against a tree to his left.

However, as he cleaned himself, the snapping of a branch alerted him to someone's presence. He turned his head toward the source. Then he frowned. There was nothing there.

He went back to washing himself. The rustling of shrubs made him look in the same direction again. There was still nothing there. His frown deepened.

Is it Enyo?

He didn't think Enyo would peek on him while he was naked. That said, when he used to take baths in the palace, several of the maids had spied on him through an eye hole in the bath house's walls. Of course, he hadn't found out about that until after Queen Alice had caught the maids in the act.

When, after another few seconds, nothing happened, Jacob went back to washing himself off.

A burst of killing intent was the only warning he had.

The world around him exploded.

Jacob gritted his teeth as he reinforced his body, covered his vitals, and rode out the blast. Heat assailed him from all sides. The concussive force would've knocked him off his feet had he not crouched on the ground. Fire scorched his skin, and even though he'd created a shield of energy over his body, that didn't stop the pain from searing through his mind.

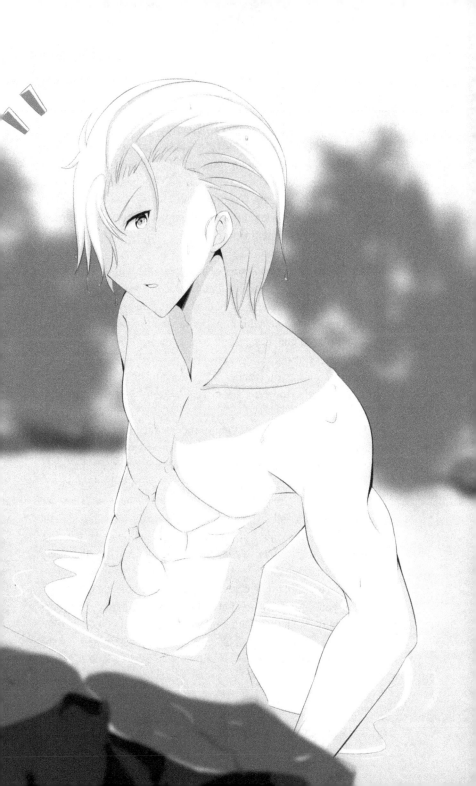

The explosion died down. Jacob stood up, casting a glance around the glade. That burst of killing intent had disappeared, but there existed a lingering hint of malcontent, a desire to harm. Whoever had tried to kill him was still there.

"I see you survived that," a voice said, echoing all around him. "I'm surprised, but then again, you are the hero who fought and defeated the Dark Lord, Alucard. I guess it's only natural that a sneak attack of this nature wouldn't work on you."

"Your astute observation is rather impressive," Jacob retorted. "Are you always this intelligent, or do you simply enjoy stating the obvious?"

"Ha ha ha! Such wit! I wonder how long that will last!"

A twinge of murderous intent. Jacob moved. The earth exploded. Fire and rock shards and water flew everywhere. Several of those shards would have hit him, but Jacob blew them apart with a couple well-placed punches.

"Impressive! Your reflexes are quite astounding."

"Almost makes you wonder if I've done this before, doesn't it?"

"Ha! Indeed. However, let's see how long you can keep this up."

The ground detonated again and again, forcing Jacob to constantly retreat. Only the flash of killing intent warned him of the danger. This allowed him to remain one step ahead of the explosions. Even so, Jacob could feel the searing heat and air pushing him back.

Jacob flipped along the ground. He landed next to Durandal, grabbing the sheath and hilt, and pulling the blade out with a sibilant hiss of steel. Another burst of killing intent. Jacob leapt to the side. The tree detonated, gouts of flame blasting off and sending fiery splinters in every direction.

"You're awfully good at running away!" the voice laughed.

"And you're awfully good at hiding," Jacob retorted. "So, does the man fighting me have a name, or should I just call you coward?"

"You may refer to me as Shade. I am an assassin sent by the Dark Council to kill you."

"How forthright of you to tell me the reason you're trying to kill me."

Despite acting nonchalant, Jacob couldn't deny that he was concerned. The Dark Council, the people who determined who would become the next Dark Lord, were after him. He could only think of one reason why they would attack now after all this time.

"You're a distraction," Jacob said. "Enyo is the one you really want."

"Heh... that's right. We don't care about you, hero. Our only concern is reclaiming the Dark Lady, who decided to go rogue for some reason. You're merely an annoyance that needs to be stepped on."

"Durandal?" Jacob whispered quietly.

"Ten meters and to left. He's standing on a tree branch."

"Gotcha."

Jacob slid into a wide stance, knees bending, sword held in a ready position near his head. He breathed lightly in, held it, then breathed out. He was facing away from the tree that Durandal said his opponent was lurking in.

"If you think I'm just a 'mere annoyance,' then you clearly don't know me as well as you should," Jacob declared. "Allow me to correct your erroneous thoughts for you."

"Please do," the voice, tinged with amusement, said. "I'm dying to see how powerful the hero who slayed Alucard really is."

"Don't worry. I will show you my power. Right. Now!"

Jacob spun around and swung his sword, unleashing a massive blue crescent wave of energy that sliced straight through the tree. A figure leapt out of it. Landing in a crouch on the ground, their black leather pants creaked as they stood up. Pale skin stood out starkly against a shirt of midnight black. Dark purple hair hung down his head, surrounding a pale face with a long nose and crimson eyes.

"So, you're my would-be assassin?" Jacob asked. "Not much to look at."

"I love that bark you've got," Shade said, his lips twisting into a bloodthirsty sneer. "And don't worry. Even if I look young, I'm probably several decades older than you."

"In that case, you probably won't be able to keep up with me, old geezer."

"Ha! We'll see."

Shade shot forward in a burst of speed, so fast that Jacob would have missed the man if he blinked. A sword shot out seemingly from nowhere. Jacob blocked it with Durandal, and the two swords struck each other in a flurry of sparks.

"Oh! Is this made of adamantine?" Durandal asked. Shade blinked. "I haven't fought against a blade made from that in a while."

Their blades locked; Shade's face came so close their noses were almost touching. "Your sword just spoke."

"You got a problem with that?" asked Jacob.

"Not at all." Shade grinned. "But you are just full of surprises, aren't you?"

"I try."

They broke apart. Jacob leapt back several meters before, with a grunt of effort, he slashed his blade down. Another blue crescent of energy flew from Durandal. It sliced across the ground, gouging chunks out of the earth. Shade wore a grin as he swung his sword. The air in front of him combusted.

Narrowing his eyes, Jacob studied the technique as his crescent wave was destroyed. Fire flared everywhere. The blue energy of his attack dispersed to the wind.

"I see," Jacob said. "Your power is explosion."

"Oh, you are good," Shade said. "How did you figure that out, I wonder?"

Jacob shrugged. "Who knows?"

"If you know what my power is, then does that mean you also know how it works?"

"Maybe."

"Then you know that I don't need to swing my sword, right? Or that I can make explosions happen anywhere? Crepitus!"

Jacob tensed just as a powerful explosion rocked his left flank. Pain seared into his flesh. His bones were rattled. He hadn't been able to reinforce his body. He could feel blisters breaking out on his skin, feel his flesh bubbling. It took everything he had not to scream.

"Oh, I guess you didn't know about that last part, did you?" Shade asked.

Jacob gritted his teeth as he realized that this person, this assassin, might be more trouble than he assumed. Had he been in shape, Jacob was sure he could have easily defeated this Shade character, but it was going to be a lot harder since he hadn't fought any true battles in years.

"It doesn't matter," Jacob said with a scowl. He sent energy into his wound. It would heal within a few seconds. "Now that I know, you won't get another attack on me like that again."

"Is that confidence or arrogance speaking, I wonder?" Shade questioned before creating another explosion directly in front of Jacob.

Having finally gotten a grasp on this man's tactics, Jacob understood that this first attack was designed to draw his attention away from the real danger. Using Linked Energy Manipulation, he reinforced his body and leapt into the flames, bursting out the other side and charging for Shade.

He sliced the air with Durandal, creating a multitude of tiny crescent waves. Each wave cut toward Shade, who used his own sword and his explosion magic to stop them. Then Jacob was there, in front of his foe, attempting to bisect him straight down the middle. It didn't work. Shade blocked it. The *clang!* of their swords echoed across the clearing.

Shade was an excellent swordsman. He used a minimalistic style that reminded Jacob of swashbucklers, and his sword was a reflection of that style. Unlike Durandal, which was a massive double-edged sword that would normally be used with two hands, the one that Shade wielded was thin, about sixteen centimeters in length, and had the unique handguard that was preferred by fencers.

Normally, such a sword would have given Shade a disadvantage in a sword fight, but his skill at swordplay was such that he wasn't hampered. His style also seemed uniquely suited to dealing with Jacob's superior strength and speed. He never took one of Jacob's attacks head-on. Every time Jacob swung Durandal, Shade intercepted it at an angle, negating most of the power behind it.

How annoying.

Jacob realized quickly that if he wanted to win, he needed to change his tactics.

Leaping backward, he avoided several powerful explosions from all sides, swerving around to dodge the ones that came from behind without looking back. There was a minute shift in the air currents just before an explosion occurred. It made predicting them easier.

"That's right! Dance for me, my puppet! Dance! Dance!" Shade laughed as he created one detonation after another.

Jacob ignored his taunts. He was no longer interested in trading banter. Instead, he put his plan into action, slamming his foot into the ground, which split open like an earthquake had struck. The split widened and lengthened, traveling toward Shade, who stumbled forward when his foot became caught in the opening.

Now!

Jacob rushed forward. Energy erupted from his feet, propelling him across the distance in less than a second.

Slicht!

He thrust Durandal forward, and the blade penetrated Shade's flesh as if it was made from hot butter. It slid in between his ribs, piercing through his organs, and jutted out of his back.

For a moment, there was silence. Shade look down at him in shock. His eyes were wide, and he was staring at Jacob like he'd suddenly become a foreign entity.

"Huh…" he murmured as blood ran down the blade. "I guess… I underestimated you some."

"Yes, you did," Jacob said.

Shade chuckled, though it was filled with pain. "It doesn't really matter if I die. We've already accomplished our mission. The Dark Lady has no doubt been taken by the other person who came with me."

"Then I'll just have to get her back," Jacob replied.

"Going so far for an enemy, eh?" Shade grinned. "I like that determination of yours, so I'll... tell you a secret. Consider it a... parting gift from one who's about to die."

Shade wet his lips. Jacob noticed that they were stained with blood.

"Myself and my companion aren't the only ones you need to worry... about. There... there are five more aside from us... they... are all powerful. Be on your guard... hero."

"I'll keep that in mind."

"Heh..." Shade's eyes were glazing over. "Killed by a hero... what an interesting way to die..."

Jacob yanked his blade out of Shade's pliant flesh. The dark clansmen toppled backward, hitting the ground with a dull thud. His eyes were still opened, but they were sightless. His body no longer drew breath.

"Partner?" Durandal said.

"I'm fine, D," Jacob said quietly. Flicking his wrist, all the blood on Durandal's sword flew off. "Let's hurry up and find Enyo."

"Right!"

Jacob ran off in the direction that he'd last seen Enyo. He hoped she was still there.

***

While Jacob cleansed himself in the stream, Enyo stood several meters away, behind a copse of trees, trying not to think about the fact that there was a half-naked man close by. The knowledge that Jacob was naught but a few meters behind her with no shirt was... tantalizing. She was ashamed of herself, but she was also curious.

She really wanted to see what Jacob looked like without clothes on.

Shaking her head, Enyo berated herself. What was she thinking?! It was not okay to let her curiosity get the better of her like this! She shouldn't be imagining Jacob's half-naked body, or wondering what would happen if she tried to join him.

I need to calm down.

Slapping her cheeks, Enyo took several deep breaths and slowed her rapidly beating heart.

Perils and numerous dangerous situations aside, traveling with Jacob had been quite fun so far. When she'd been little, she had imagined what it would be like to journey alongside the hero, fighting evils and saving people. She had conjured all kinds of scenarios. She had imagined the conversations that she and the hero would have, imagined how their relationship would evolve into something more.

It was good to know that some of what she'd imagined back then was happening between her and Jacob right now.

Enyo sighed as her heart finally slowed. She felt better, and now that she was thinking clearly, her thoughts once more returned to curiosity.

Maybe... just a little peek?

She really did want to see what he looked like underneath his clothes. It had been too dark, and she had been too nervous, during their first meeting to really look at him.

Creeping over to the trees, Enyo was prepared to peek out from behind one—

"Enyo?"

—when a voice spoke behind her.

Enyo didn't yell, not because she didn't want to, but because she was already busy chanting for a spell.

"Tenebris. Umbra—Fellis!"

Standing before her was a woman whose skin was nearly translucent. Her pale body was covered in dark clothes, shorts, and a vest. They did little to hide her skin, or the notorious curvature of her hips and bust. Yellow eyes were surrounded by hair like dusk. Strapped to her side was a whip.

"Hello, Enyo." Fellis smiled. "It's good to see you."

"It's good to see you, too. I haven't seen you in so long!"

Fellis was Enyo's former maid, the one who'd taken care of her and told her stories of Jacob's travels after he'd been summoned. Even years before then, this woman had taken care of her.

Enyo remembered nothing of her mother. From as far back as she could remember, Fellis had raised her, brought her up, taught her right from wrong, and told her not to give into the demands of others if it meant compromising her own beliefs. One could even say the woman before her was her surrogate mother.

"I see that you have been doing well," Fellis said. "How is traveling with the hero?"

"It's everything I imagined it to be," Enyo admitted, holding a hand to her chest as if to encase the warm feelings in her heart. "Even though he tried to pretend he doesn't care, Jacob is such a kind person. Every day, I'm learning something new about him. He's a wonderful man."

"I bet he's really handsome, too," Fellis added with a knowing grin.

Enyo's cheeks suddenly felt warm. It was true. She thought that Jacob was handsome, with his dirty blond hair that partially fell into his face, his youthful features, bright blue eyes, and powerful arms. She would be lying if she said that she hadn't wondered what it would be like to be held by those arms. Growing up, one of her biggest fantasies had been marrying the hero and starting a family.

Shaking her head to dispel these thoughts, Enyo refocused her attention onto her former maid. "What are you doing here, Fellis?"

"I came to warn you," Fellis said, her expression suddenly turning grave.

"Warn me? About what?"

"About the danger you're in. The Dark Council has realized that you're no longer in the darklands. They've sent six assassins to reclaim you and dispose of the hero, should it become necessary."

A thrill of fear jolted through her body, but it wasn't fear for her. It was fear for Jacob. She needed to warn him!

Turning around, Enyo was prepared to rush through the trees, Jacob's nakedness be damned, and warn him of the danger.

She would never get the chance.

Before she could take even a single step, her mind suddenly froze. If she had to describe the feeling, it would be like a lock had been placed on her thoughts, making it impossible to move.

Wha... what?

"Mind Manipulation," Fellis said behind her. Footsteps reached her ears before her former maid walked into her field of vision. "You know about my magic, right? It's the ability to manipulate the mind. It's quite the powerful ability, if I do say so myself, though I can only manipulate people who are weak-willed, or people whose thoughts are in disarray, such as a woman who is frantically worried about the person they love."

Fellis shook her head.

"Oh, Enyo. You're supposed to be smarter than this. You should know to never turn your back on someone that you haven't seen in years. There's no telling whether or not they are still your ally."

If she could have, Enyo would have gritted her teeth. This situation was so frustrating. Even more than that, she felt betrayed and hurt, so much so that it was a nearly physical pain in her chest, as if her heart had been stabbed by a blade coated in poison.

"W... why?"

It was just a single word, but it carried so much meaning.

"I'm surprised you can still talk," Fellis said. "As for why... well, let's just say that the people who the Dark Council have sent are not a group that I am particularly enamored with. I've managed to... cajole the aid of one of those people, but he is the most weak-willed of the bunch. There are still five others, and they won't hesitate to hurt you in order to get what they want."

Did that mean Fellis was doing this to protect her? If so, then that did make her feel a little better, but knowing that Fellis was trying to take her away from Jacob, the one helping her achieve her goal, still hurt.

"Well, in the end, my reasons don't really matter," Fellis continued. "It doesn't change the fact that I'm taking you away from the man you love."

Enyo tried not to blush. She knew that Fellis was saying that to throw her off guard, to keep her from being able to counteract the mind manipulation. However, it wasn't like her words didn't have a grain of truth to them. She didn't know if she loved Jacob, but she wouldn't deny her attraction to him, just like she couldn't deny that she'd harbored a crush on the Jacob the Hero ever since his summoning.

I... need to calm down.

Just then, an explosion ripped through the air, and a massive pillar of steam and smoke rose above the treetops.

Fellis sighed. "I guess that idiot isn't as weak-willed as I thought. I told him not to fight the hero unless there was no other option, but it looks like he's decided to disobey me. Perhaps his battle lust overwhelmed my mind manipulation." After a moment, she shrugged. "Well, I suppose it doesn't really matter. Let him and the hero fight. I have what I came here for."

As Fellis turned back to her, Enyo realized that she would be in big trouble if she couldn't break free of the mind manipulation. Calming her mind wasn't working. That meant she needed to take more drastic measures.

Battle lust.

Enyo had always hated her battle lust. It was her battle lust, more than anything else, that marked her as a member of the Dark Clan. When she was younger, she had believed that the hero would hate her because of it. Considering the hero was human, and they and the Dark Clan were at war, it was easy to imagine that being the case.

Then she'd finally met Jacob, and he hadn't hated her for her battle lust. In fact, he didn't even seem to care. Enyo doubted that Jacob even realized how much that meant to her. Thanks to him, she felt like her battle lust was a part of her that she could now accept.

It was a good thing. Right now, she needed that battle lust more than anything.

Enyo called up her love of battle, her enjoyment of spilling her enemy's blood. She conjured image of herself slaying her foes, of crimson pools and flashing daggers, of dark magic and the cries of her enemies. She felt it coursing through her, the insatiable desire for battle.

She broke free of the mind control.

"Caligo. Halitus. Nebula. Domo. Inimica."

A dark fog shot from Enyo's hands, billowing out like a blanket overtaking the coast during a muggy summer morning. Whatever the fog touched died. The grass decayed and withered, trees crumbled as all the moisture and life was sucked out of them.

"Tch!" Fellis clicked her tongue as she leapt back. "So, you've broken through my mind manipulation, have you. That was a poor move on your part. Had you just come back with me, this whole situation would have been a lot easier."

"Don't give me that," Enyo snapped. "You should have known that I would never agree to just go with you, especially after you used your mind manipulation on me."

"I was doing that for your own protection."

"I don't need to be protected!"

More fog poured from her hands, undulating as several tendrils were created and went after Fellis, who went into a series of back handsprings.

Explosions in the distance let Enyo know that Jacob was still fighting. She tracked Fellis's movements, seeking to end this battle so she could travel to her companion's side. This fog was a powerful toxin that aged whatever it touched. If she could just drive away Fellis, then it would be enough for her to leave and find Jacob.

As if to repudiate her thoughts, Fellis unclipped her whip and lashed at the fog, dispersing it. Enyo frowned as the whip remained pristine. It must have been made from a powerful material that was magically resistant.

She was about to create more. Before she could, Fellis lashed out with her whip again. This time the attack was aimed at her!

Leaping back several times, Enyo watched as chunks of earth were gouged out. She'd be in trouble if any of Fellis's attacks hit her.

"Mortem. Mors. Malevolentia. Displodo. Conflo. Fulgo."

There was a tug at her navel as she pulled more magic from her reserves, and then a flame darker than the sky at midnight flared into existence on her right hand. A malevolent aura wafted from the flame. Most dark magic had this feeling, though only the powerful spells gave off such a strong malignance.

"Are you really going to use such a powerful spell on me?" asked Fellis. "You might actually kill me with that."

"I have no intention of killing you," Enyo said. "But I'm not going to let you stop me either."

Fellis smiled. "That's some resolve you've picked up. Very well, then. Fight me with everything you have. Prove to me that you're capable of protecting yourself and accomplishing your goals."

"Sorry," a voice suddenly whispered in their ears. "I hate to break up this touching bloodbath between a woman and her servant, but I'll be taking the Dark Lady now."

A dark shadow appeared behind Fellis, who cried in pain and arched her back as if something had stabbed her. Enyo opened her mouth to scream, but then she felt a sharp sting on the back of her neck. Everything became blurry. The world was spinning. Darkness was creeping everywhere, crowding around her. She couldn't—

***

Jacob arrived in the clearing where he'd left Enyo before going to cleanse himself. The ground was burnt, several trees looked like they had been turned to cinders, and there was a body lying in the middle of the clearing. Enyo wasn't there anymore.

Walking up to the body, Jacob looked down at the woman. She was a dark clansman. Her skin was so pale as to be nearly translucent, and her hair was the color of dusk.

Kneeling, he studied the woman further. She was staring listlessly at the sky. He thought her dead at first, but then he noticed she was still breathing. Her chest rose and fell in time with her breath. It was like she simply wasn't there.

With a frown, he turned to the woman over, onto her stomach, and that was when he discovered the problem. Protruding from her back was a black dagger. However, it didn't look like a normal dagger. There was an etherealness to it that made him think it wasn't real, that it was some kind of illusion. He reached out to touch it, but then hissed and jerked his hand back when his skin began to blister.

"Is that a malum dagger?" Durandal asked. "I haven't seen one of those in centuries! Why, the last time I saw one was during the great war five centuries ago between the Dark Council and the White Council. These things are supposed to be rare. I wonder what it's doing inside of this woman."

"Someone clearly stabbed her with it," Jacob said. "Is there any way to safely remove it?"

"Not really. You just have to grin and bear it." Durandal paused, and then added, "You should be able to protect yourself by coating your hand in energy, though that could also cause a severe backlash. The dagger may explode and blow the woman up."

"That's great. Thank you for that insightful knowledge."

"You're welcome."

"That was sarcasm."

"How mean!"

Despite being sarcastic, Jacob didn't have any better ideas. Enyo was missing, and he needed to know where she'd gone.

Coating his hand in energy, causing it to glow a bright blue, he reached out and grasped the hilt. Darkness crackled. Tendrils of energy skittered across the blade and up his arm. He ignored it, along with the tingling feeling of his arm going numb, and pulled the blade out.

The woman woke up with a startled gasp. She jerked, then flopped onto her back. Her eyes, no longer sightless, looked around frantically. Then they landed on him.

"You're... hero..." she rasped.

"Easy. You shouldn't speak yet," Jacob said. "You had a malum dagger piercing your back. Take a moment to catch your breath, and then tell me what happened."

"No... time... here... come..."

Realizing that she wanted, he leaned over, allowing her to reach his face with her hands. The moment she touched his face, however, images flooded his mind. He saw a man with chalk white skin and completely white eyes appear behind Enyo. He saw Enyo collapse into the man's arms before he disappeared. Then he saw a younger Enyo practicing magic, listening to stories about him, grinning broadly as she declared to someone that she was going to marry "the hero" one day. He saw and saw and saw, until, with a sound like shattering glass, he saw no more. He was back in the clearing, and the woman before him was pale and unconscious.

Jacob held a hand to his head. He had a bad headache. However, he knew that he couldn't afford to remain there. If the visions that this woman had shown him were true, then Enyo had been taken by a dark clansman. He needed to find this person before they could return to the darklands.

This day has just become a whole lot more complicated, didn't it?

Jacob sighed as he lifted the woman into his arms and raced toward the nearest town.

If he was going to chase the person who had kidnapped Enyo, then he needed answers.

He had a feeling that this woman could provide them.

✳✳✳

It took Jacob far longer to reach Deterion than he wanted. Truth be told, he hadn't even wanted to return to Deterion at all. Lack of options forced him to return. However, the chances of Enyo's kidnapper having come here, or indeed, even traveling this way, were so slim as to be non-existent.

Jacob had to rent out a room at one of the taverns, and though he'd gotten some weird looks for carrying an unconscious woman around, no one had stopped him. The fact that he'd acted so unconcerned probably helped. Now, sitting in a small room, he waited for the woman to wake up.

"Do you think she's really gonna help us, Partner?" asked Durandal.

"I don't see why she wouldn't," Jacob said. His arms were crossed as he stared at the woman, who lay on the bed, unmoving save for the rise and fall of her chest. "She gave me those visions for a reason, and I believe that reason was to help rescue Enyo. Mind Manipulation, huh? What a frightening ability."

Jacob had seen far more than just who had attacked Enyo. He'd been given a glimpse into her life as a child. While it might have been a mistake, something that happened because the woman hadn't been in her right mind, he believed otherwise. She had shown him that part of Enyo's life to make him realize how much that young woman meant to her.

Though showing me a vision of a younger Enyo saying she'll marry me was a bit odd.

"But still... this woman is a member of the Dark Clan," Durandal argued. "She could have shown you those visions to make you think she was on your side, and then she'll stab you in the back when you least expect it."

"No..." Jacob shook his head. "There's no reason for her to go that far. Remember the fight with Shade? They were after Enyo from the beginning. The only reason I was attacked is because I would have tried to stop them. Since Enyo is now in their possession, there's no reason for her to show me all that to try and earn my trust."

"You're right," the woman spoke up. Her eyes were open, revealing yellows eyes as she turned her head to him. "There isn't."

"I'm glad you're up," Jacob said. "How are you feeling?"

The woman twitched as if surprised. "I am fine. Tell me, hero, why have you not gone after Enyo?"

"Because I don't which direction her kidnapper went in," Jacob said. "I know that he is traveling to the darklands, but I need to know the route if I am to intercept them."

"And so you were hoping I would help you," she deduced.

"You have no reason not to."

As silence ensued, Jacob studied the woman before him. Her shorts were hugging her hips, leaving all of her long legs on display, and her vest conformed to her figure and showed off a generous amount of cleavage. From her clothing and the whip at her side, he deduced that she was a seduction specialist. Her Mind Manipulation magic only confirmed this.

"What makes you think I'll help you?"

"Are you really going to play the 'I might be working against you' card now?" Jacob asked. "The longer we spend talking, the more time Enyo's kidnapper has to escape."

The woman sighed. "You're right. I apologize. My response was a habit."

"It's fine." Jacob stood up as he waved her off. "Do you think you're fit to travel?"

Trying to sit up, the woman winced several times before fully managing it. "I believe I can. However, if I end up slowing us down, you can feel free to leave me behind."

"Considering how important you are to Enyo, I don't think I could possibly abandon you."

The woman smirked. "You really are a hero, just like you were portrayed in the stories I used to tell Enyo."

"I'm no hero," Jacob said. "A real hero would have never abandoned the people who relied on him. I'm just a kid who was forced into an unenviable situation. However, this is neither the time nor the place to discuss my sordid past. We need to leave. I have one more stop that I need to make before we can go after Enyo's kidnapper."

"Then let's go," the woman said. "By the way, my name is Fellis."

He nodded. "I'm Jacob."

"And I'm Durandal," Durandal said.

… A moment of silence.

"Did that sword just talk?" asked a flabbergasted Fellis.

"Ignore the talking sword," Jacob groused. "There are more important things to worry about."

"Right you are," Fellis said.

Their first stop was *Dolton's*, the blacksmith shop where he and Enyo had ordered a pair of daggers to be made. He'd already cashed in the reward for the cockatrice. Since cockatrices were considered a fairly dangerous monster, the money he had earned was enough to pay for the daggers, though he would have very little left over.

Dolton must have sensed his haste. He didn't even bother berating Jacob for bringing Durandal into his shop. Fortunately, Durandal also seemed capable of reading the mood. The sword remained silent.

"Here you go." Dolton handed Jacob a rectangular box with clasps on it. "These are the daggers you ordered. You're lucky I had no other orders on hand. It allowed me to work on them non-stop."

Jacob undid the clasps and lifted the lid. Resting on a soft purple cushion, with long blades and short handles meant for one hand, were two daggers that glinted obsidian in the light. They were simple daggers. There was no real ornamentation to them. That said, Jacob could tell from the sharpness of the blade and the quality of the folding techniques used, that this was a weapon only the best blacksmiths could make. Running along the blade were several runes meant specifically for Magic Channeling.

"Thank you," Jacob said, closing the lid and tucking the box underneath his arm. "I really appreciate you making these so quickly."

"You're welcome," Dolton said. "Now, it looks like you're in a hurry. Go help that friend of yours. She's in trouble, right?"

It didn't surprise him that Dolton had reasoned out why he was in a hurry. Enyo wasn't there but a new woman was, he hadn't set Durandal outside, and he was in a rush. It was easy to conclude that his companion was in danger.

"Thank you," Jacob said, waving to Dolton as he raced out of the store with a still somewhat weakened Fellis following behind him. As he slowed down to let the Dark Clan member catch up with him, he turned his head and asked, "Do you know how to find the person who took Enyo?"

"I do," Fellis said, nodding. "Without a doubt, he will be taking the road through the Jörmungandr Mountain Pass."

Jörmungandr Mountain Pass, so named because of the powerful monsters that resided there, which looked similar to the legendary serpent itself, was one of several passes that lead through the Tenebrae Mountains. It was an incredibly dangerous route. Fraught with dangers that couldn't be found anywhere else, only the strongest and most powerful warriors could traverse it and come out with their lives intact.

When Jacob had left his companions during the war against the Dark Clan, that was the pass that he took to reach the darklands.

"That's two weeks travel from Deterion," Jacob murmured.

"The one that we're after, Wraith, can travel through shadows," Fellis said. "His magic is Shadow. He'll be able to get there within a week."

"Then we'll need to procure a method of transportation." Jacob sighed. This was just what he needed: more work. "A horse isn't going to cut it. They're not fast enough. We need something that flies. A griffin or a drake would be ideal, but where are we going to find one of those?"

As if summoned by his need, a familiar group of knights walked past them, their shining armor plates clinking together as they walked up to citizens and spoke with them. No doubt they were asking about the whereabouts of himself and Enyo.

"Friends of yours?" asked Fellis.

"No, but they're timing is fortuitous," Jacob said. "Come on. If they're here, then their drakes are likely in the stables."

"We're going to steal a drake, huh?" Fellis grinned. "What kind of hero steals from others?"

"I think I've already mentioned that I'm not a hero," Jacob said. "I'm just a guy who wants to save his companion."

Having used the stables here before, Jacob led Ellis to them, traveling past several numerous buildings. The stables were located on the top level near the outskirts of the city. There were two: one for flying creatures and one for land creatures. They were traveling to the one for flying mounts.

There was a person guarding the stables. It was just a young boy, however, and so Jacob walked up to him and tossed the lad the last few coins that he possessed.

"Thanks for all your hard work," he said to the boy.

The boy looked at the coins, and then gave him a toothless smile. "Thanks, Mister!"

He and Fellis stepped into the stables. The scent of hay, manure, and unwashed animals filled the air. Jacob ignored this as he strode past several empty stalls.

There weren't very many mounts. Aerial beasts were expensive. Not only were most of them vicious and therefore required extensive training, but they were also rare. Drakes, griffins, and other tamable flying creatures could only be located in certain parts of Terrasole.

Standing in several stalls, their four legs ending in a set of giant clawed feet, were six drakes. Armor plating hung from their muscular physiques. Horns jutting from either side of their head curled behind them, giving them a sort of demonic appearance. Most of them had green scales, signifying them as wind drakes, but one of them had red scales—a fire drake. That must have been the paladin's.

"Fellis, can your Mind Manipulation affect animals?"

"It can," Fellis said, stepping forward. "Hold on just a moment while I work my magic."

Jacob stood back while Fellis walked forward some more, alerting the drakes to their presence. They craned their necks to look at the woman confidently striding toward them. Several growled. Fellis merely smile. She reached out her hand, muttering words that he couldn't hear under her breath, and while it looked like the drakes were going to bite it off at first, they soon settled down and allowed her to pet them.

"All done," Fellis said.

"Nice work." Jacob walked up to the fire drake, which acted quite docile, and placed a hand on its muzzle. "Let's mount up on this one and move out."

"That sounds like a grand idea."

Before either of them could actually commit to their actions, the door to the stables burst open, and a familiar man clad in silver armor glared at them.

"I thought I had recognized you from somewhere," the paladin shouted as he pointed an accusing finger at Jacob. "You're the ruffian who attacked me while I was trying to apprehend that criminal!"

Jacob swore as he leapt onto the drake's back. He reached out his hand, which Fellis took, and then he pulled her onto the mount with him.

"I leave this to you," he said to Fellis.

"Got it!"

Using her ability to control the drakes via Mind Manipulation, she immediately ordered the other drakes to attack the knights. The beasts charged at their masters. Several knights ran out of the stables as they were attacked. Only the paladin and two other braves souls remained. They tried to wrangle the drakes, to force them into a state of calm, but it was no use. Under Fellis's mind control, the drakes had no choice but to obey.

Grabbing hold of the reins, Fellis directed the fire drake out of the stables. It rushed past the three knights, slamming one with its tail and head-butting another.

"Hold it, you fiends!" the paladin shouted. "I said stop!"

"Sorry, but my companion is in danger," Jacob said. "I'll return your mount to you after I've rescued her."

"Hya!" Fellis cracked the reins, and the drake burst forward, knocking the paladin aside before it rushed outside.

Jacob felt his stomach drop as the drake took flight. He closed his eyes as the loud flapping of massive wings echoed in his ears, mixing with the howl of the wind. The loss of traction on his boots made his feet tingle. He didn't need to open his eyes to know that they were far above the ground.

"What's wrong?" Fellis asked. "Don't tell me the big hero is afraid of heights."

"I'm not afraid of heights." He scowled. "Being this high up with nothing to keep me from such a long drop just makes me uncomfortable."

"Is that so? And yet you're still flying to rescue Enyo?"

"Of course I am. Enyo is my companion."

"Is that all she is?" asked Fellis.

"What do you mean by that?" Jacob cast Fellis a suspicious glance.

"I mean: is Enyo just a companion to you, or is she something else, something more?"

Jacob knew what Fellis was referring to. She was asking if he thought of Enyo as someone he wanted to be with in a more intimate fashion, a lover or even as a potential wife. He didn't know how to answer her, so he changed the subject.

"This guy we're after--Wraith, I think you called him. What's he like?"

"Wraith is one of the more dangerous assassins currently working for the Dark Council," Fellis informed as she pulled hard on the reigns, changing the drake's general heading. "I mentioned it before, but his magic is Shadow. Basically, he has the ability to manipulate any shadow regardless of whether or not he is touching it. He can also travel between shadows so long as the shadows are touching, making sneaking up on people quite easy."

"That certainly sounds like a troublesome opponent." Jacob narrowed his eyes. "But I've fought worse. He's not going to take Enyo."

"Speaking of Enyo... I know that now isn't necessarily the time, but you should know that Enyo has been in love with you for a long time now."

Jacob tried not to blush, but he could feel heat rising to his cheeks. "I don't see how such a thing could be possible. We only met around a month ago."

"My apologies." Fellis shook her head while subtly redirecting the drake. "When I said that she was in love with you, I meant she fell in love with Jacob the hero. She fell in love with the stories that I told her of you."

He could accept that more readily than her being in love with him. After the war's end, there had been many girls who'd professed their love. Of course, all of them had been in love with the hero, not Jacob. It seemed a little odd for the daughter of the Dark Lord, slain by his hand, to love Jacob the Hero, but, well, this was an unusual world that he lived in.

"However, just because she fell in love with the hero you, that doesn't mean she doesn't feel the same way about the real you," Fellis continued. "It might be impertinent of me to say this, but I think you should talk with her about her feelings sometime. Enyo is an oddly compassionate young woman, especially for a member of the Dark Clan. Right now, I believe that she is burying a lot of her feelings to help you and not be a burden, but that's not healthy."

"I suppose I could agree with you on that," Jacob said, sighing as he tried to block out the howling wind. "It's not good to ignore your own feelings. I could certainly talk to her. However, are you saying that after we rescue her, you're going to just let us go?"

"Of course not," Fellis said. "Since my original plan of hiding her away failed, I've decided to join the two of you. I don't know what you are hoping to accomplish yet, or what your goals are, but I have protected Enyo since she was a little girl. I'll continue to do so for as long as I'm needed."

It seemed Enyo wasn't the only compassionate Dark Clan member. Of course, he knew from experience that not all members of the Dark Clan were evil. Most, in fact, were just regular people who had a predisposition for darkness based magic. Still, though, those kinds of dark clansmen and women did seem to be in the minority.

"That's fine," Jacob said. "The more help we can get, the better off we'll be, especially since what Enyo and I are trying to do is dangerous."

"I thought that would be the case." Fellis released a deep breath as though resigned. "Really, that girl, I have no idea what she was thinking, leaving the sanctity of our home and running off on her own like that."

Jacob didn't think Enyo was thinking when she ran away. He didn't say anything, though. Truth be told, he had other things on his mind.

Talk about her feelings for me, huh?

Jacob looked up at the sky. The evening sun was beginning to set. It would be dark soon, and if they wanted to make good progress, they would need to reach the next town before nightfall.

Hold on, Enyo. I'm coming.

***

Enyo was jostled awake when something shook her. Blinking several times, she tried to figure out why the ceiling over her head was shaking so much. Also, why did the ceiling look like nothing but a simple cloth? She didn't remember any of her beds ever having a canopy.

It wasn't until she became more alert that she realized a few more facets about her situation—namely, the fact that she couldn't move her arms.

Looking down, Enyo was shocked to discover that her arms and legs had been completely bound. Strange black threads wrapped around her body, ethereal but strong. They pinned her in place.

Another jostle that made her body shake caused Enyo to finally realize what was happening. She was in a wagon, being taken somewhere, though she knew not where.

How did this happen…?

She remembered. It wasn't very clear, but she remembered fighting Fellis, remembered preparing to fight with everything that she had, but during the fight, someone had snuck up behind Fellis. Enyo didn't know who they were. However, she'd instinctively called out a warning to the woman, right before darkness had engulfed her.

Someone must have snuck up behind me...

It was odd, though. As a member of the Dark Clan, she had a strong sensitivity to negative intentions. When someone desired to harm her, she could feel it, and, in certain cases, she could even sense the location of the one who intended her harm.

Whoever had attacked her, she had not sensed their intent to harm.

That frightened her.

Enyo winced as she was shaken again. The sound of wheels rolling against the ground stopped, leading her to believe that she was no longer moving. Did that mean she'd get to find out who her attacker was? She hoped so. She would at least like to put a face to her enemy.

The fabric of the wagon parted to reveal the outside. It was dark out. The sky had turned into a twilight banner of stars, though that banner was currently being obscured by a pale man with chalk-like skin and a handsome face. He had long hair, pointed ears, and, perhaps oddest of all, his eyes were entirely white.

"I see that you're finally awake, Dark Lady," the man said.

Enyo jolted. She remembered being called that once before, back when she was really young. It happened the one time that her dad had taken her out of the mansion. They had met a man whose entire body had been hidden in darkness, as if the light abstained from him. That man had called her "Dark Lady" back then, too.

"Who are you?" she demanded.

"My name is Wraith." The man bowed low. "I apologize for the improper accommodation, but since we are currently in transit, there is not much to be done about that. Please bear with it until we reach the darklands."

The darklands?!

Now she understood; this person must have been working for the Dark Council. There couldn't be any other explanation. Yet, if that really was the case, why, then, had he stabbed Fellis? Was it because he desired to be the one who claimed the glory of returning her to the darklands? She didn't know. She wasn't even sure if it mattered.

Fellis...

Despite what her maid had done, she hoped the woman was all right.

"I have no intention of returning to the darklands," Enyo said.

"That is unfortunate." Wraith shook his head as if disappointed. "I was ordered to bring you back, you see? So there is no way I could release you, which means that you are going to the darklands whether you like it or not. Now, then, please keep quiet until we pass the upcoming village."

As he finished speaking, something dark wrapped around her mouth. Enyo released a muffled shout. It didn't do any good. Whatever this thing was, it completely muffled her voice.

"Do not bother yelling. That cloth over your mouth was created from shadows. Since I am connected to all shadows, it means that I can send your scream to any shadow of my choosing. No one near that town is going to hear you, so you shouldn't waste your breath."

The fabric fell back, and Enyo heard receding footsteps. The wagon jolted a little, then it started rolling again, making her teeth rattle as the wheels hit numerous bumps on the road.

I need to get out of here...

She needed to escape from this man. She couldn't go back to the darklands—no, she wouldn't go back. Enyo didn't want to return to that place, which was filled with the despair of her people. She wanted to go back to Jacob. She wanted to be with Jacob and start a new life somewhere else, in a world far from this one.

Looking at the shadows that were binding her, Enyo thought about the best method of escaping. Shadows were weak against light magic. She could easily break these bonds, but if she did that, then she would be outed as a light magic user.

No one but Fellis, her father, and Jacob knew that she could use both light and dark magic. When her father had found out about it, he had told her to keep it a secret. She was to tell no one. Of course, she had told Jacob, but that was different. He was a hero, and what's more, she needed to earn his trust, so she couldn't afford to keep secrets from him.

I don't think I have much of a choice. If I want to get out of this, then...

Enyo closed her eyes and chanted. She didn't worry about the man hearing her. He was apparently sending her voice somewhere else.

"Lumos. Luminous. Lucidus."

She felt the tug on her navel as light burst from her body like an oil lamp catching fire. The shadows holding her evaporated instantly, and Enyo didn't waste time scrambling to her feet and jumping from the wagon. Hitting solid ground, she stumbled forward after losing her balance. However, she quickly regained it and began running away.

A shadow appeared in front of her. It rose into the air as if it had physical mass, and then it took the shape of a person. The shadows soon fell away to reveal Wraith. The dark clansmen was staring at her with an intense frown, as if she was a puzzle that he couldn't solve.

"How did you escape from my bindings?" he asked. Enyo said nothing. "You refuse to speak? Very well. This is a most troubling situation that we now find ourselves in. I am supposed to bring you in alive and unharmed, but if you can escape from my bindings, then it makes holding you much more difficult. And you probably won't agree to come with me quietly, will you?"

"Of course not," Enyo said. "What makes you think I'd ever agree to return to the darklands, especially with someone like you?"

"Yes, that is the answer I expected." Wraith suddenly disappeared. Then, with his voice echoing all around her, he said, "It looks like I have no choice but to hurt you. Do forgive me, Dark Lady."

Enyo didn't know where the man was going to appear. Behind her? To the left? The right? There was no telling where he would show up, but it didn't really matter. He wouldn't be able to use his shadow magic if she destroyed the shadows around her.

"Lux. Lumin. Luminous. Accendo!"

Light engulfed Enyo's body, brightening the entire area, bathing the land around her in radiance. All of the shadows were burnt away. They disappeared as if they never were.

Wraith screamed as the shadow that he'd been hiding in was destroyed. He covered his face with his hands, rolling along the ground as steam rose from his body. She narrowed her eyes. Being a person who controlled shadows, he must have been physically weak to light as well.

"Ugh... agh! I can't believe it... you're a light user?!"

"That's right," Enyo said proudly. "I'm a light user."

"There's no way! One who bears the title 'Dark Lady' couldn't possibly be a light magic user!"

"I don't know much about this 'Dark Lady' business, and I don't really care. If you don't like the fact that I can use light magic, then return to the darklands and leave me alone already!"

"I cannot do that." Holding a hand to his face, Wraith stood warily to his feet. "Your light magic is all the more reason I must return with you in tow. We must exorcise this blasphemous power from you immediately!"

"That's never going to happen!"

Enyo clapped her hands together and chanted once more.

"Candidus. Lucidus. Aduro."

As she moved her hands apart, light gathered between them, until a small orb was formed. The orb grew in brightness. It was so bright that Wraith raised his forearms to protect his face. While her foe was distracted, Enyo pushed her hands out, launching the orb toward Wraith at speeds that he couldn't match.

The orb struck his chest and detonated. Whiteness. The entire world became a world of white. Enyo had to close her eyes, lest she be blinded by the light that erupted from the attack. When the light died down, Enyo lowered her arms and opened her eyes.

Wraith was gone.

She sighed in relief.

"Hmph. I'm surprised Wraith was defeated so easily. Then again, light magic is his greatest weakness," a female voice said, though Enyo couldn't tell where it was coming from.

"Who's there?" Enyo demanded. "Are you another lackey of the Dark Council?"

"I resent being called a 'lackey,'" the woman said. "It is true that I obey the will of the Dark Council, but I only do so for personal reasons. Once I have what I want, the council can go die, for all I care. Now, why don't you come with me... little girl," the voice whispered right next to her ear.

Enyo spun around and leapt backward. No one was there.

"Tsk. Tsk. I'm not over there, dear child," the voice said from behind her again. Enyo spun around, only to find that no one was there, again.

Is she using magic?

"Where are you hiding?" Enyo demanded to know, which caused the woman to laugh.

"Now why should I tell you something like that? Doing so would ruin my fun. Besides, unlike that idiot, Wraith, I am not keen on being blinded or blasted with that light magic of yours."

Did that mean she was another shadow user? No, specialized magic like that was rare within the Dark Clan. She'd never heard of two people sharing the same kind of unique magic. But if she wasn't a shadow magic user, then how was she able to hide so well?

"Lux. Lumin. Luminous. Accendo!"

Light exploded from Enyo's body like radiant waves of energy. They covered the land around her in luminescence, evaporating all of the shadows in her vicinity. She expected the person hiding to suddenly appear like Wraith had. She expected them to be in pain from her light magic.

That didn't happen.

Pain shot through her left shoulder like a searing bolt of lightning, making her gasp as she stumbled forward and brought her right hand to her shoulder. Something warm and wet became stuck to her hand. Pulling it back, Enyo gaped when she saw crimson liquid covering her hand like paint.

"W-what is… how…?"

"Are you wondering how I injured you?" The woman laughed again. "I'd be happy to tell you. However, I'm on something of a time schedule. So sorry. Maybe next time."

Enyo was given no time to retort as something crashed into her back, sending her stumbling forward. Before she could get too far, another something hit her in the chest, leaving her gasping in agonic asphyxia. It felt like her ribcage had been crushed!

"What's wrong? Not going to fight back?"

Enyo would have retorted, but something hard clipped her shoulder, sending her spinning to the ground. She landed with a harsh thud. Pain traveled up her shoulder as it was jarred from the impact, but she had no time to recover as something large slammed into her back.

"Ah… ah…" Enyo tried to scream, but all that came out was a series of agonized rasps. Her vision was going white. Pain overrode every one of her senses.

"Oh, you poor dear. It looks like you fell down and got injured. Here, let me help you up."

As if gravity had suddenly increased, Enyo found herself be smashed against the ground. She would've screamed as the feeling of her bones being crushed slammed into her like a tidal wave. She couldn't. She couldn't even breathe. Her chest was being compressed. It felt like her body was being flattened by a stampede. Everything hurt!

"Ah!"

The pressure suddenly ceased. Groaning, Enyo tried to get up, but her body wasn't working. She couldn't even move her arms.

Boots appeared in front of her face, black and high-heeled. They were open toed, so she could see the perfectly manicured nails, which were painted the same black as the boots. She tried to lift her head, to raise it and look at her assailant. It was impossible. Her body wouldn't respond to her commands. She felt numb.

"Look at you," the woman that she had been fighting said, scorn clear in her voice. She spoke like she was drinking poison. "I cannot fathom how someone so lacking in talent could possibly be the Dark Lady of our clan. To think that you are the one who's going to give birth to our new Dark Lord is shameful. Hmph! Truly, this world is filled with blasphemy."

Enyo cried out as a sharp heel dug into her cheek.

"Be grateful that I am supposed to take you in alive. Were it not for the Dark Council's orders, I would have already disposed of you."

Even though the pain was horrific, Enyo pushed past it and tried to think of a way out of this situation. Her body wasn't moving, but she still had her mind. Also, her opponent had just revealed herself to gloat. There had to be some way she could take advantage of that... fact...?

That's it!

"..." she mumbled.

"What was that?" The heel left her back. A shadow cast the stars in darkness. "Why don't you speak a little louder?"

"Lux. Lumin. Luminous. Accendo!"

"GYAAA!"

Light burst from Enyo's body like fireworks during a celebration. She couldn't see what the result of her attack was, but she could certainly hear the incredible width of breadth of the woman's swearing.

"You little cunt! How dare you do this to me!!! I'll kill you!!"

Enyo felt a moment of satisfaction at getting the better of her adversary—too bad it was only a moment, because the next thing she felt was pain as something hard slammed into her side. The world spun around. Her back squealed in pain as she crashed back into the ground. The stars hung above her, but she only saw them for a moment before they were blocked out by a face.

It was a gorgeous face, admittedly. White skin. Blood red lips. Seductive purple eyes. The face that appeared before her was the kind that most men would have killed people over, and in fact, it wouldn't have surprised her if this woman had gotten people to kill for her. Right now, however, that face was marred by an ugly snarl full of hatred.

"I hope you've enjoyed your life so far," the woman spat. "I might not be allowed to kill you, but I will take great joy in making you wish that you had been killed."

Enyo would have loved to say something witty, but she'd already lost her ability to speak. She'd never been so injured in her life. Even though the pain had faded to a dull ache, she could tell that her body was a wreck. She no longer had the strength to so much as talk.

The woman snorted as she stood back up. "Pathetic wench. I am going to enjoy teaching you your place."

As Enyo prepared herself for what could only be more pain, a loud shout reached her ears.

"ENYO!!"

In that exact moment, multiple things seemed to happen at once. The ground that she was on exploded, the woman who'd been hurting her screamed in agony, and a pair of strong arms picked her up. A familiar scent drifted into her nose. She recognized it, this masculine smell. Beneath the sweat and scent of steel, it was the fragrance that she had come to associate with comfort.

Enyo didn't know when it happened, but as she felt herself being carried off, she fell asleep, secure in the knowledge that she could leave the rest to Jacob.

✳✳✳

Jacob couldn't remember the last time he'd been this worried. Enyo was unconscious, her body covered in blood and bruises. Crimson liquid trickled down her mouth, and her face was smeared with sweat and dirt.

The area around Jacob was a mess, remnants of the battle that Enyo had fought. Several meters away was a large pillar of earth, which rose from the ground, a monolithic reminder of what had happened to his companion.

There was a mighty flap next to him—the drake, which kicked up dust and wind as it landed on the ground. Fellis alighted from the mount and rushed over to him.

"Jumping from the drake while it was in mid-flight was reckless," Fellis said. "Aren't you supposed to be afraid of heights?"

"I'm not afraid of heights. I just don't like them."

"So you say, but…" Fellis trailed off, shrugged, and then cast a concerned gaze on Enyo. "Is she okay?"

"She'll be fine. I'll make sure of it."

Jacob set Enyo on the ground and placed his hands on her, one on her forehead and the other in the center of her chest, right against her beating heart. His hands glowed a light blue.

"What are you doing?"

"I'm regulating her chi," Jacob said, frowning in concentration. "By regulating and boosting her chi with my own, I can help her own body speed up the healing natural process."

"I see…"

"You didn't understand any of that, did you?"

"Nope."

As they spoke, a woman walked out from behind the pillar. She limped forward, her lips split into a snarl. Her black dress was in tatters. Burns marred her pale skin and some of her hair had been burnt away, ruining the seductive beauty that she had once possessed.

"Fellis," the woman hissed out the "s" of Fellis's name like it was a curse. "I knew that you couldn't be trusted! When the Dark Council hears about this—"

"I don't care if the Dark Council hears about this," Fellis cut off. "I never planned on handing Enyo over to them. You think your words are going to scare me?"

"Tch! I've always hated you, you fucking bitch."

"There's the pot calling the kettle black."

Jacob finished regulating Enyo's internal energy. There was nothing left for him to do. The rest was up to her.

Standing up, he turned to face the woman who'd caused his companion so much pain. He was surprised at the amount of hatred he felt for this woman. However, he couldn't deny that, right now, he really wanted to bash her face in until it was nothing but a bloody smear.

"I don't know what your Dark Council wants with Enyo," he said, and his voice sounded harsh and grating even to his own ears. "Truthfully, I don't care. The moment you hurt Enyo, you made yourself my enemy. You're not going to get the chance to tell them about Fellis's betrayal. I'm not letting you get away."

The woman shifted her attention from Fellis to him. She blinked once. Then she smiled.

"Oh, my. What a handsome young man," she purred, her change shifting as though the sight of a male caused her entire emotional paradigm to change. "How would you like to come with me and—"

She wasn't able to say anymore.

Because Jacob had just smashed his fist into her face.

It was like a thunderclap, echoing across the vast plane. The air distorted where his fist connected with her left cheek, blasting out from the point of impact with a loud *boom!* What followed was the woman being launched off her feet and sent shooting backwards like a falling star. She slammed into the large earth pillar that she had created, blowing a hole straight through it and causing the entire thing to crumble like a house of cards.

Jacob didn't even bother looking to see if she was alive. He'd felt her neck snap with his punch. That combined with the impact when she hit that pillar meant there was little chance of her having survived.

Fellis whistled as Jacob walked back over to Enyo. "Remind me never to get on your bad side."

Ignoring the remark, Jacob knelt back down and tenderly scooped Enyo into his arms. He didn't want to move her because it could affect the healing process, but they couldn't afford to stay there. They needed to get to the next town. It would be better if Enyo could rest on a bed anyway.

"Please take us to the nearest town," he said to Fellis. "After that, let the drake return to Deterion."

"Very well." Fellis smiled as she mounted the drake again. "Hop on. Just be sure to keep a tight hold of Enyo. I don't want her falling off."

Jacob nodded as he climbed onto the drake. He glued himself in place with chi, and, as Fellis took hold of the reins, he held Enyo close to his chest.

Feeling the labored breathing of his companion, Jacob thought about the Dark Council assassins that they had met so far.

He could only wonder about what sort of disaster would strike them next.

CHAPTER 5 - CHAMPIONS OF THE DARK COUNCIL

Vicus was a village located nearly two dozen leagues from Deterion. It was smaller than Altus and Deterion, and the architecture that could be found there reflected that. All the buildings were made from wood and possessed thatched roofs. They appeared sturdier than the constructions found in most small villages, but there was no denying their quaintness.

After arriving at the village, Fellis sent the drake they had stolen back to its master. Meanwhile, he had carried Enyo to the nearest inn. He'd received some strange looks for carrying a woman who was unconscious and covered in bruises, but that was all. It wasn't like this sight was unusual. Most of these people probably thought they were victims of an attack.

Monster attacks happened quite frequently to the unwary.

The room that they had rented had two beds. It was small, but that suited Jacob just fine. His only real concern was how they would work out sleeping arrangements, though he imagined that he would be sleeping on the floor.

Since Fellis was now with them, Jacob had stepped out of the room while Fellis stripped Enyo of her clothes and bandaged her wounds. Rather than stand outside, he made himself useful and went downstairs to grab some food for them. He had a few gold coins left. Fellis was done dressing Enyo's injuries when he returned.

"That energy manipulation thing that you did is really impressive," Fellis said as she picked at her food—steamed potatoes with two chicken legs. "Most of her bruises had already vanished by the time we arrived here, and the few that remain are healing up more quickly that I had anticipated."

"Linked Energy Manipulation is hands down the best practical skill a person could ask for," Jacob boasted. "Not only does it allow me to enhance my own strength, but it also lets me manipulate the energy found within others."

"Ah." The way Fellis's eyes widened told him that she understood what he was talking about now. He guessed she'd been under the assumption that his powers were some type of magic. "That is indeed a fortuitous skill to have. I had no idea there was someone left in this world who knew how to use Linked Energy Manipulation."

"By the way," Jacob continued, "don't you think it's time you told me about the Dark Clan members that we faced off against? It won't do if we fight them again, and I'm in the dark about who they are and what sort of magic they possess."

"Yes, I suppose I should tell you about that, shouldn't I?" Fellis sighed.

Jacob walked over to the bed that Enyo was resting on and sat down, ignoring the way the mattress sunk underneath his added weight. He looked at Enyo. Her eyes were closed, her mouth was partially open, and her face looked peaceful. The bruises that had covered her face were gone, leaving behind unblemished porcelain skin.

"The Dark Council has decided that they want to reclaim their 'Dark Lady,' in other words, Enyo. To that end, they have chosen seven champions, who have turned this mission into something of a competition." Fellis finished her meal and set the empty plate aside. "I am one of the seven that was chosen, along with Shade, Wraith, and Heart, the woman whose face you caved in with your fist."

At the mention of how he'd practically destroyed that woman's face with a single punch, Jacob shrugged. "She upset me."

"Indeed," Fellis said, her expression conveying a hint of amusement. "In any case, aside from myself and those three, there are two others: Nemesis and Darkness."

"That's six."

"Excuse me?" Fellis looked startled.

"I said that's only six," Jacob repeated. "Who is the last one?"

"I..." Fellis hesitated, then shrugged. "I'm not sure. The last one was selected by Lust, but I was not made privy to who she chose."

That didn't invoke pleasant feelings, but Jacob decided to ignore the unknown champion for now. He would cross that bridge when he got to it.

"What can you tell me about them?" Jacob asked.

Enyo shifted on the bed, seemingly trying to make herself more comfortable. She mumbled several times and smacked her lips. Then she settled down once more.

Fellis shrugged. "Not as much as I would like. I don't know a whole lot about those two. Nemesis is a very large man who wields two scimitars. I do not know what his magic is, but his skills at dual-wielding is nothing to scoff at. Darkness I know even less about. She's never been the talkative type."

"So, we've got two more enemies that we don't know much about, which means we're essentially going to be fighting blind."

"Pretty much."

"Great. That's just what I need: more unknowns."

"As someone who once fought his way through the darklands and defeated the Dark Lord himself, I imagine fighting against opponents with unknown magic is something you're used to."

"Just because I've fought against unknown opponents before doesn't mean I like to do it, or that I want to do it again," Jacob retorted. "Anyway, I guess we'll just have to take them as they come."

"I suppose so."

Jacob finished eating his meal, and then set the empty plate on top of Fellis's. He thought about what they should do from now on, but without knowing when, where, and how these last two enemies would strike, he couldn't formulate a solid plan. In the end, he would be fighting a reactive battle.

Enyo shifted some more, drawing his attention. His companion had suffered quite a bit at the hands of that woman. Remember how he'd seen Heart torturing Enyo for her own sick amusement pissed him off. His blood boiled just thinking about it.

"You're quite protective of her," Fellis said. Jacob glanced up. "Of Enyo, I mean."

"I guess." Jacob ran a hand through his hair. "Speaking of Enyo... why have I been getting the feeling that you want me and her to become intimate?"

Fellis smiled. "I don't know what you're talking about."

"Don't play coy with me," Jacob snapped. "Back when we were chasing after Enyo and her kidnapper, you talked about how Enyo was in love with the hero, and then you went on to suggest that I speak with her about her feelings. You wouldn't have done that unless you wanted us to get together for some reason."

Fellis was silent for a time, and Jacob had no issue letting that silence become prolonged if it meant she would eventually answer him. During this silence, his eyes were once more drawn toward Enyo. Several bangs had fallen into her face. Jacob reached out and gently brushed the bangs away.

"You already know what is required of the Dark Lady, or rather, you know what the Dark Council makes those with the title of Dark Lady do," Fellis said. "From the moment she was born, Enyo's fate has been to birth the next Dark Lord once her father was felled. However, doing so is a death sentence."

"What?"

In response to what was undoubtedly his flabbergasted expression, Fellis offered a bitter smile. "Giving birth to a Dark Lord requires untold amounts of magical power, far more than what any normal person would have."

Dark lords were born with insane amounts of magical power. If someone were to put it in averages, then a single dark lord would equal an army of about 5,000 paladins. The power they wielded was on a level that few people could ever reach. Jacob still sometimes found it amazing that he'd been able to defeat Alucard in single combat.

"Impregnating the Dark Lady is not done through normal means. It is done through a ritual that creates a life. This ritual involves all seven members of the Dark Council sending their power into the Dark Lady. However, receiving that much power from seven of the most powerful Dark Clan members in the world doesn't come without a cost. Likewise, giving birth to a being with the power of those seven is a death sentence. All dark ladies are essentially sacrificial lambs whose only purpose is to give birth to the next Dark Lord. Once their purpose is done, their dead bodies are tossed aside."

Ignorance is said to be a bliss, but Jacob, having experienced quite a few hardships thanks to his ignorance, had believed otherwise —until now. Learning this new piece of information made him sick to his stomach.

He hadn't known anything about how dark lords were created. It had always been one of those things that everyone just accepted. Every generation there was a dark lord and a hero, they would do battle, one of them would die, and the process would repeat itself with the next generation. This was how it had always been, and no one had questioned it.

Learning the truth was hard.

"I see." Jacob pressed a hand to his face, rubbing his eyes as if they'd suddenly become sore. "So, the reason you want me to get with Enyo is because if she and I are together, you believe the Dark Council will leave her alone?"

"Not quite," Fellis corrected. "It's not enough for you to just be 'together.' You and Enyo need to be sexually active."

Jacob was glad that he had finished eating, or he would have choked on his food at those words. "W-what?"

"The Dark Lady has to remain pure for the ritual to work," Fellis explained. "Part of the ritual involves the act of 'staining' the Dark Lady's purity. If the Dark Lady isn't pure, then the ritual won't work properly."

"So... the Dark Lady needs to be a virgin for the ritual to work?" Jacob asked.

"Yes."

"I'm not sure I understand," Jacob confessed. "Why does she need to be a virgin?"

"Because of the dark nature of the ritual," Fellis patiently explained. "Rituals like this involve perverting the nature of people. The power necessary to fuel the ritual is created by staining those who are pure in mind, body, and heart."

"Is that also why Enyo wasn't allowed outside of her home when she was younger?" he asked. "To keep her pure?"

Fellis crossed one leg over the other and nodded. "Yes. By keeping her contact with others, especially men, to a minimum, the Dark Council ensures her purity."

Jacob still didn't understand, but perhaps that was because he was human. The nature of the Dark Clan often eluded humanity. It was at least part of the reason their two sides were always at war. They just didn't understand each other.

That didn't matter to him, though. He didn't like the idea of Enyo being used in such a ritual. Throughout their journey, she had been nothing but kind and helpful. She'd put up with his act when they had been gathering information on the Phantasma Forest, she'd protected him when he'd been poisoned, and she'd defeated Agatha. Enyo was an invaluable companion now, and he considered her to be a good friend.

He couldn't say he loved her because he didn't know what his feelings were anymore. At one point, he had thought he loved Alice, but after she allowed the hyenas known as the White Council to take advantage of them, whatever feelings he might have possessed had turned into resentment.

That said, he couldn't deny that, from a purely physical standpoint, he was attracted to Enyo. He thought she was gorgeous. However, thinking that someone was physically attractive wasn't the same as being in love.

Fellis suddenly standing up made Jacob snap out of his thoughts and look at her. She smiled as she grabbed the plates. "I think I'm going to take these down to the barkeep."

"Okay."

Walking out of the room, Jacob's last glimpse of Fellis was the door closing behind her. Then he was alone with Enyo.

"This is a fine mess I've gotten myself into," he said to himself.

It seemed like no matter where he went or what he did, trouble always arouse. He wondered if this was the curse of a hero, or maybe it was his own personal curse. Was he destined to always face dangers and troubles in this world?

"I'm sorry about Fellis," Enyo said, her voice a soft whisper.

"Oh. You're awake." Jacob looked down. Enyo was staring back at him with half-lidded eyes. "How are you feeling?"

"Like I got beaten up by an old hag."

Jacob grinned. "I don't know how old she was, but you did get beaten pretty badly." His lips twitched, the smile left, and a frown took its place. "I'm sorry. This only happened because I was careless."

Enyo shook her head. "Please don't apologize. I'm the one who should be saying sorry. I came to you for help, but I never told you everything."

"Are you talking about the ritual to create a new dark lord?" he asked.

"Yes." Enyo closed her eyes, and her body sunk further into the bed with a boneless quality, as if she was so exhausted that staying awake required more effort than it was worth. "I didn't tell you about the ritual because I didn't want you to think I was trying to make you fall in love with me."

"Fellis did say that you were in love with the hero version of me," he said.

"It is true that I fell in love with the stories that Fellis used to tell me," she admitted. "However, I know that you aren't the same as the person who I heard about in the stories of you. You're different than him."

"Does that disappoint you?"

Enyo shook her head. "On the contrary, the you that I kept hearing stories about always seemed unreal, like you were larger than life. The Jacob who I met that night at the pub felt a lot more real, more attainable. If it's you, I feel like I can stand by your side rather than look up at you as you're raised on a pedestal."

To stand by his side. He'd never heard someone say that before. Not even Alice had told him that she wanted to stand by his side as an equal.

"Is that really all you want?" he asked.

Enyo smiled tiredly and, raising her hand, she reached out. Jacob only realized a few seconds later what she wanted, and he clasped her hand in his. The tired smile on her face became just a few shades brighter, which might have been due to pink hue spreading across her cheeks.

"The only thing I want," she began, "is to spend the rest of my life with you in the world you came from."

He stared at Enyo, unable to comprehend her answer. It was so simple that he couldn't help but think she had an ulterior motive.

Jacob had spent his entire life in Terrasole learning that people couldn't be trusted, that, if it meant getting what they wanted at the expenditure of his trust, they would betray him without hesitation.

The White Council had abused his trust, Alice had abused his trust, and he didn't even know where his old companions were. It was only natural that he wouldn't trust Enyo at her word. At the same time, he wanted to.

He really, really wanted to.

"I see," Fellis said as she entered the room. "So that is what your goal is. You are seeking to accompany Jacob to his original world."

"Fellis..." Enyo muttered.

"I'm glad to see that you are awake." Fellis's smile was far more tender than anything Jacob had seen from the woman thus far. "I apologize for trying to fight with you. I had not realized that you already had such a well thought out plan."

"It's okay," Enyo murmured. She looked about ready to fall asleep again. "I figured you had a reason for trying to stop me. I'm sorry I never told you what I was planning."

Fellis sat down on the other side of the bed, and, leaning over, she placed a kiss on Enyo's forehead. The sight reminded Jacob of his mom. Back before he was summoned to this world, she used to kiss him on the forehead just like that.

"Get some rest, Enyo," Fellis said. "You're still recovering and need your sleep."

"Right..."

Enyo sighed as she closed her eyes. Her body relaxed, her grip on his hand slackened, and her arm became limp. Despite this, Jacob remained holding her hand.

"I believe we should get some sleep as well," Fellis said.

"Yeah," Jacob agreed. "You can take the other bed."

Raising an eyebrow, Fellis cast him an inquiring glance. "Oh, are you planning to sleep on the floor, or is your intention to slip into Enyo's bed once I'm asleep?"

"I'll take the floor," Jacob said, unbothered by the woman's teasing. "But I plan to remain here for a little while longer."

Fellis sighed. "You're no fun."

"I say that all the time," Durandal said.

"Both of you should be quiet."

It wasn't long after she slipped into bed that Fellis fell asleep, her breath evening and becoming deep. Jacob stayed awake. He held Enyo's hand, unsure of why he didn't feel like letting go.

Visible through the window, a thousand stars twinkled like specks of white on a pure black canvas.

The plan that Jacob and Enyo had come up with after retrieving the gate key was to travel toward Alysium, sneak into Avant Heim, and use the otherworld gate to escape to his original world. Their original plan had taken something of a nose dive after all of the trouble they had in the Phantasma Forest. Somehow, instead of ending up closer to Alysium or even back in Altus, they had landed themselves on the other side of Terrasole.

Despite this initial series of setbacks, they had decided to continue their journey. Since Vicus, the city they found themselves in, was located north east of Avant Heim, they needed to travel south west. This would take them through several major cities, including Tellus Caelum, the second largest city in Terrasole.

Tellus Caelum was a massive city. It sprawled out for kilometers in all directions, and there appeared to be little rhyme or reason in the construction of its structures. Numerous styles of architecture mixed together to create a smorgasbord of styles. Gleaming towers stood next to squat homes, cathedrals sat beside bars. It was a liberal mess. The city was like a maze. There were so many twists and turns that only the people who'd lived there their whole lives could navigate it.

The cobblestone streets were filled with pedestrians, thousands of people walking along the walkways while carriages and carts moved down the road. They looked through store windows, chatted with each other in front of restaurants, and gossiped while standing before street signs and vendors.

Jacob strode alongside Fellis and Enyo. Both of them looked quite out of place amongst the crowd, with their pale skin and unusual hair and eye color. Most people in this city had fair to dark skin, and their hair was either brown or blond, while their eyes of the standard range of colors for humans.

It might have also had something to do with their ensemble. Enyo was wearing leather pants that hugged her hips, a white skirt with cuts on either side to allow for freedom of movement, black knee-length boots, and a brown leather corset over a sleeveless red shirt. Her daggers were strapped to the small of her back.

Meanwhile, Fellis was decked out in what looked more like the bondage outfit of a fetishist. Her cleavage was exposed by the V-cut that went all the way down to her navel, and she was wearing black heeled boots. Her taste in fashion was similar to many other dark clanswomen that he'd met. It made him wonder if all women of the Dark Clan enjoyed outfits like this.

Enyo must be a black sheep of the clan.

It was fortunate there were so many people. The crowd kept others from getting a really good look at them.

Leading them through the streets, he sought a place where they could rest. It wasn't quite late, but it was definitely getting to the point where he wanted to at least rent out a room.

There were several taverns and inns, but from just a glance inside of them, he could tell that most were filled to capacity. It took them nearly twenty minutes to find a tavern where they could rest their weary legs in.

The Boar's Head was an older tavern. Despite that, the exterior had a well-maintained appearance. The walls were made of brick, and a glass window allowed people a glimpse inside. Red tiles made up the roof, which was shaped like a spiral instead of the standard triangle shapes he usually found on buildings.

He, Enyo, and Fellis entered through a red doorway, stepping into a well-lit room with numerous tables and booths. Most of the tables were already occupied. Jacob pushed his way through the crowd, his leather boots thudding along the wooden floor as he wove between tables. Several men catcalled when they saw Enyo and Fellis. The catcalls died off, however, when Fellis sent them a glare that promised death. Jacob smiled when several men who'd been eyeing Enyo with lust in their eyes suddenly paled.

Serves them right.

There was an empty booth near the back. He slid into one side of the booth. Fellis sat on the other, while Enyo slid in on his side. The warmth from Enyo's thighs made him aware of her proximity.

Fellis ordered an ale from the bar wench, a young woman with red hair, green eyes, and a false smile. Jacob and Enyo ordered a water. Neither of them liked to drink, and both of them remembered what happened the last time they drank.

"How much further is Alysium?" asked Fellis.

"It's about one month's travel from here," Jacob said. "Once we leave the city, we'll come upon the Jovis Bridge. We'll cross that and continue traveling until we reach Alysium."

"I still don't see why we can't grab some drakes or a griffin and just fly there." She leaned back, crossed her arms, and sighed.

"Because we don't have enough money," Enyo pointed out. "Also, wouldn't flying there be more conspicuous? I mean, most people can't afford to buy a flying mount, right? If we arrive at Alysium on a couple of drakes or a griffin, everyone is going to spot us, and then we'll be in trouble."

"I guess," Fellis said.

This woman was surprisingly lazy. She didn't like traveling on foot, often complaining about how much her feet hurt as they walked from place to place. When they slept in a tavern, she'd sprawl herself out on the bed and pass out. Her snores could also wake the dead. It was kind of like listening to a dragon snorting fire. Despite this, she was quite reliable in a fight, which he was grateful for.

Sometimes, you had to appreciate the little things.

"Fellis?" Enyo said.

Putting down her drink after taking a long gulp, Fellis looked at her charge. "Yes?"

"I was wondering... have you given any thought as to what you're going to do once Jacob and I travel to his world?"

With a thoughtful frown, Fellis appeared to ponder the question before shrugging. "I haven't thought that far ahead. Honestly, once you leave, I won't have much left to live for."

"Then why don't you come with us?" Enyo suggested.

"Come with you?" The expression on Fellis's face, the way her eyes had widened as if she'd never thought of Enyo's idea before, almost made Jacob laugh. "I don't know if that would be a good idea..."

"Why not?"

"Because we don't even know if it's possible for someone from this world to travel through the gate, for one," Fellis pointed out.

"Which reminds me, what do you plan on doing if it turns out that you can't cross over?"

"I…" Enyo hesitated. "I'm not sure…"

Biting her lip, she looked at Jacob. Her gaze made him remember their conversation a few weeks ago. It also made him feel conflicted. More than anything, Jacob longed to return home. He was sick and tired of this world, which had forced him to fight for a people that he wasn't a part of. He wanted to see his mom and dad again. He wanted his mom to hold him and his dad to take him for rides on his motorcycle. He wanted to go back to where he belonged…

… But he didn't want to leave Enyo.

In the two months since they had first met, Enyo had become an irreplaceable part of his life. During the days where they walked from place to place, he and Enyo would talk for hours on end. At night, they would stay up late telling each other stories. When they were battling monsters, he could always trust her to have his back. He didn't want to part with her.

"If…" Jacob swallowed. "If it turns out that you can't cross over, I'll stay here."

"Wha—you can't!" Enyo shouted. Several people looked their way, but most went back to their drinking.

Fellis agreed before he could say anything. "If you decided not to leave just because we couldn't, it would negate all of the effort Enyo put into helping you."

"I guess…"

Enyo smiled as she placed her hand over his. "Thank you for saying that. It makes me really happy, but even if I can't go with you, I would like you to at least return home. It's where you belong."

Liar…

He wanted to call her out because he knew, without a shadow of a doubt, that she was lying. They'd had many conversations. Most of them revolved around Jacob's world. She would always ask him questions about his world, about its people and the places he'd visited. The way her eyes would sparkle as he spoke, as if she was imagining what it would be like to live in his world, was a clear indicator that she wanted to go with him more than anything.

"Let's cross that bridge when we get to it," Jacob said at last.

"That reminds me, I don't think I've ever seen the gate key before," Fellis said. "It's supposed to open the gateway to another world, right? Is it just a key, or is it some kind of mystical device?"

"That's right," Jacob said. "We haven't shown it to you, have we?"

Fellis shook her head. Reaching into his pouch, Jacob felt around until he'd grasped the gate key, and then pulled it out. Fellis studied the object, with its long handle and gem on one end, and the strange blade-like shape on the other. It didn't look anything like a key.

"I've never seen writing like that before," she murmured in reference to the archaic symbols written all over the key's surface.

"I've only seen them once before," Jacob admitted as he pocketed the key. "It was the day the White Council summoned me to this world. The writing was on the circle that I found myself standing in when I was summoned to Avant Heim."

"Hmm…"

"I have a question," Durandal suddenly spoke up.

"What is it?" asked Jacob.

"If it turns out that Enyo and Fellis aren't able to travel to your world, does that mean I won't be able to either?"

No one had an answer to that.

It was still too early for them to fall asleep, and Enyo professed that she really wanted to see more of the city. They rented out a room. Once the barkeep had given them the key, they traveled outside to do some exploring.

The day was spent wandering the city. Enyo looked through almost every store they came across, her eyes glittering like a child who'd been told that every day was her birthday. They checked out shops, bought treats at street vendors, and enjoyed the many sights.

Tellus Caelum was an artisan city, meaning it was home to many artists, including architects. This was, in fact, part of the reason the city's architecture was so mixed. There were numerous architects hoping to make their mark on the world, and this city was their testing ground.

Aside from architects, there were also painters, sculptors, musicians, and playwrights. As they wandered the street, he, Enyo, and Fellis saw numerous shows being put on; people played music, painters were drawing portraits, and there was even a sculptor working on a statue in the middle of a street.

Enyo gazed at it all. Her head twisted and turned as if she were trying to take in everything at once. The smile on her face lightened his heart.

Time passed, and midday became evening. Jacob, Enyo, and Fellis traveled back to *The Boar's Head*, passing through the bar and heading up the stairs, where several doors sat. Their room was the last door on the right. It was a basic room with two beds and a small bath. They needed to call the bar wench to draw the bath for them. Jacob took his last. The water was freezing, but he didn't mind.

Later that night, as the moon waxed across the sky, Jacob drifted into a light sleep. He was in his own bed while Enyo and Fellis shared one. A cool breeze blew in through the open window. Jacob, who never slept with covers on because he could get tangled in them if he moved too quickly, shivered as goosebumps broke out on his skin.

Thump. Thump. Thump.

Footsteps made him twitch. They were soft, nearly silent. Had his sleep been any deeper, he would have never heard them.

An assassin?

Jacob had been attacked by assassins many times in the past—too many times to count. It wouldn't have surprised him if this person was an assassin. However, just who they were there to assassinate was another matter entirely.

Enyo? No, the only people who employ assassins are the Dark Clan and the dregs of human society.

The Dark Clan was trying to get Enyo to return. They wouldn't assassinate her. On the other hand, humans barely knew that she existed. Those who did recognize her as a thief, so they would want to capture her alive to interrogate her.

They could be after Fellis.

It was a strong possibility, given that Fellis was now a traitor to the Dark Council. Killing her would also mean one less person protecting Enyo. That would make it easier for the last two champions of the Dark Council to kidnap her, but...

What is that rustling noise?

The noise coming from the assailant made it sound like they were rustling around their bags. That was... odd. They didn't have anything of value there, except for...

Shit!

Jacob leapt to his feet, and, using the bed as a springboard, he tried to kick the thief.

Unfortunately, they must have heard him. The thief ducked low. Jacob sailed by, twirling around until his feet touched the wall. Then he bent his leg and launched himself at the thief again.

The thief leapt backward as Jacob tried to land an axe kick on their cranium. Their jump took them all the way to the window sill, which they hopped onto without hesitation.

Jacob only had a short glimpse of the person. Covered from head to toe in black, he could make out nothing save for their burning amber eyes. The only thing he could see aside from that was the shape of their decidedly male figure, lithe yet masculine. The perfect physique for a thief or assassin. Grasped firmly within this person's hand, glinting like a coruscating gem, was the gate key.

"Damn! Hold on there, you bastard!"

Jacob rushed toward the window, but it was already too late. The thief had jumped. Placing his hands on the windowsill, Jacob could only swear as he saw the person hopping from roof to roof, their figure getting smaller and smaller.

"Jacob?" Enyo with a yawn, making it clear that she'd woken up. "What's going on? What are you doing out of bed?"

"There's no time to explain!" Jacob turned around and rushed to grab his clothing, which he hurriedly put on, saving Durandal's sheath for last. "Hurry up and get dressed! Someone just stole the gate key!"

"What?!" Enyo and the now wide awake Fellis shouted.

"Hurry up and get dressed!"

The two hopped out of bed, threw their clothes on, and then they were leaping out of the window in chase of the thief.

Racing ahead, Jacob looked back at the two. "I'm going on ahead! I'll hold him off while you two catch up!"

After receiving a nod of acknowledgement, Jacob faced ahead and, channeling his energy through his legs and feet, shot forward at speeds so fast his cheeks peeled back. Tears formed in his eyes as the wind slapped his face. He didn't even pay attention to the discomfort. The entirety of his being was focused on catching up to the thief.

The thief soon came in sight. However, their figure was blurry and indistinct, even when he drew closer. Growling, he put on more speed in his effort to catch up. As he neared them, held out his hand, channeling energy to create a glowing orb of blue light, which he launched at the thief.

They vanished right before the orb hit them.

What?!

A soft whistling from behind made his ears twitch. He turned around. There was a flash of light as something flew at him. Unsheathing Durandal in one smooth motion, he knocked the projectile aside.

There was another projectile hidden in the shadow of the first. He tried to dodge, but he was too slow, and the weapon penetrated his left bicep.

"Grk!"

Gritting his teeth, Jacob yanked the weapon out. Blood leaked down his arm, creating trails of crimson that fell onto the roof. Standing on another roof about two meters away, a lone figure clad in darkness stood. It was the thief.

How did he get behind me?

"I see you are confused," a voice said, though it didn't come from the thief. This voice was female.

Jacob calmed his racing heart. He couldn't afford to lose his cool.

"Confused? Yes, I suppose you could say I'm a little confused, though that has more to do with the creepy ventriloquist voice than anything else. Wanna do me a solid and reveal yourself?"

"Oh, my. What an interesting wit. For that alone, I suppose it would behoove me to show myself to you. Very well, Boy."

A person appeared before him, flickering in and out, as if she was made from light particles or not all there. Her body then solidified. Jacob blinked.

Her crimson tresses reminded him of a violent conflagration as they swayed in the breeze. They surrounded her pale face, complimenting her ruby red lips while contrasting with her viridian eyes. The dress that she wore was sleeveless. It was a midnight gown that trailed down to her feet, fitting her like body paint. She was lithe, with a supple bosom, a thin waist, and shapely hips. A slit running across the left side displayed tantalizing hints of bare leg.

"It's a pleasure to finally meet you, hero," she said, her eyes smiling at him. "My name is Darkness, and you're going to be my new puppet."

Jacob stared into Darkness's vibrant green eyes, which held an iridescent sheen.

It was the last thing he saw before the world was consumed by darkness.

Enyo was gasping as she chased after Jacob. While she was in excellent shape from constant training, she didn't have the ability to enhance her muscles like he did. Running beside her, Fellis was gasping as if she'd been running at top speed for ten days straight.

"H-how fast… is this boy?" she rasped.

To that, Enyo didn't have an answer.

They continued running, hopping from roof to roof, until they finally caught up with Jacob. Enyo cleared the gap between buildings, landing in a crouch. She stood up, prepared to travel over to Jacob, but then she stopped.

There were two other people with him. One of them was a man covered in darkness, with amber eyes and pale skin hidden behind a mask. The other was a woman of such beauty that Enyo found herself feeling self-conscious. The woman wore a midnight dress with no sleeves and a notorious gap that traveled all the way down to her navel. Her red hair, viridian eyes, and ruby lips gave her a familiar appearance. Enyo thought she had seen her somewhere before.

"Oh, my," the woman said. "It seems you've caught up with us, and so quickly, too."

"Are you the person who stole the gate key?" Enyo demanded to know.

"No, that was not me," the woman said. "That was my companion, Nemesis."

Nemesis? Enyo frowned as the woman gestured to the man standing beside her. However, while all she felt was confusion, Fellis suddenly paled.

"Enyo," she said, her voice containing a hint of warning. "Be very careful around these two. That's Darkness and Nemesis, the last two assassins sent by the Dark Council to apprehend you."

Darkness clapped. "Bravo, Fellis. Excellent job in figuring that out. Yes, you are correct." Darkness's ruby lips twisted into a pleasantly unpleasant smile. "We're here to take you back home, Dark Lady. I do hope that you'll cooperate with us."

"I'm not going back!" Enyo declared, though most of her attention was focused on Jacob, who hadn't said a word since they arrived. "Jacob? Why aren't you saying anything? Why are you just standing there?"

"The hero can't hear you, dear," Darkness said. "He can't hear anything except my voice." She gazed at Jacob with a hungry look that made Enyo sick to her stomach. "Isn't that right, my hero?"

"Don't worry. I'll protect you."

"What? Jacob?" Enyo gawked. What was going on? Something had obviously happened to her friend, and it was clear to her that this woman was responsible. Mind manipulation? No, this seemed like something else. "What have you done to Jacob?"

Darkness looked hurt. She placed a hand against her bosoms, as if Enyo's words were an arrow piercing her heart.

"What makes you think I've done anything? Perhaps the hero has simply been charmed by me."

"As if Jacob would ever find you charming," Enyo spat. "You've clearly cast some kind of magic spell on him. Return him to me this instant!"

Placing a hand on her cheek, Darkness said, "Such a demanding girl, you are." Then, in a feminine voice that made Enyo think the woman was mocking her, she continued, "Jacob, that person is attacking me! Please take care of her!"

"Don't worry, I'll protect you from her," Jacob said, turning around to face Enyo.

"Jacob, stop this! Can't you see that woman is controlling you!" Enyo said.

Scowling, Jacob shifted into a standard swordsman stance. "I don't know who you are, but I'm going to make you pay for trying to hurt my friend."

"Hurt your friend? Jacob, that's not your friend! I don't know who you think she is, but she's trying to control you!"

"Shut up! You don't know what you're talking about!"

Enyo flinched, but she didn't give up. She opened her mouth in an attempt to make him see reason. However, before she could speak, Fellis interrupted her.

"It's no using trying to call out to him," she said. "He's not in his right mind. The only thing we can do is—"

"Nemesis," Darkness called. "Take care of the traitor, please."

"Yes."

Nemesis leapt at Fellis without warning, claws appearing on his hands, which he used to try to slash her apart. He missed when Fellis leapt back, but he wasn't deterred. He leapt after her as the woman disappeared from the rooftop. Enyo heard the *clangs!* of clashing steel recede into the distance.

Be safe, Fellis...

"Jacob," Enyo called out. "You don't need to do this! Snap out of it!"

Darkness laughed. "He's not going to listen to the words of a villain! Jacob, please take care of her for me, but leave her alive. I think we should question her to find out what she knows."

"That's a good idea, Enyo," he said.

W-what did he call her?

Enyo wasn't given any time to speak out before Jacob was on her. He moved so fast that she'd barely seen him, like he was a bolt of lightning. Durandal slid out of its sheath with a hiss as he swung his blade. She did her best to block it with her daggers, but the attack was so powerful that she was lifted into the air and sent sailing backward.

As her feet hit the tiles, she slid across the roof, skidding until she was at the lip of the building. She almost fell off as her left foot slipped. When she looked back up after making sure she was secure, it was to find Jacob standing right in front of her, Durandal raised and ready to slice her apart.

"I'm sorry!" Durandal cried. "But my partner isn't in control of his actions right now!"

The sword came down. Enyo did the only thing she could think of. She fell backward and kicked off the roof, soaring over the side building. Luckily, there was a rope used for drying clothes hanging between the buildings. She grabbed the robe with one hand, cut it with the dagger in her other hand, and swung down to the street below.

Jacob followed her, dropping off the building and landing in a crouch.

Enyo raced down the empty road, Jacob hot on her heels. He launched several blue crescent attacks her way. She dodged, juking left and right to avoid them. Each attack gouged chunks of cobblestone from the road. She eyed the long slash marks that traveled through the street with apprehension. She'd be killed if even one of those hit her.

I need to do something. I need to snap him out of this!

Something was wrong with Jacob. That said, she didn't know what was wrong with him. It was definitely some form of mind control, but there were several methods of controlling the mind. Fellis had taught her a few of the ways. There was mind manipulation, which was Fellis's magic, but there was also charm magic and illusion magic. Charm magic did exactly what it sounded like. It charmed a person into being someone's slave. Illusion magic was the ability to project illusions into a person's mind, making them see things and think things that weren't real.

Jacob had probably fallen for one of these two magics. As strong as he was, his strength meant nothing in the face of this type of magic. They didn't affect the body. They affected the mind. What made these two magic types so insidious was that it didn't matter how strong, be it mentally or physically, a person was. Everyone was affected the same way.

Another crescent wave of energy cut the air near her, and Enyo threw herself out of the way, letting the attack hit a wall. She winced as the wall exploded. Scraps of brick flew in every direction. There were shouts coming from inside of buildings now. People were turning on their lights and coming to the window to see what the commotion was about.

I need to leave this place before people see us.

Turning down a corner, Enyo raced into an alley. Jacob followed her. He didn't fire off any more of his crescent attacks. She could hear Durandal screaming at him.

"What are you doing, Partner?!"

"What do you mean, 'what am I doing'? I thought that would be obvious. This person tried to hurt Enyo. It's only natural that I fight them."

It's just like when he was with that woman. He called her Enyo.

That meant Jacob thought that woman was her, which lead her to believe that he was being affected by an illusion and not a charm. Charms worked under the principle that the person who'd been charmed had an irrational love for the one who charmed them. Illusions placed false images and thoughts into a person's head.

For example, creating an illusion to make someone think you were someone else.

The sound of running feet drew closer. She looked back. Jacob was closing the distance between them. He was already right behind her, swinging the screaming Durandal. She ducked underneath the blade, feeling the air being sliced as it passed her. Several strands of her hair were cut. They fluttered away as she leapt back up and continued to run.

Ragged breathing. Heart pounding. Jacob swung his blade, tearing through a wall like it was made of parchment. Her heart nearly leapt into her throat as she realized that he was actually trying to kill her. It felt like her chest was being pierced by a dagger.

He really... thinks I'm his enemy!

All the while, Durandal screamed. "What the hell are you doing?! Get ahold of yourself, Partner! That person isn't your enemy!"

"You've been tricked, Dur. That woman has cast an illusion over your eyes!"

"I don't have eyes!"

Enyo burst into another open street, Jacob hot on her heels. His sword was a flash of light. Enyo raised her daggers and crossed them in front of her. She clenched her teeth when her arms protested as Durandal slammed against them with the loud *clang!* of steel ringing against steel. The attack was so powerful that her feet left the ground.

She sailed backwards, slamming into the road. Yelping, she rolled along the ground like a doll thrown by an angry child. When she stopped rolling, she groaned and picked herself up.

Jacob was already running toward her.

He's too strong!

Enyo had known that Jacob was a powerful swordsman. Many of the stories about him told of his unprecedented strength, and she'd seen his power in action before. However, it was one thing to hear and see the strength of a person. It was quite another to be on the receiving end of that person's power.

"This is the end for you," Jacob said, raising Durandal above his head, ignoring the blade's protests. "I'll make you regret trying to fool me!"

Enyo knew that she needed to do something. Jacob would kill her if she didn't. But what could she do? Magic? Would magic even work? Also, she didn't want to kill him. What kind of magic could she use that wouldn't—

Binding!

"Religo. Revincio. Restringo."

A circle appeared underneath Jacob. Dark threads shot from the circle, latching onto Jacob's arms, legs, and torso. The threads tightened to restrain him. They were unable to fully stop him, however, as Jacob merely grunted and ripped through the threads pure brute strength. Gritting her teeth, Enyo chanted some more.

"Conteneo. Confuto. Conpesco."

More threads shot out from the circle and bound Jacob, wrapping around more of his body, covering it in darkness. Even with all of the bindings keeping him in place, Jacob still pressed forward. The black threads were tearing. It wouldn't be long before he was free.

Enyo needed to do something, and quick.

She stood up and, barely thinking about it, rushed at Jacob before he could break free. The arm holding Durandal had already broken its bindings. He raised it into the air as if to split her head open. Enyo placed her hands on either side of Jacob's head, pulled him down, leaned up, and kissed him.

Time stood still. Enyo had closed her eyes, so she couldn't see what Jacob was doing. A loud clattering rang in her ears, followed by an indignant squawk. A pair of hands settled on her hips. They were large, masculine and calloused, yet warm and gentle. Jacob's lips were rough and chapped, but she didn't really care. Enyo tried to pour all her feelings into her kiss.

She pulled back and looked up. Jacob was gaping at her, his mouth open and his eyes wider than she'd ever seen them. At the same time, he wasn't attacking her anymore.

"Are you... back to your normal self?" she asked.

"Uh... I think so," he muttered, raising a hand to his lips. He was still staring at her. "You just kissed me."

Enyo felt heat rise to her cheeks and ears. She looked down at the cobblestone floor. "S-sorry."

"Don't be," Jacob said. "It's not like I disliked it or anything..."

She looked up at Jacob, who was looking everywhere but at her. Under the pale glimmer of moonlight, she could see the redness of his cheeks.

"Oh... well, um, okay."

"Right..."

They both stood there in awkward silence, neither of them speaking because they didn't know what to say. Enyo was embarrassed by her own actions. She really hadn't thought this through, and now she'd ruined the atmosphere between her and Jacob. There was no way things could go back to the way they had been after this.

"Anyway," Jacob continued, "we should, um, go and help Fellis. I'm sure she's in trouble by now."

Enyo shook off her embarrassment and nodded. "You're right. Fellis was fighting that Nemesis guy. She'll need our help."

The two took off again in search of their comrade. It wasn't hard to discover her location. All they had to do was follow the clashing of steel.

Fellis was still fighting on the rooftops, leaping from buildings as she and Nemesis clashed in a series of sparks. Every time she landed on a roof, she'd leap off again. Then she'd swing her steel-tipped whip at Nemesis, who would knock it aside with his claws.

"We need to get up there," Enyo said. "Jacob?"

"On it."

Jacob scooped Enyo into his arms, bent his knees, and jumped. The air around them whistled. Enyo wished she could have enjoyed the moment. It was too bad they were in a combat situation.

His leap took him above many of the buildings. He landed in a crouch, then set her down. Enyo looked around, her head turning until she spotted Fellis' and Nemesis' battle not too far off.

"Let's go!" she said.

"You two aren't going anywhere," a voice said behind them.

"Close your eyes," Jacob warned. "She puts illusions on you through eye contact."

Enyo closed her eyes, even though the part of her that was wary wanted to leave them open. She trusted Jacob, however.

"I see you figured out my power," Darkness said.

"It wasn't hard to figure out." While she couldn't see him, she could imagine the nonchalant shrug Jacob gave the woman. "Once Enyo broke me out of the illusion, I realized what happened. Since you and I were never in physical contact, the only way you could have put one on me was through eye contact."

"Such an admirable deduction," Darkness purred. "It really is a shame that I have to kill you. You'd have made the perfect toy."

"This toy would have broken you in two if you tried to play with it," Jacob said, and his words were followed by the sound of boots sliding along tile.

"This toy seems to be quite full of himself," Darkness murmured. "It sounds like I'll need to teach him a lesson."

"Enyo," Jacob whispered.

"Yes?"

"I want you to go help Fellis. I can handle Darkness."

Enyo wanted to look at Jacob, but it was kind of hard with her eyes closed, and she knew not to open them. She also understood that time was of the essence. They didn't have time to argue.

"Be careful," she said.

"Don't worry." She could almost hear the smile in his voice. "I'll be fine."

Turning around, Enyo opened her eyes. She ran toward the edge of the building and leapt to the next one.

The sounds of clashing steel soon echoed behind her.

✳✳✳

It didn't take long to spot Fellis. Sparks flashed as she and Nemesis fought along the rooftops. Fellis was doing an excellent job of keeping Nemesis at bay. She shuffled along the roofs, lashing out with her whip to keep him from getting close. Nemesis would knock her attacks aside, but they were just a distraction, which she took advantage of to put some distance between them.

However, no matter how good a job Fellis was doing at keeping Nemesis back, it would only be a matter of time before he closed the distance so long as she kept on the defensive. Enyo knew this to be true. What's more, it looked like Fellis was having trouble ensaring Nemesis with her Mind Manipulation magic.

Knowing better than to get mixed up in the battle, Enyo followed them from a distance. She didn't want to get in Fellis's way. At the same time, she also had to help her former maid. That meant using long distance attacks to distract and help defeat Nemesis.

Fellis was already leaping from another roof. Nemesis tossed something at her, which Enyo only saw as a brief flash of light. It was knocked away by Fellis. She lashed at it with her whip, and then she attacked Nemesis, who knocked aside her whip with the claw attached to his left hand. It all happened so fast that Enyo was barely able to keep up.

And then something shocking happened. Fellis was going in for another attack. Her whip soared toward Nemesis, who did not block this time. In fact, he didn't do anything. Enyo didn't know why—until the whip passed right through him. Nemesis's body seemed to flicker before disappearing.

W-what? Where did he go?

It took Enyo several seconds to spot Nemesis, but when she did, shock rippled through her as she called out to her friend. "Fellis! He's behind you!"

Fellis looked at her. That was a mistake. Nemesis came in behind her, and Fellis screamed, her back arching. Enyo stared, horrified, as her friend's back was slashed apart by five claws.

"No!!"

The woman stumbled forward, teetered, and then fell onto the roof and rolled down it. With fear gripping her heart like an icy fist, Enyo raced forward. Her desire was to catch Fellis before she hit the ground. She'd never get the chance because Nemesis appeared in front of her seconds later.

Reacting on instinct, Enyo yanked her daggers from their sheaths and took up a defensive stance. She expected him to toss those projectiles again. That was why she became surprised when he dashed at her, closed the distance, and attacked her using hand-to-hand combat.

Enyo felt the swishing of air as Nemesis threw a punch that she ducked under. Shock ripped through when she found a knee heading for her face, but she avoided it by throwing herself backwards.

Her back hit the tile wrong. She gasped as pain shot through her spine. Coming back up, she avoided Nemesis's incoming punch by tilting her head, allowing the fist to whiz by her. Then she attempted to stab him through the chest.

In that moment, just before her dagger could hit him, Nemesis flickered and vanished.

What?!

Pain shot through her body as something stabbed into the base of her neck, sending her stumbling forward. Her legs gave out. She fell onto her knees, then she had to press her hands to the roof to keep from falling on her face. Even so, her arms shook fiercely as they, too, threatened to fail on her.

"Do not bother trying to move," Nemesis said in an emotionless voice. "I just used my acupuncture needles to stab the nerve endings in your neck. It's blocking all signals generated from the brain to the rest of your body. You should already be starting to feel numb."

She was feeling quite numb. Her feet, her calves, her shoulders, all of it had gone numb. Enyo was holding herself up through willpower alone.

Fortunately, her mouth still worked. "You… killed Fellis…"

"Of course," Nemesis said. "Fellis was a traitor to our kind. The only thing a traitor like her deserves is death."

Enyo gritted her teeth so hard she tasted blood. This person had killed someone that she loved, the woman who'd had the largest hand in raising her. She might have been considered a traitor of the Dark Clan, but that didn't matter, because Fellis had never been loyal to them anyway. Her loyalty had been with her, Enyo, and so as far as she was concerned, Fellis had never betrayed anyone.

You can't betray a people that you were never loyal to.

"Lux. Lumin. Luminous. Accendo!"

Enyo felt the tug as magic was pulled from her. Light exploded from her body like an incandescent star detonating in the night sky. She heard a scream. Nemesis. He must not have been prepared for her attack. Gritting her teeth as she fought against the wave of numbness, using her light magic to heal whatever she could of her damaged nerves. The tug on her navel grew stronger as she pulled more magic into her task, chanting several spells under her breath. Slowly, feeling returned to her body, and, with shaking limbs, she climbed to her feet.

Nemesis, blinded by the sudden but intense blast of light, was stumbling backwards. He didn't seem to have realized that she was no longer helpless. Picking up her daggers, she rushed toward Nemesis and thrust both weapons forward.

She expected to stab him through the chest.

What happened was that Nemesis disappeared.

Having already fallen for this trick once, she spun around, already preparing to counter whatever attack came her way. No attack came. Nemesis stood on another roof. His eyes were now closed, and he seemed agitated.

"That was a surprising attack," he said. "I had no idea that you used light magic. However, now that I know, I'm not going to let you get a second attack on me."

We'll see about that.

Enyo had finally figured out his magic. Line of sight teleportation. Basically, it was a very linear method of teleporting from point A to point B. Of course, this also meant he could only move in a straight line, and only to places where he could see.

She'd heard from Fellis during training that once someone had discovered what kind of magic their opponent used, the battle was already half-finished. If she knew the magic, then she could come up with a counter.

"Ustulo. Uro. Torro."

Black flames burst into existence, engulfing her hand, which she moved in a quick slashing motion. The flames raced forward in a crescent similar to Jacob's attack. They reached Nemesis and went straight through him, her foe's body flickering before disappearing altogether.

Enyo was already reacting. She placed her hands on the ground, palms flat, fingers splayed, and chanted.

"Umbra. Premo. Religo. Nox!"

Several magic circles appeared on the roofs all around her. Ancient scripts written in an arcane language formed letters and words within the circles. As the circles began to glow with a dark purple light, thick bindings of a purest black shot out. Most of them hit nothing. However, a scream from behind alerted her that one of her circles did get something.

With her hands still on the roof, she turned her head and gazed at Nemesis as several black flames shaped like ribbons latched onto him. His flesh was burned where they touched. As more wrapped around him, more of his body was lit on fire. Loud screams tore from his throat as his skin hissed, bubbled, melted, and then evaporated. Pretty soon, nothing remained of Nemesis. He was gone.

Fellis...

Enyo didn't hesitate to rush down to the street now that her foe was gone. She raced across the cobblestone and knelt beside her former maid.

Fellis's wounds were grievous. The claws had shredded a good portion of her back, leaving five long claw marks. It also looked like her left collar bone had fractured when she hit the ground, and her arm was bent at an awkward angle. However, she was still alive. Her chest rose and fell in ragged gasps.

"Medeor. Medico. Medicor."

Threads of light shot from Enyo's fingers, tiny strings that stood out starkly in the dark night. They attached themselves to the claw marks. Then the threads slowly wove through them like a doctor stitching a wound shut. Sweat beaded on Enyo's forehead as she concentrated on the threads, which slowly repaired the damage done. Little by little, centimeter by centimeter, the wounds healed.

The first thing that she repaired was the internal damage. Her spine had been gouged, and several of her muscles had been torn.

Her breathing grew heavy as she used even more of her magic. While using magic in and of itself did not make one tired, the focus required to cast certain spells was mentally exhausting. Healing was a particularly strenuous art. A healer couldn't just chant some words and expect magic to do the rest. It required more focus than most, lest she want it to be an indiscriminate spell, which could do more harm than good.

J-just a little more...

The organs and muscles had been repaired; she could see the last bit of torn muscle fibers slowly being stitched together by numerous threads of light. Now all she needed to do was fix the damaged skin. Pouring more magic into her threads, Enyo held her breath as she carefully healed all the damage, intently observing the skin as it slowly closed as if it had never happened.

"There," she muttered, wiping the sweat from her forehead. "All done."

Enyo wasn't given much time to congratulate herself as, seconds later, she noticed all the light coming from the inside of the buildings around her. The lights were followed by shouts.

Knowing better than to remain, Enyo stood up. It was a struggle. However, she put her all into clambering to her feet. After which she grabbed Fellis and lifted the woman before, half-dragging and half-carrying the woman, she left the area with ponderous, slow footsteps. She needed to leave quickly.

I have to find Jacob.

***

Jacob was having a lot more trouble than he'd originally anticipated. Sure, he was fighting blind, but he'd fought blind plenty of times in the past. He had honestly expected the fight to go his way from beginning to end.

He was beginning to regret his moment of egotism.

"To your left!" Durandal warned.

Jacob spun around and swung Durandal in a wide arc. The *clang!* of his blade hitting several projectiles resounded across the rooftops. He wasn't sure what kind of weapons this woman used, as he still had his eyes closed, but from the speed and weight, he judged them to be fairly standard throwing knives.

They're probably laced with poison.

The air that night was chilly. The combination of the night's cool air and the sweat plastering his clothes to his skin caused goosebumps to break out. Despite this, Jacob maintained his calm, knowing that half of the battle would be won so long as he remained composed.

"Oh, my. But you are an able young man, aren't you?" Darkness laughed. He frowned as her voice echoed all around him. She was quite the ventriloquist. "I really do regret not being able to make you my toy. Think of all the fun I could have had."

Why was it that every dark clanswoman outside of Enyo and Fellis vulgarly talked about making him their toy? Seriously. This was like the ten thousandth time a dark clanswoman had said this to him. During his travels through the darklands, he couldn't fight against one woman without them saying something to this effect.

So annoying.

"Sorry, but I'm not into become the plaything to an old hag," Jacob responded calmly.

"Arrogant little shit!" Darkness growled, and he could practically hear the snarl in her voice. "I give you compliments and you pay them back with insults? I take back everything I said about you. I'm going to enjoy killing you!"

Jacob would've smiled if that hadn't given him away. This woman was just like most of the dark clan assassins he'd fought in the past—arrogant, boastful, and prideful. The weakness of most assassins like this one was that they didn't take insults well. It was a common trait among the prouder dark clan members.

"You ready, Durandal?" asked Jacob.

"I'm about as ready to cock block this wench as I'll ever be."

"I… didn't need to know that."

"Left!"

Spinning around, Jacob heard the whizzing of several projectiles. He knocked them away with Durandal.

"Right and slightly behind!"

He swung his sword again, rotating in the direction Durandal told him to. Steel clashed as he batted at the projectiles, hitting it hard enough to send it flying off.

"She's on your flank!"

Jacob continued listening to Durandal's advice. With his sword tracking Darkness's movements, there was no way she could get the drop on him. Even if his sword was sentient, Durandal couldn't be placed under an illusion, since it lacked the mind necessary to fall sway to one. That meant she couldn't rely on her normal tricks.

"That sword of yours is an annoyance!"

"Isn't he, though? I keep telling him that as well. I'm so glad you understand."

"What are you doing, empathizing with the enemy? What kind of partner are you?"

"The best kind."

"Would you two shut up?!!"

As the woman became more annoyed, her attacks became even sloppier and easier to deflect. It was his hope that she'd eventually become so frustrated she would make a mistake. If she did, then he could capitalize on it and strike her with a decisive blow.

"Directly in front!"

Jacob leapt back. He felt something sharp swish past his nose. It looked like she was getting bolder, or maybe she was becoming impatient.

"Left!"

He spun around and slashed at his left flank, striking something metallic. It wasn't a projectile. It weighed more. A sword, then. The air in front of him shifted, and he followed the currents, using them to predict the attacks. Left. Right. Right. Duck. Left. Block. Metal clashed. The sound rang heavily in his ears.

The air shifted again.

"She's to your right now!"

Instead of meeting her blows head on, he moved backward. Something cut in front him, in the space where he'd been standing. The sound told him it was a projectile.

"Stop moving around, you little brat!"

"She's moving behind you now!"

Spinning on the balls of his feet, Jacob slashed at the woman as she tried to get behind him. He could tell that she was there. Her footsteps were giving her away. With his eyes closed, his sense of hearing was enhanced, and he could easily hear the way she clunked around in those heels.

Just a little more.

"On your port!"

Jacob spun. He slashed. More projectiles were felled.

"Your flank!"

She came in close, attempting to pierce his guard with a surprise attack. He blocked, twisted his wrist, then tried to bisect her. He missed.

"Forty-five degrees!"

"Left! Your left!"

"Behind again!"

"Turn clockwise!"

No matter how many times Darkness attacked, Jacob was able to defend. No matter how she tried to surprise him, Durandal warned about it beforehand. Of course, Durandal was just a distraction. His sword wasn't what she really needed to worry about.

Movement to his left. She was close, and she was closing the distance quickly. He waited until the last second, then spun around, knocked aside her blade, and thrust his sword forward. The air shifted as she tried to dodge. She leapt back, but he'd already channeled his energy into Durandal and let it loose to extend his reach.

"A-ah…!" a pained cry, a feminine gasp. The sound of footsteps stumbling backward.

Jacob opened his eyes. Darkness stood near the edge of the building. Her face was twisted with pain, blood leaking down her lips. She'd placed a hand against her chest, from which blood leaked. His last attack, the energy projectile shaped like a thrust sword, it had pierced right through her chest.

She was going to die shortly.

"H-how?" she asked. "Your sword… he didn't tell you where I was that last time…"

"He didn't need to," Jacob said. "He never needed to. I could tell where you were at all times right from the very beginning."

"A distraction…" Her eyes were glazing over. "Now I see… h-how cunning… I can… see… why you defeated the…"

She was unable to finish that sentence. Jacob watched as her body, finally unable to continue functioning, gave out and fell off the ledge. He walked over to the lip of the building, slowly moving until he was leaning over to look down. Lying on the ground, sprawled out and with her limbs twisted in unusual directions, Darkness stared sightlessly at him.

Jacob stepped back. Darkness disappeared from his sight. As shouts began to ring out from people becoming aware that something had just happened, he decided that it was time to disappear.

He needed to find Enyo and Fellis.

✳✳✳

The death of two dark clan members had caused a huge ruckus in the city. It wasn't just because two dark clan members had been killed, but also because they were dark clan members and they had been killed by someone or something stronger than them. What kind of security did their city possess that a pair from the dark clan could infiltrate them so easily? What sort of monsters were lurking around at night that could kill people from the dark clan? Since the two deaths were announced that morning, the city had been in a state of perpetual fear.

Jacob was thankful that Tellus Caelum was such a large city, as it meant he and his companions were able to move from the eastern side of town to the west, away from where the battle had taken place. However, while changing locations had been a great idea, there were still problems. The biggest issue right now was that the city had been under lockdown since the bodies of Darkness and Nemesis were discovered.

Tellus Caelum was a city surrounded by a large gate and a moat. The only way into or out of the city was through one of four gates, which were located on the north, west, east, and south sides of the city.

Because the city was so large, it had been divided into four sections based on the four cardinal points. Each of the four districts was named after a specific and powerful monster. The north was dragon, the south was tortoise, the east was cockatrice, and the west was minotaur. Of course, it wasn't like the four districts differed all that much from each other. This was just a way of helping people figure out where they were.

It was the day after their fight with the dark clan assassins. Jacob sat at a table with Enyo and Fellis, slowly sipping from a glass filled with a beverage called milk coffee. Enyo sat on the opposite side, not looking at him. Fellis sat between the two, making the last point of a triangle at their round table.

"There are a lot more knights patrolling the city now," Fellis observed as she sipped her beverage. Jacob didn't know what it was called, but steam wafted from her cup. A kind of tea, maybe?

"The knights are on high alert because of Darkness and Nemesis," Jacob said. "We probably should have hidden their bodies after defeating them, but it wasn't like we'd been given much time. Had we done anything besides leave immediately, we would have been caught, and I don't envy the idea of trying to escape from a horde of knights and paladins after what happened."

"Hm... true. I wasn't all that up for running either," she agreed.

Of course, Fellis had been unconscious at the time. She couldn't have run anyway.

"Enyo? How are you feeling?" Fellis asked suddenly.

"W-what?" Enyo said, looking up.

"I asked if you were feeling well. You've been spacing out a lot this morning."

"Oh, yes. I'm fine." Enyo looked away. Her cheeks were stained red.

Jacob wanted to sigh, but he didn't want her to know how stressed he was. Enyo had avoided him after they'd met up. He didn't blame her. She was probably embarrassed by what had happened, by what she'd done to him.

Last night, he and Enyo had shared a kiss, though it might have been more accurate to say she kissed him. He was grateful. Really. Thanks to her, the illusion that had been cast on him broke, and he'd been able to pay Darkness back for making him almost kill Enyo. At the same time...

Her lips were really soft.

It was maddening, but he'd been unable to get that kiss out of his mind. Last night, after they had moved to a new inn and fallen asleep, he had been plagued by dreams of Enyo and her kiss. He wanted to feel her lips on his again. More than that, he wanted to initiate their next kiss.

Taking a sip of his drink, Jacob carefully put his thoughts of Enyo, kissing, and his newfound awareness of her as a woman, out of his mind. There were a lot more important things to think about.

"We need to come up with a plan to escape from this city," he said at last. "The longer we remain here with all these knights, the greater the chances of Enyo being recognized become."

Even now there were posters with her face on them all over the city. That was why, unlike him and Fellis, she was still wearing a cloak with a hood. They couldn't afford to let people see her face. This was especially true now that all of these knights were patrolling the town.

"I don't disagree with you," Fellis began, "but how are we going to escape from the city with so many knights hanging around? If we act suspiciously, we'll be spotted for sure."

It was no surprise that Tellus Caelum, being one of the larger cities, had a large garrison of knights stationed there. Jacob didn't know how many there were. However, he did know that a standard garrison normally held around four squadrons. If they went with that number, then there would have been at least forty-eight knights stationed in the city.

Since Tellus Caelum was much larger than most cities, they probably had closer to several garrisons, and each garrison likely had around seven or eight squadrons. Just looking at all the knights passing by as they patrolled made him realize that there were a lot more stationed here than in a normal city.

They would need to be careful.

"We can at least do some scouting," Jacob answered. "When we leave, we'll be doing so by passing through the north gate. That's why I found us another inn located in the Dragon District."

"Then what are we going to do?" asked Fellis. "Pretend to be a couple of tourists? Maybe you and Enyo could pretend to be a married couple on a honeymoon, and I, your lovely chaperone."

While Enyo hid her face further into her head, Jacob tried to slow his rapidly beating heart.

The idea of being a couple, or even just pretending, did have appeal, both on a practical level and a personal one. At the same time, he wasn't sure it was a good idea. His feelings for Enyo were too jumbled right now. He hadn't sorted them out, and they didn't have time to sort them out in this situation.

He was about to tell Fellis what a bad idea it was—

"I... don't mind."—when Enyo spoke first.

"Hm?" A grinning Fellis placed her elbows on the table, leaned forward, and set her chin on the butt of her hands. "What's this? Is Enyo finally taking the initiative?"

"It's not that," Enyo said, though her blush said otherwise. "I just think that your idea is a good one. That's all."

"If you say so." Fellis glanced at Jacob, her grin still in place. "What say you, hero?"

Jacob needed to actually think about his answer. He didn't know how useful he'd be if he and Enyo were in such close contact. At the same time, it might be a good idea to get these issues out of the way quickly. They were going to be together for the foreseeable future, and that meant working closely together, so it would be better if he sorted out his feelings now while he had the chance.

There was no telling what might happen in the future.

"It would make a good cover..." Jacob glanced at Enyo. "However, we should really do something about your cloak."

"Is something wrong with my cloak?" Enyo asked, frowning.

"You mean aside from the fact that it makes you look completely suspicious?" Jacob asked. Enyo blushed.

"It does make me think you have something to hide," Fellis added. "If I didn't know you, and I saw you walking around the north gate while the city was under lockdown, I would assume you were up to something bad."

Enyo's cheeks turned an even deeper shade of red. "I get that, but what can I do? It's not like I can take my hood off. Everyone will see my face."

"We could always dye your hair," Jacob suggested.

"Fweh?" was Enyo's intelligent response.

"That's not a bad idea," Fellis agreed.

Durandal, fortunately, said nothing. A talking sword was too conspicuous for such a public place.

After paying for their meal, Jacob took Fellis and Enyo through the streets. His destination was an apothecary.

Apothecaries were the places where herbalists and potion makers sold their products—medicinal herbs, healing potions, antidotes, and so on. Jacob had spent a lot of time in apothecaries when he was younger. Journeying to defeat the Dark Lord had required that he and his comrades keep constantly stocked with medical supplies.

Aside from medical supplies, apothecaries were also the place where people could go to get their hair dyed.

Jacob didn't know when dying one's hair had become popular. He remembered seeing several times people who used to have black or brown hair suddenly having blond hair like him. They had been trying to emulate him, he later learned.

As they entered the apothecary, the scent of several dozen ingredients assaulted his nose. It wasn't a pleasant smell, though it wasn't horrible either. Still, his nose wrinkled as he was assailed by various scents. He glanced at the potions and ingredients lining the shelves that sat along the walls. Many he recognized, like newts and frog eyes and monkshood, but there were a few that he couldn't name.

The sound of their footsteps along the hard-wooden floor must have alerted the clerk to their arrival. A bored-looking man raised his head from where it rested against a counter in the back. He glanced at Jacob, then at Enyo. He frowned when he couldn't see her face.

Then he looked at Fellis.

Jacob almost snickered when a blush spread across the young man's face. Not that he blamed him. It wasn't every day that a woman wearing what looked like strategically placed leather straps walked into your store.

"C-can I help you?" he asked.

Fellis took the lead, walking to the front with an exaggerated sway in her hips. Jacob and Enyo hung back, watching as the poor man's face turned into a bonfire of color. He must have been a virgin.

"I do hope you can," Fellis said, leaning against the counter. "You see, my friend over there is very insecure about her hair color, so she wants to get it dyed. We were hoping your apothecary had hair dyes that we could use. Think you can help us?"

Placing her hands on the counter, Fellis leaned over, and from the way the man's eyes popped, he was getting quite the view.

"I-I think we... have something... w-what color are you, um, looking for?"

Jacob felt kind of bad for the man. He was clearly not used to someone like Fellis putting the moves on him. However, he also knew that Fellis was doing this so the man wouldn't focus on Enyo.

"I hadn't realized she was so good at seduction," Jacob remarked.

"Fellis excels at all manners of combat, including seduction," Enyo said, glancing at Jacob before looking away.

Jacob ran a hand through his hair. They needed to clear the air between them, but he honestly didn't know how to do that, or rather, he didn't know what to say yet. He was still unsure about his own feelings. The fact that he didn't have time to explore those feelings didn't help.

Fellis continued to tease the skittish lad until he said something about checking the back, and then ran through a door behind the counter. Chuckling in a self-satisfied manner, Fellis turned around, leaned against the desk, and winked at them. Jacob rolled his eyes while Enyo gave a small smile.

The man returned seconds later. He was carrying several vials.

"Um, so, ah, these are our... hair dyes." He placed the vials on the counter. "W-which, um, which one do you—does your friend want?"

"That is a very good question," Fellis said, turning her head to look at them. "Enyo, do you have a color preference?"

Enyo's thinking face was pretty cute, Jacob admitted. "Um, why don't we go with something simple, like… black?"

"Black?" Fellis sighed. "How plain." Enyo pouted, causing her to wave a dismissive hand through the air, as if she was swatting flies. "All right. All right. We'll go with black."

After paying for the hair dye, he, Enyo, and Fellis left the shop and walked to their next destination. Since their new inn didn't have its own bath, they needed to dye Enyo's hair at one of the local bathhouses.

Bathhouses were a popular commodity in Terrasole. They were essentially massive baths where dozens of people bathed together. The idea behind the bathhouse stemmed from the idea that by being naked with a bunch of other naked people, they were baring their souls to each other, which would foster friendship.

Jacob didn't really get it, but he had been born in the United States, not ancient Greece.

Bathhouses were separated by gender. Jacob heard that they used to be unisex, but after an incident several decades ago, it was changed to keep people from getting too… rowdy.

It wasn't the first time Jacob had ever been in a bathhouse, but it had been awhile. After putting his clothes in a box and placing a towel around his waist, he headed inside.

Since bathhouses were meant to hold dozens of people, it didn't surprise him that this one was quite large, easily spanning two dozen meters. There were already about a dozen people there. They ranged from old men to young children. He frowned.

I really don't want to be here… I should have stayed at the inn.

He walked into the bathhouse. Durandal wasn't with him, having been left with his clothes. His feet padded against the rock tiles. Jacob tried to ignore the stares of others as he sat down on a stool and began cleaning himself. When taking a bath, it was important to cleanse yourself first. That way people didn't spread filth when they climbed into the water.

After cleaning himself off, Jacob sat in the steaming water as far from everyone else as possible. With luck, no one would notice him, and he'd be able to remain that way until—

"Excuse me," someone said as they sat down next to him.

Jacob groaned. *This is great. Some idiot's gonna sit by me. What the heck did I do to deserve this? I don't want to talk to people while I'm naked.*

"It's been a hectic day, huh?" the other man said.

Someone please kill me.

"Yeah," Jacob muttered unenthusiastically.

The man sitting next to him had dark hair, dark eyes, and a chiseled face. Jacob put him at twenty-something years old. From his build, muscular without a trace of body fat, he was either a warrior of some kind or a blacksmith. His hands were also calloused from wielding either a sword or hammer, lending further credence to Jacob's theory.

"I can't believe how much they've had us patrolling the city," the man continued. "I'm not even a part of the garrison here, but they've been working me like a dog." A self-deprecating chuckle issued from his mouth. "Then again, I did offer myself and my squad when I learned of what happened. I guess I only have myself to blame."

Jacob perked up. "You're a knight?"

The man nodded. "I'm a paladin, a captain of the Drakon Squadron, to be exact."

This city didn't have a drake squadron. Also, now that he was looking at the man more closely, he did seem vaguely familiar. Jacob thought he remembered seeing this face somewhere before…

"What's a member of the Drakon Squadron doing in Tellus Caelum?"

"I'm chasing after a pair of criminals," the man admitted.

"Uh huh…"

"I'm also looking for a man named Jacob Stone," he continued. Jacob suddenly felt more uncomfortable than he had been several seconds before. "However, the trail for him has gone cold." The paladin looked at him. "Speaking of, has anyone told you that you're the spitting image of Jacob?"

"It's been mentioned once or twice," Jacob said, keeping his cool. "My friends were always jealous because I look like the hero. Course, I had to dye my hair first."

"I can't say I blame them." The paladin nodded as if he agreed with Jacob's non-existent friends. "Ever since I first saw Jacob several years ago, he's been my hero and the person I've aspired to become like."

"Is that so?"

"Yes. It's been a long-standing dream of mine to one day stand side by side with him, fighting evil for the sake of the kingdom."

How lovely. Not only was he sitting next to some dude when he just wanted to be left alone, he was also sitting next to a sycophant, who just so happened to be unknowingly chasing after him and Enyo. This was just what he needed to make his day complete.

While Jacob contemplated smashing his face against the wall, the paladin continued talking. "Ever since that parade at the end of the war, I've strived to become a knight worthy of fighting alongside Jacob. I want to become a person who helps protect people like him." He paused. "By the way, I don't think I ever got your name?"

"It's… Jake," Jacob said.

"Even your name is close to his. Now I really am jealous. My name is Caslain, by the way."

"A pleasure," Jacob said, even though all he wanted to do was gouge his eyes out. This entire situation was beyond ridiculous.

At least he doesn't seem to realize who I am. He probably doesn't suspect that a wanted criminal or his hero would be bathing in a public bathhouse.

As he listened to Caslain jabber on, his thoughts went to Enyo and Fellis. He hoped they were having a better time than him.

***

Fellis had somehow managed to secure a room for them. Enyo didn't know how she'd done this, though she suspected that Fellis's Mind Manipulation magic had been involved.

Enyo sat in a chair that tilted backwards. There was a bowl of water behind her, which would be used in the hair dying process. Fellis was untangling her hair so it would be easier to dye.

"It really is a shame that we're dying your hair," Fellis said as she ran her fingers through Enyo's locks. "You have such beautiful hair."

"I don't think my hair color really matters all that much," Enyo said.

"I bet Jacob will be sad once you no longer have your natural hair color, too."

Enyo didn't say anything at first. She was busy trying to master her blush. "I... don't think that will be the case."

"Why not?"

"Because he... I don't know if Jacob even feels that way about me."

"Have you asked him about his feelings?"

"Oh, I-I could never—"

"Why not?"

Enyo tried to come up with an answer. Sadly, the only answer she could think of was, "Because it's embarrassing."

"Well, with an attitude like that, it's no wonder you two haven't gotten anywhere." Fellis hummed as she had Enyo lean her head back. "Speaking of, is there a reason you've been avoiding looking at him since this morning?"

An excuse lay on the tip of Enyo's tongue. She paused, however, when she realized that Fellis might actually be able to help solve her dilemma.

"I... might have kissed Jacob last night."

Fellis stopped moving her hands for a moment, though she recovered with admirable swiftness and began putting the dye in Enyo's now wet hair. "I see. That is indeed a big step. However, now I'm even more confused as to why you two aren't more intimate."

"It was kind of a spur of the moment thing," Enyo admitted. "Jacob was being controlled by an illusion, so I needed to break the illusion."

"I understand. You injected him with your light magic."

Illusions were a rare branch of magic. However, they were not entirely unknown. Having been trained by Fellis, who was knowledgeable about illusions, Enyo had learned that there were several ways to break out of one.

The first was for the person under the illusion to recognize it, and then break out by causing themselves physical pain. The pain would force the foreign energy inside of their mind to vanish, breaking the illusion. The second was for someone with the opposing element to inject their magic into the person who was under the illusion.

In other words, that she had been able to break Jacob out of the illusion had been a case of luck. If Darkness's magic hadn't been a subcategory of dark magic, she wouldn't have been able to break him out.

"What do you think I should do?" asked Enyo.

Fellis hummed as she rinsed Enyo's hair in the bowl of water. "I suppose that would depend on what you want to have happen. Are you looking to form an intimate relationship with him beyond that of mere companions?"

"That… would be nice," Enyo admitted.

"Then maybe you should ask him about his feelings," Fellis said.

"I can't. I already told you it's embarrassing." The bowl was removed and Fellis began to gently towel Enyo's hair off. "B-besides, if we did talk about our relationship, I'd rather he be the one to bring it up."

"Sit up please," Fellis instructed. Enyo did as told. The towel returned to her hair as Fellis continued speaking. "If you want him to speak to you about his feelings, you're going to be waiting for a long time. Do not forget that right now we're in an unusual situation. We're on the run, with people from both sides coming after us. Jacob doesn't have time to think about things like love or romance, not when there is already so much on his plate."

"I know that," Enyo muttered.

"If you know that, then you should also know that Jacob is a man," Fellis countered. "Most men aren't prone to talking about their feelings during the best of times. Waiting for him to bring up how he feels about you while we're in the middle of enemy territory is like trying to teach a dragon to speak English. Not happening."

"Then are you saying I should do nothing?" Enyo asked.

"I'm not saying you should do nothing." Fellis finished drying off Enyo's hair, then presented her with a small mirror. "I'm saying that you should at least clear the air between you two. If things go on in this awkward state, you're going to be distracted, and we can't afford any distractions in our current situation. By the way, what do you think?"

Enyo looked at herself in the mirror. Her hair was now pitch black. It was so dark it seemed to absorb light. She brushed several strands that fell in front of her face, and then sighed.

"I think I liked my original hair better," she declared.

"So do I," Fellis said. "This hair is just too plain. We're lucky it washes out easily."

Twirling a strand of hair between her fingers, Enyo couldn't help but agree.

"Now, then, let's go and meet up with Jacob," Fellis continued, her face splitting into a grin. "I bet he's sick of waiting for us."

***

Jacob had gotten sick of listening to Caslain, so the moment he was able to, he slipped out of the bathhouse, got dressed, and waited in the lobby for Enyo and Fellis to return. He fortunately didn't have to wait long. A few minutes after he exited the men's side, his two companions came out of the female side.

Enyo's hair was midnight black.

"What do you think?" Fellis asked as Enyo blushed and made a face that all but screamed she wanted to hide somewhere.

"Honestly," Jacob breathed out deeply, "I think her original hair color was a lot prettier."

Enyo froze. Her eyes were wide like an animal staring down the mouth of a fire breathing dragon. Traveling from one side of her face to the other was a fierce red blush.

"I said the same thing," Fellis admitted.

"Still, this should help. No one is going to recognize you with black hair."

It was a well-known fact that the thief who stole from Queen Alice had pink hair. Not only was it in the description, but someone had actually taken the time to make the posters in color, and every poster had Enyo with pink hair. The fact that the drawing wasn't very accurate further helped ensure that no one would suspect her.

They walked out into the street, for once, Enyo went without her hood. No one batted an eyelash at her. Of course, given the recent string of events, two girls and one guy walking around wasn't that interesting.

There weren't many people in the street right now. With the two confirmed dark members and their deaths, a lot of people were staying indoors. It wasn't everyone as there were still a good few dozen people wandering around. However, there were no longer several hundred-people crowding the walkways.

"Are you ready?" Jacob asked Enyo.

"Ready for what?" Enyo asked in return. Jacob stared at her. Enyo blushed as her eyes went wide. "O-oh. Right. Yes, um, I'm ready."

"Then let's do this. Just remember to play it cool." Jacob offered his arm, which Enyo took after another moment. "Fellis, would you mind following slightly behind us?"

Fellis smiled. "Don't worry, hero. I've been a maid for several years now. I know how to play the part."

"Right."

Jacob led Enyo down one of many cobblestone streets, their destination the north gate. His companion had a tight grip on his arm. She felt tense. A glance out of the corner of his eye revealed that she

was moving stiffly, like someone who had both of their legs broken and was trying to walk with a pair of splints.

"Relax," Jacob leaned down and whispered into her ear. "You look like someone who's been paralyzed from the waist down. Remember, right now you and I are a couple out for a stroll before dinner. You need to be more natural."

"I'm sorry," Enyo said. "I guess I'm more tense than I usually am."

Going off a hunch, Jacob asked, "Is it because of the kiss last night?" Enyo's cheeks suddenly turned so red he thought her face might catch fire. "So that's it."

It was only natural that she would be thinking about last night. He'd been thinking about it as well. The kiss had plagued his mind. In truth, he'd been unable to get his mind off it since it happened.

"Sorry," she apologized. "I know that now's not really the time."

"No, now may be the perfect time," he rebutted. "It might be best if we talk about this right now while we still have the chance."

"R-really?"

"Yeah…"

He'd been thinking about it while trying to ignore Caslain's ramblings. As much as he didn't want to deal with this right now, he knew that they might not get another chance. What's more, neither of them could afford to be distracted by their own insecurities. While Jacob was worried about how this would change their dynamics, he knew that something needed to be done or their team work would suffer.

"So, um…" Enyo started.

"I want you to know that I do like you," Jacob decided to go with outright honesty. Seeing Enyo's blush made his own slight embarrassment worth it. "I'm saying this now because I don't want you to think that I don't like you, or that I don't want to be with you in a more, uh, intimate manner."

Several meters behind them, Fellis appeared like she was trying to listen in without getting caught. He ignored her. Enyo was gazing at him with an uncertain gleam in her eyes.

"So... you do like me in... that way?"

"Yes," Jacob confirmed. "However, I think we should wait before doing anything."

"What?" Enyo blinked, her expression suddenly unsure. "I'm not sure I understand. Not do anything?"

Pausing for a moment, Jacob thought about how best to explain himself. He wasn't good at expressing his feelings. Rather, he was reluctant to because he'd become so used to holding them in.

Durandal was mercifully silent.

"Right now, you and I are on the run, we're trying to sneak into Avant Heim and activate the otherworld gate to travel to my world. We have enemies after us from all sides and even a single slip in judgement on our part could mean certain death. We don't really have the time to be exploring a relationship. We can't even do the things that most people who are in a relationship do because we're constantly on the run."

He'd been thinking about this for a while now. Ever since Fellis had showed him those visions, he'd been trying to think of what he should do, of what his own feelings were, and how he should respond to them. This was the answer that he came up with.

"That's why I want us to wait," he continued. "Once we reach my world, you and I will be free to do what we want. We'll be able to go on dates, have conversations that don't involve our potential death, and do things that regular couples do. I think that will be the best time for us to explore and deepen our relationship further."

Jacob waited for a moment, to see if Enyo would say something. When she didn't, he became worried.

"Is that... okay?"

"Oh! Um, yes. That's fine." Enyo smiled at him. "Honestly, I am a little disappointed, but I also understand what you're getting at. Now's not the time for us to do anything. We've already got our hands full, right?" Enyo hugged his arm a little more tightly and rested her head on his shoulder. "I… don't mind waiting until the danger has passed."

Jacob knew that Enyo was disappointed, or maybe he was pushing his own sense of disappointment onto her. He did feel guilty. He'd like to offer her more, but it was neither safe nor healthy to explore a relationship while on the run. If he was going to give this relationship thing a try, then he wanted to be able to give Enyo all of his attention and not just the token attention he could give right now.

They kept moving through the streets.

The north gate was called such because it sat on the northern side of the city. Surrounded by high rising walls made of massive bricks. Two cylindrical towers were situated on either side, connected by an arched bridge that ran over the gate, which was a massive construct made of thick wood. Jacob knew that beyond the gate itself, there was a drawbridge. The only way to drop the drawbridge was to pull the lever located inside one of the towers. He didn't know which one.

"That's a lot of guards," Enyo murmured.

Indeed, there were at least sixteen guards stationed there. He could see two on either tower, two guarding the gate, two more guarding each door making for a total of four, four standing on the arched bridge, and another four patrolling the wall. Who knew how many more were inside of the towers themselves.

"Getting past them isn't going to be easy," Jacob said.

The problem, as he saw it, was that they couldn't knock each guard out one at a time. Everyone would see them. Then it would all be over. Strong as he, Enyo, and Fellis were, they wouldn't be able to beat that many people without causing unnecessary destruction and death.

Jacob wanted to avoid killing innocent people.

"Maybe we should wait for the lockdown to end?" Enyo suggested.

"If I may intrude," Fellis said before Jacob could. "Waiting for the lockdown to end could have even more disastrous results. The longer we remain here, the greater the chances of someone catching us are. Even if no one knows exactly what we look like, it's only a matter of time before we're found out."

"We also have to be wary of the Dark Council," Jacob said. "I don't know if Darkness and Nemesis reported us to the Dark Council..." He trailed off and glanced at Fellis.

"There's a chance," she admitted. "We were technically supposed to contact them once we had apprehended Enyo, but I don't know how many of them did. Then again, Darkness and Nemesis did find us pretty easily, so the Dark Council may have a way of tracking us."

Mysterious and elusive, few people knew of the Dark Council even among the Dark Clan itself. Of the few who did know, no one knew who the Dark Council members were, or what powers they possessed. It was perfectly feasible that someone among them was tracking his, Enyo's, and Fellis's movements.

"I get what you're saying," Enyo said at last. "I'll admit, I'm not as experienced in these matters as either of you."

"That's probably a good thing," Durandal said quietly. Jacob tapped the sword on the hilt, a reminder that he needed to keep quiet in public.

"Let's head back to the inn, we can come up with a plan to open the gate there."

Still keeping in character, he, Enyo, and Fellis moved off, wandering down the street. As they rounded a corner, they almost ran into Caslain. The man was wearing his armor now. It was easier to see the resemblance between this man and the one who's drake he and Fellis had stolen back at Deterion.

"Oh, pardon me—ah, Jake! I apologize. I hadn't realized it was you," Caslain said, smiling.

Jacob returned the smile with an uneasy one of his own. "It's fine."

"Are you out for an evening stroll with your betrothed?" Caslain asked politely.

"That's right." Raising his free hand, he gently placed it over one of Enyo's. It might not have been acting, but the redness that spread across his companion's cheeks helped add credence to his claim. "I guess you're on patrol?"

"That is correct," Caslain said. "Which is why I must apologize again. I've not the time to speak now. Please forgive me."

He waved the man off. "Don't worry about it. Keep up the good work."

"I shall do my best."

Giving a salute, Caslain glanced momentarily at Fellis with furrowed brows, and then he shook his head and left. Jacob tracked the man as he disappeared around the corner of a building.

"Hey," Fellis started, "isn't that…"

"Yes," Jacob said. "That's the guy we stole the drake from. He's also the one Enyo and I fought in Altus."

"Is he really?" Enyo asked. "I never got a good look at him because it was so dark and everything was happening so quickly."

"Yep, that's him," Jacob said dryly. "I'd recognize that manner of speech anywhere."

"He was very loud," Durandal added.

The group moved on. As they started walking, Jacob froze as something descended upon him. It was the feeling of eyes watching him. There was someone observing them, and they didn't feel quite human.

He looked up, toward where he felt the source, but there was no one there.

"Jacob?" Enyo inquired curiously.

Jacob shook his head and smiled. "It's nothing. Let's keep going."

While she still looked unsure, Enyo nodded, and, together with Fellis, they walked back to the inn.

Did I imagine that feeling? he asked himself before shaking it off.

It must have been his imagination.

JOURNEY OF A BETRAYED HERO VOL. 1

CHAPTER 6 - LUST

After they returned to the inn, Jacob had given Enyo the gate key. His reasoning was that it would be a good idea to keep it on one of them at all times, but he wasn't responsible enough to hold it. Enyo had protested. Fellis agreed. Since the gate key had been in his bag when it was stolen, they had eventually reached the consensus that Enyo would hold the gate key.

She had not been pleased.

A plan had been concocted to escape from Tallus Caelum. Using Fellis's Mind Manipulation magic, they would "convince" all the guards to leave. Fellis had told him that she couldn't use her mind magic for mass manipulation, which meant they needed to get each one alone. Fortunately, Fellis had been trained as a temptress.

Later that night, Jacob, Enyo, and Fellis left their inn through the window, taking to the roofs and going straight for the north gate. The guards were all still there, though they had been shifted out for new guards. As they knelt on the roof of a nearby building, Fellis clicked her teeth.

"Some of those guards are female," she muttered bitterly.

"Is that a problem?" asked Jacob.

Fellis sent him a flat look. "Yes, that's a problem. I can't seduce women."

"Why not?" asked Enyo.

"What do you mean 'why not?'" Fellis gave her the flat stare.

"It would be hot if you did," Durandal said suddenly. "What?" he asked when everyone glared at him. "You all were thinking it, too."

"Look," Fellis sighed, "I have no talent at seducing members of the same sex. Darkness might have been able to do that. In fact, I'm sure she could, but I can't. I don't have the right mindset."

"Couldn't you still use your Mind Manipulation on them?" Jacob asked.

"Maybe." Fellis bit her lip. "It depends on how strong their will is. There's a reason I didn't just manipulate Enyo when I was trying to take her away from all this. If a person has enough willpower, they can resist my manipulation. I can still dominate their mind, but it takes more time. Men are easier to manipulate because I seduce them at the same time. They're too busy thinking with their dicks instead of their heads. Women are different. Since I have no talent at seducing them, especially if the woman is straight, it takes a lot longer to manipulate them."

That was troubling, but it was nothing they couldn't handle either. Even if it would make everything a bit harder, they couldn't really afford to give up.

He sighed. "All right. Here's what we'll do. Enyo, I want you to play the part of an innocent young girl who's seen a suspicious character lurking around. Go up to them, convince a few of them to follow you. I'll keep them still while Fellis dominates their mind."

"I think I can do that," Enyo said.

With a plan in place, they left the rooftops and snuck up to a corner that was just out of the guard's sight. Enyo took a deep breath, squared her shoulders, and then ran out into the street, her appearance the definition of a frantic young woman.

"Guards! Guards! I found a strange figure over that way! He tried to attack me!" she said, sounding every bit the frightened girl as she pointed in the direction that he and Fellis waited.

"Did you teach her that?" Jacob asked.

"Nope," Fellis said. "She learned that all on her own. Not bad, right?"

"I give her a five out of ten," Durandal muttered.

"Quiet, you," Jacob whispered.

"A strange figure?" The guards looked at each other, nodded, and then looked back at her. "Show us where this person is!"

"He's this way," Enyo said. "Follow me!"

The guards followed Enyo. Jacob and Fellis disappeared, hiding in the shadows. Enyo appeared around the corner seconds later, and then the guards did. One of them was a female, so Jacob snuck up behind her and captured her in a strong hold. One hand went against her mouth, muffling her screams. The male guard turned at the slight sound, but Fellis was already in front of him.

"Hey there," she said. "I hadn't been sure when my colleague told me about how attractive you are in uniform, but now that I've seen you, I'm forced to believe her."

"Uh... what?" The man blinked rapidly several times. His eyes were zeroed in on Fellis's chest, which was emphasized when she squeezed her arms together.

The woman in Jacob's grasp tried to shout something, but her voice no longer worked. Jacob was already disrupting the flow of her energy with his Linked Energy Manipulation. Her entire body had been paralyzed.

"Do you think you can do me a favor?" Fellis continued. "I'm in need of a big, strong man like you. I don't think there's anyone else who can do the job."

"W-what do you need?" the man asked. He seemed to have forgotten all about Enyo and the mysterious figure that she had spoken of.

Fellis grinned as her eyes glowed. "I need you to do everything that I tell you to."

The guard's face slackened. "Yes, Mistress."

"Good." Fellis patted him on the cheek. "Just wait here a moment."

"Yes... Mistress."

Fellis walked around the man and went over to Jacob's prisoner, who stared at her with frightened eyes.

"Don't worry," Fellis said, smiling. "This won't hurt a bit."

Jacob watched from behind as Fellis's eyes picked up an ethereal glow. He waited, unsure of what he was waiting for. Looking at his prisoner, he saw that her eyes were glazing over. Fellis eventually sighed and straightened back up.

"You can let go of her now."

Jacob did as instructed. The woman didn't move.

"Nice job," Jacob said. "To both of you. Enyo, that was some pretty good acting."

"Thanks." Enyo beamed. "I've never done that before. It was kind of exhilarating."

"What should we do with these two?" Fellis asked, hitching a thumb at the two mind-controlled guards.

"Have them return to their posts. We want to keep everyone from getting suspicious."

After Fellis ordered the two guards back to their post, he and Enyo and the temptress used side streets and alleys to travel to the other tower. Like the first one, there were two guards there. Both of them were male, fortunately.

"We're counting on you, Fellis," Jacob said.

"Good luck," Enyo added.

"Show me sexy times," Durandal just had to say. "Owch!" the sword muttered when Jacob smacked it on the hilt.

Fellis strolled out from behind the building with a seductive sway of her hips. Jacob and Enyo watched as she waved the two guards down, speaking with them and ensnaring them with her seduction before taking control of their minds. As she worked her magic, Jacob looked up. The guards patrolling the wall had noticed her, and a few had stopped to watch. They could be trouble.

"I didn't think about how to deal with those ones," Jacob muttered.

"What?" asked Enyo.

"I was saying we might run into trouble if those guys on top of the wall become suspicious."

"Oh…"

Fellis returned a few seconds later, having thoroughly dominated the minds of both men. There was a satisfied smile on her face. A contentedness surrounded her. For whatever reason, it reminded him of a kitten after drinking its first bowl of milk.

"Did you find out which tower the lever was in?" Jacob asked.

"It's in this one," Fellis answered. "There's a basement level where the lever is located."

"I'm guessing there's a guard protecting it?"

"Yes." Fellis nodded. "I asked those fine gentlemen over there, and they said that there are four more guards inside of the tower."

Jacob rubbed his head. Four more guards were four guards more than he wanted to deal with. That said, it didn't look like they had much of a choice. If they wanted to escape from this place, they would need to take out those guards.

"Should we fight?" asked Enyo, sounding excited. It must have been the bloodlust of the Dark Clan.

"I don't think fighting is going to be a good idea," Jacob said. "There's way too many of us to take out all at once. If we start fighting them, there's also a good chance they'll call for reinforcements."

"Oh…" Enyo's shoulders drooped.

"Don't look so down, Enyo," Fellis said. "There will be plenty of chances for us to fight people. Right now, getting out of the city without getting caught is what's important."

"I know that…"

Jacob tried to think of the best method for sneaking into the tower, opening the gate, and lowering the drawbridge. Unfortunately, he couldn't see any of his ideas working. All of them ended in combat when he replayed each scenario in his mind. It was vexing, to say the least.

While he was thinking this, a loud scream rent the night air. The sound, a piercing wail unlike anything he'd heard before, echoed across the area, a threnody of terrified voices all screaming as if something horrible beyond belief was happening. It didn't take long for Jacob to realize where those screams were coming from.

"That came from inside of the tower," Jacob muttered.

The guards standing on the wall were already making their way into the tower. They disappeared one by one. Jacob, Enyo, and Fellis remained outside, unsure of what to do before, just like the first time, more shrill cries echoed from inside of the tower. The two guards standing outside, who'd been told to ignore everything happening around them, stood in place like statues.

"Jacob?" Enyo said in a questioning tone.

"Damn it," Jacob swore. "Let's go!"

Since the guards patrolling the wall were gone, it was easy for them to slip inside. The two guards who Fellis had under her mind magic didn't even bat an eyelash.

Jacob's eyes slowly adjusted to the dim lighting. They were in a spiral stairwell. The stairs on his left lead up and the ones on his right lead down. More screams echoed from beneath them, so he, Enyo, and Fellis headed down. As they ran, the lights from torches on the walls cast eerie shadows along the ground.

They burst into the lower level, and Enyo gasped when they entered the room to see what appeared to be the end of a massacre. Bodies lay strewn across the stone tiles. There was no blood; however, all the bodies reminded him of dried out corpses. Their skin was brown, rail thin, and wrinkled. He couldn't see much of their bodies, but their faces were gaunt, their cheekbones hollow. Even their eyes were staring at nothing as they bulged from dried-out sockets.

In the center of this scene stood a woman. Her beauty was beyond compare. The sleeveless dress she wore barely went past her hips, showing off her toned thighs and shapely calves, which were covered by a pair of black boots. The front of her dress had strange cut out design that went down all the way to her navel, exposing her taut stomach and the inner swell of her large breasts. Slender shoulders moved into deceptively strong arms and delicate fingers, which were currently clenched around the neck of a female guard.

Her mouth was open wide, as did the mouth of her victim. Something white and ethereal emerged from the guard's mouth, the woman herself kicking and gurgling. Reminiscent of ectoplasm, the white essence traveled out of her mouth like a snake and moved into the mouth of the pale-skinned woman, almost like she was eating it.

Jacob was so shocked that it took him a full ten seconds to realize that the woman was eating the guard's soul. As he continued to watch, the guard slowly withered away just like the other ones that were laying haphazardly across the floor.

What kind of magic is that?

"Mm," the woman moaned as she discarded the now soulless husk. "That was a delectable treat. A perfect snack before the main course." The way she smiled at him did nothing to put Jacob's mind at ease. "Welcome, hero, Fellis, Dark Lady. My name is Lust, and I'll be your murderer tonight."

✳✳✳

"L-Lust?" Fellis stuttered as she took a step back.

"You know this person?" Jacob asked.

"Know of her would be more accurate." Fellis eyed the one calling herself Lust like a wild animal might stare at a predator. "Lust is the name given to one of the Dark Council's seven members."

"The Dark Council?" Enyo sucked in a breath. "Then this woman is…"

"That's right," Fellis said. "If this woman really is Lust, then she is one of the seven most powerful Dark Clan members in the entire world."

That wasn't good. Jacob had never faced a Dark Council member, but from what Fellis told him, each member of the dark council was about as strong as the Dark Lord—maybe even stronger.

"Fellis," Lust said in a mockingly sad tone. "I would like to say that I'm surprised to discover your traitorous intentions, but the truth is that I've known about the protective feelings you have for Enyo since the beginning. It really is too bad. All this time you thought you were protecting her when what you were really doing was playing into my hands."

"So, what?" Fellis asked. "Are you saying everything I've done up to this point has been by your design?"

"More or less," Lust said. "There were a few things that I hadn't anticipated, such as all of the Dark Council's champions being killed off. However, I think it works better this way. With them gone, the only champion now alive is you, the one that I chose, which means none of the old codgers on the council will even know what happened here until it's too late."

This Lust lady seemed to enjoy talking a lot. He wondered if she was just that narcissistic, or if her loose lips were there by design. Was she hoping to accomplish something by letting them know all this?

"Enyo, Fellis," Jacob grabbed their attention. "When I tell you to, I want you both to run back up the way we came."

"W-what?" Enyo gawked at him. "You can't mean you want us to leave you alone with this woman."

"Yes, that's exactly what I'm telling you."

"But—"

"Enyo, this is not a battle that can be won through superior numbers," Jacob said. "I'm going to have to go all out to beat this woman, but I can't do that if I'm worrying about you two."

"He's right," Fellis said. "I'm not strong enough to go toe to toe with a member of the Dark Council, and while you have the power, you lack the experience. Jacob is the only one among us who has a chance of beating her."

Enyo bit her lip in indecision. She looked at Jacob, who could only gaze at her out of the corner of his eye, to keep her and their enemy in sight. Lust didn't interrupt them. If anything, the smile on her face said that she was amused by their conversation.

"Promise me that you'll be okay," Enyo said at last.

"I can't make that promise," Jacob said. He wasn't going to lie. "However, I can promise that I'll do everything in my power to come back to you."

"I guess... that's about as good as I can expect," Enyo said.

Jacob shrugged in a helpless manner. "I won't make a promise that I don't know I can keep."

"I understand," Enyo said softly.

"Good. Then get out of here."

With nothing left to say, Jacob shot from the ground, closing the gap between him and Lust. Durandal slid from its sheath with a soft hiss. He slashed the sword at Lust, but it was blocked, not by another sword, but by a set of black claws that appeared to have been created from darkness itself.

"Have you finished saying your last goodbyes?" Lust asked, her lips twisting into a venomous smile. "Aren't I kind for letting you speak without interruption? I thought it would be nice to allow you a few seconds to get your feelings sorted out."

Jacob heard the sound of receding feet behind him. Enyo and Fellis were already gone. That meant it was time to get serious.

"Goodbyes are only something that should be said when you're parting permanently." Jacob grunted as he used Linked Energy Manipulation to increase his physical prowess. "Someone like you isn't strong enough to keep me from returning to them."

His muscles flexing, Jacob shoved his sword against the woman's claws. Lust was sent flying backwards. She slammed into the wall. Cracks appeared, spreading out from the center of impact. Jacob, unwilling to leave it at just that, thrust Durandal forward as he charged at her.

A dark shield sprang up in front of Lust, but Jacob had already prepared for something like that, and he sent a surge of energy through his blade. The tip of Durandal struck the shield. The shield shattered like a thousand broken glass fragments, and Durandal continued forward, stabbing into the wall as if it was made of bread.

Lust wasn't there.

Knowing better than to just standing there, Jacob pulled Durandal out of the wall and moved. He was just in time. Several spears made of darkness shot out and pierced the wall, perforating it. A few of the spears changed direction and tried to attack him, but

Jacob swung Durandal, releasing a wave of energy that sliced them apart.

He stopped moving when he was standing right next to the gate lever.

"You're quite strong," Lust complimented. "Linked Energy Manipulation, is it? It's been almost five hundred years since I fought against someone who could use that."

"Is that so? That probably means you're rusty," Jacob taunted.

"Indeed." Lust stretched her arms above her head. Her chest popped out of her dress, but Jacob ignored the obvious attempt at seduction. "However, it's not been so long that I don't remember the weaknesses of someone who uses Linked Energy Manipulation."

Jacob kicked the lever before setting himself in a combat stance, feet sliding shoulder width apart, Durandal held in a two-handed grip, shoulders squared. This battle was not going to be easy.

"I think you'll find that all of the weaknesses you're thinking about have been stamped out this time."

A delightful curve made Lust's already gorgeous face somehow even more enchanting—in the same way King Cobras were enchanting. "Oh, is that so? Then why don't you prove it to me?"

"I will. Right. Now!"

Jacob rushed forward. Several spears made of darkness tried to impale him, but he dodged them with ease, jinking and juking around the attacks. This woman was a dark magic user, and her magic seemed to be Darkness. She could probably create lots of weapons and shields from darkness. With that in mind, so long as he kept moving, it would be harder for her to stab him. He was only two meters away now. Just another second and—

The earth beneath his feet exploded as several tree-like tentacles shot from the ground. Jacob was forced to stop his advance and cut the tentacles with Durandal. The sword sliced through what he could only assume were vines with ease. As the vines fell to the ground, Jacob prepared to close the distance.

That was when the vines exploded.

Jacob didn't cry out as his body was engulfed in flames, though the pain as intense. As he flew through the air, he spun around and unleashed his energy. A loud boom echoed across the room as the flames were put out. Jacob twisted his body around further, landing on his feet and skidding along the ground.

Channeling energy into his sword, he swung Durandal at Lust, who laughed as she weaved around his attacks with the grace of a dancer. Each of his crescent blades destroyed a section of the wall behind her. A large hole soon formed. No one was outside in that area, but it would only be a matter of time before more people came here to see what the commotion was about.

I have to finish this quickly.

"Tell me, hero, do you know what my magic is? Have you figured it out?" Lust asked. Jacob remained silent. "No? That's too bad. By the way, you might want to look behind you."

Jacob did not look behind him. Instead, he rolled along the ground. Several loud explosions went off at his back. The earth rumbled as he came up to his feet. There were several deafening roars as the roof where he'd been standing collapsed. He ignored even that and, sending more power to Durandal than usual, unleashed a massive wave of blue energy that crashed into Lust—or it would have, if she hadn't cut it apart with a blade of darkness.

Her retaliation was swift and brutal; swiping the air with her left hand, several balls of fire appeared in the air. They flew at Jacob like crossbow bolts. He slashed one apart with Durandal, only to yelp when the fireball exploded and sent him skidding backwards.

The sound of ground breaking echoed behind him. Jacob spun around. Durandal cut the air. The thick vines that sprouted from the ground and tried to grab him evaporated as he unleashed a blast of energy at them.

"Partner, this chick is really strong—and I have no clue what's going on here!"

"And you think I do? Just keep cutting!"

Jacob didn't understand what was happening. So far, Lust had used three different kinds of magic: Darkness, Fire, and Plant. People were only able to use one type of magic, or, in the rare cases like Enyo, who had a dual affinity, two types. Someone being able to use three different magic types was unheard of.

I need to know more.

He didn't have enough information to make any conclusions yet, which meant he needed to hold out and observe Lust further. If he could just figure out her gimmick, then he could beat her. He was sure of it.

"Let me guess, you're trying to figure out what kind of magic I'm using, correct?" Lust laughed. "I'm sorry to say this, but you'll never be able to figure it out. Speaking of magic, you might want to dodge."

Jacob leapt backward as a beam of light melted through the roof, struck the floor, and incinerated the stone tiles. Jacob and Durandal were both gawking.

"She can even use light magic?!"

"I'm really not liking this woman, Partner!"

"Yeah, well, that makes two of us!"

Lust giggled. "You and your sword really are an amusing. It's funny, but in all my years of being alive, I have never once met a talking sword until today. I guess even one such as myself can be surprised on occasion."

"I'm surprised someone who has lived as long as you has never seen a talking sword before," Jacob taunted.

Rather than get upset at essentially being called old, Lust giggled. "Yes, it is quite disappointing. I'm glad that I had the chance to see one now. Thank you for that."

"You're so welcome," Jacob said, his voice thick with sarcasm. "You know that my only reason for being here is to show you my super awesome talking sword."

Jacob didn't let the woman respond as he unleashed another wave of destruction. The ground in front of him was torn apart, fragmented stone flying at Lust like projectiles launched from a ballista. Lust seemed neither bothered nor worried. Jacob found out why seconds later when a wall of darkness appeared before her. The fragments and energy wave struck the wall, which undulated for a moment as if it was elastic. The fragments broke, the energy dissipated, and the wall suddenly transformed into several dozen spears that came hurtling at him.

Peeling his lips back in a snarl, Jacob swung Durandal again—a vertical slash that tore through the spears and split apart the ground. This time, Lust did not block his attack. She leapt aside, allowing the gigantic wave to tear straight through the wall. It not only went through this wall, but it continued on to destroy the hallway on the other side.

Lust looked at the collapsed hall, listened to the sounds of destruction as his wave of energy continued, and then looked back at him.

"I can see now why Alucard lost to you. You have an impressive amount of energy for one so young."

"Lady, this isn't even a one-hundredth of the power I possess," Jacob declared as he shifted into a one-handed grip. "Allow me to show you just how much power I have at my disposal."

Jacob didn't give Lust a chance to respond. He'd been keeping his power carefully locked away, for fear that unleashing it would hurt others, but now he unlocked the restraints that held it back. Like a flood it came. It swept over him, this power. However, he didn't drown. Rather, he allowed himself to flow with the surging tide of energy, using it to fuel his own body.

With his entire body encased in energy, Jacob blasted off the ground, which exploded underneath him. He was on Lust in seconds. She raised her arm to block his swing, her entire limb encased in light energy. Durandal met her forearm. From the point of impact and spreading outward was a massive blast of wind. Lust screamed as the attack sent her flying backwards, out of the hole Jacob had made.

Jacob followed as Lust destroyed the roof and leapt into the open air. He leapt out of the tower, which rumbled and shook before, like a house of cards, the entire thing collapsed. Screams echoed all around. Soldiers were going to converge on their location soon. He needed to finish his battle with Lust quickly.

He unleashed another blast of energy at Lust, a giant tornado of blue destruction instead of a crescent wave. It slammed into Lust, who was sent flying.

She smashed through a building several feet away. There was a large gaping hole where she'd busted through it. As he stalked forward, she walked out of the hole, blood trickling down her scalp.

"I've figured out your power," Jacob said as she stopped several meters from him. "You're not a dark magic user, or a light magic user. Your magic is to steal the magic of others."

Despite being bloodied and bruised, Lust smiled. "That's correct. My magic is called Drain. I drain the life force of people by sucking it out of them, and once I've drained every last drop of life they have, their magic becomes my magic."

A dark aura appeared around Lust, purple wisps of miasma that wafted off her like violent streamers. The air around her had become heavy. Jacob felt the pressure of her magic from where he was standing, though he shrugged it off.

"Do not think that this battle is won just because you know how my magic works," Lust said. "You may know how I can use other people's magic, but you don't know what types of magic I have at my disposal. I've been doing this for over five hundred years. I have more magic in my fingertips than you have comebacks."

Jacob narrowed his eyes. "We'll see about that."

The moment of ensuing silence only lasted until their battle began anew.

Their clash caused the very atmosphere to tremble.

***

Enyo ran behind Fellis. They had already escaped the tower. The drawbridge was down, likely because Jacob had lowered it sometime during his fight. Behind them, explosions went off like fireworks. If she turned her head, Enyo knew that she would see the two massive auras of clashing energy from the fight between Jacob and Lust.

Of course, she and Fellis had other things to worry about.

"Ignis! Flamma! Impes! Ustrina! Incendium!"

A fireball crashed into the ground half a meter to their left, detonating with concussive force. Enyo felt the heat wash over her back. It was too far away to do any damage, but having something explode so close to her and not seeing it was nerve wracking.

She and Fellis were running down the cobblestone street. She didn't know how far they'd run. It felt like they'd been running for hours, but she could still see Tallus Caelum in the distance, so it couldn't have been more than a few minutes at most.

From the moment that she and Fellis had run across the drawbridge, they'd been chased by several knights. She didn't know how they had responded so quickly. Indeed, considering the battle that was going on between Jacob and Lust right now, she would have expected them to let her and Fellis go in the confusion.

That hadn't been the case. Now they were running for their lives. What made it worse was that they had no way to lose them. Everything was open plains here. There was no forest, no trees, not even so much as a large shrub.

A roar from above alerted her to more trouble. Enyo looked up. Several drakes were practically on top of them.

I have a bad feeling about this...

She couldn't hear any chanting because they were so high up, but she could tell they weren't going to just fly above her without doing anything. Her foresight proved to be a blessing. Seconds after they appeared, magic rained down from the drake riders—lightning, fire, wind, light. Enyo was left with no option but to chant a spell.

"Finis. Sepio. Opsideo."

A dome of light appeared around her and Fellis. The barrage of different magic spells slammed into her shield, which shook as it was assaulted. Fortunately, the people attacking her did not have the sheer power that she did. The shield held up against the barrage, and when the assault ended, she dismissed the protective dome and kept running.

"We need to lose these people," she shouted at Fellis.

"Undoubtedly," Fellis agreed. "Unless you think you can take them on from a distance?"

Enyo might have been able to take on one or two people at range, but she didn't have the ability to fight off multiple opponents like that. She shook her head.

"Then let's keep going," Fellis said. "Jacob said there was a bridge up ahead."

Thinking about Jacob made her remember how they'd left him to fight off Lust. She hoped he was okay.

More magic spells came at them, but she and Fellis either dodged or blocked accordingly. Enyo tried to use her magic sparingly. She might have had a lot of magic at her disposal, but there was no telling how much longer they would have to fight. It was better to conserve energy for when they really needed it.

A mountain appeared up ahead, and before the mountain, slowly becoming more visible, was the Jovis Bridge. Like Jacob had described it, the bridge was large. It spanned across a massive ravine that was even bigger than the one in the Phantasma Forest. As they neared it, she realized that it was a standard bridge made of wood and rope. There was a noticeable curve, and it swayed as a strong breeze blew across the ravine.

"I'm not sure I want to go across that," Enyo said.

"That's too bad," Fellis countered. "We really don't have much choice."

"I know that," Enyo grumbled. "I was just saying…"

As more attacks flew by, she and Fellis raced onto the bridge. Her heart leapt into her throat as the bridge rocked back and forth. She grabbed onto the ropes and tried to ignore the fact that she was running across a rickety bridge, with a several hundred-meter drop, and that the ropes were burning her hands because she refused to slacken her grip.

Following behind Fellis, they made it about three-fourths across the bridge before they had to stop. The drake knights who'd been following them had flown to the other side and landed. Now they were blocking their path. The man in front, the same one who'd been hounding them this whole time, stood with his sword poised and a self-righteous expression on his face.

"Thieves! I demand that you surrender yourselves now! Do so, and I will guarantee you safety and a fair trial."

This man clearly didn't know how the world worked. Safety and a fair trial? She and Fellis were members of the Dark Clan. What's more, she had stolen the gate key. Even she was not naïve enough to assume they would be given a fair trial after this. As for safety, well, Enyo had faced more assassination attempts than most people were capable of counting to.

"I hope you have a plan, Fellis," Enyo said. "Because I have no idea what we should do."

"That would depend. Do you trust me?" Fellis asked.

"I have always trusted you." Enyo's immediate answer.

"Good. Then, please wrap your arms around my waist and hold on tight."

Enyo didn't hesitate to do as she was told, even though she suddenly felt wary, like her former maid was about to do something incredibly stupid. She was right. Almost as soon as her arms were secured around Fellis's waist, the woman lashed out with her whip. The steel tip sliced straight through the ropes that held the bridge together.

Enyo barely had a chance to open her mouth before a sudden feeling of weightlessness overcame her. Her stomach leapt into her throat. Her feet were tingling. The wind rushed by her, howling on all sides like vicious, snarling animals. Enyo thought she was going to be sick—no, she was sick. Everything blurred by, making her eyes swirl. She wanted to puke. The ground was getting closer. She couldn't breathe. She was—

Cold. Enyo felt coldness seeping into her bones, her skin, her everything. The weightlessness was still there, but a sense like she was being yanked in a random direction accompanied it now. She wanted to breath, but her lungs wouldn't let her take in any air. It took her a moment to realize why.

Water!

Opening her eyes, she realized that she and Fellis were underwater, with a strong current pulling them. The coldness seeping into her bones was freezing water. The reason she couldn't breathe was because water was filling her lungs.

Enyo struggled to break the surface. Fellis wasn't helping her for some reason, so she was left to do the work alone. She kicked her legs while keeping a firm grip on Fellis. Her lungs burned, her chest ached, and her body felt like lead, but she did her best to ignore these feelings.

Her head broke the water's surface, and she inhaled a deep, grateful, lungful of air. Fellis was weighing her down. Her friend and former servant wasn't moving at all.

"Fellis?" She coughed as she struggled to keep her head above water. "Fellis?"

The woman still didn't respond. Enyo couldn't see Fellis's face. Water was splashing in her eyes, and she was doing all she could not to get sucked back under.

Realizing that she couldn't afford to stay as she was, Enyo kicked feet. She couldn't fight the current, which was stronger than her legs, so she moved sideways, across the current. There was a rocky ledge several yards away. It was covered in vines and other things that she could grab onto. However, it was also wet and slippery. She grabbed a vine, only to have it slide from her grasp. It didn't help that Fellis was keeping her from being able to stay above water.

Come on... come on... yes!

Enyo felt a moment of triumph as she grabbed onto a vine and wrapped it around her arm. Unfortunately, climbing up proved harder than she thought it should have. In the end, she was unable to climb up unless she wanted to let go of Fellis. The vine slipped from her grasp, and the current pushed her away.

Enyo was swept along.

***

Magic clashed with energy. Pillars of darkness rose into the sky before they were sliced apart by blue crescents that rent the very air itself. Massive balls of blue energy burst apart as they were pierced with spears of darkness.

Jacob leapt backwards as several serpentine-shaped magical attacks tried to latch onto him. Unleashing another burst of energy, he blasted away the attacks before they could reach him, and then he sent his own attack at Lust, who countered by slicing the air in front of her, cutting the wave in half.

Nasally gasps escaped Jacob's mouth as he ran, avoiding a series of earth spikes that jutted from the ground, trying to impale him. He leapt into the air. There was a giant fire bird there to meet him. Lust must have set this trap in advance. Scowling, he hacked the bird-shaped flame apart with impunity and landed back on the ground.

A lapse appeared in the battle.

He and Lust had been fighting for over fifteen minutes, far longer than most battles took to conclude. It was a testament to this woman's prowess that she barely had a scratch on her. Her clothes were scuffed, ripped in some parts, and she had a few cuts here and there along her legs and arms, but nothing beyond that.

"You're holding back," Lust declared. Her expression was narrowed, as if she was angered by this fact.

Jacob grimaced. "You can't expect me to use all of my power here. If I did that, this entire city would be in shambles."

Thus far, Jacob had been able to limit damage to the city to this one section near the wall. No attack had strayed too far, no magic cast had gone near the city itself. While the area around him was covered in pitfalls, scorch marks, cracks, and wreckage, everything beyond the fifteen-meter zone of their battle was pristine.

"Ho?" Lust grinned. "So, you are protecting the people of this city, then? How admirable of you to protect a people that you've already forsaken. Still…" Lust raised her hand and a crackling orb of lightning appeared, hovering before her palm. "… I don't much care for these people."

Jacob felt all the air get driven from his lungs. "What are you doing?!"

Lust grinned. Jacob tried to charge toward her, but it was too late. The orb fired off. It blasted into a building, destroying it completely. It didn't stop there, however. The orb shot through another building, and then another and another. Jacob could only watch in horror as several dozen buildings were decimated in half as many seconds.

"Wha... why?" Jacob asked, turning back to Lust. "Why did you do that?"

"Are you really asking me why?" Lust scoffed. "You, a hero, should already know the answer to that."

Of course he knew. It was the same reason that Alucard had been so willing to massacre others, even his own people. This woman was just like him—no, she was even worse. Alucard's desire had been obvious: the domination of the continent. This woman? She was just testing him. She wanted to fight him at full power, and for that reason, she was willing to massacre people.

"Fine," he ground out. "If that's how you want it, then I won't hold back anymore."

There was no warning, no great surge of power that foretold Jacob's next attack. One moment, he was standing a dozen meters from his opponent. The next he was right in front of her. Being so close, his sword already swinging, Jacob had just a split second to see the way Lust's eyes widened before he sliced her in half.

Lust burst into flower petals.

"What?"

"Ha ha ha! Yes! This is what I was looking for!" a voice rang out.

Jacob turned around. Lust was standing on an undemolished roof. She leered down at him from her position on high, her lips peeled back in a face-splitting grin that revealed her pearly white teeth. He wanted to punch those teeth out.

"Come on, hero! Show me the power that defeated the Dark Lord!"

The challenge was issued, and Jacob responded to it. He swung Durandal down, unleashing a wave of energy that sliced through the ground, struck the building, and demolished it. Lust had not been hit. She leapt into the air at the last second, laughing like a maniac—until Jacob shot into the air like a cannon, appeared over her head, and struck her in the face with a heel drop.

Jacob felt nothing but the utmost satisfaction as he watched Lust hurtle toward the ground. When she slammed into the earth, upheaving the road and gravel as cracks spread along the surface like an endless spinneret, he smiled.

At least, he did until a massive beam of darkness shot from within the expanding cloud of dust. The attack slammed into him, causing his mind and vision to go white. His skin burned. His body boiled. It felt like he was being melted from the inside out.

He gritted his teeth and poured out more energy, creating a thick layer of chi that surrounded him like a fiery aura. The pain lessened, though the damage had already been done.

Lust was down below. She was bleeding profusely from a wound to her head, and her left arm was limp, hanging at her side like a wet noodle. Despite that, she wore a grin that reminded him of Alucard when they had fought.

That smile enraged him all the more.

Roaring out his anger, Jacob swung Durandal at the woman. There was no massive beam of energy this time. The swing was purely one of strength. A storm of force-like wind was created from the swing. It slammed into Lust, who merely laughed as she thrust out her hands as if that would protect her.

Roots shot from the ground, the massive roots of a tree that could have been thousands of years old. Each one was as thick as he was wide. They converged around her, protecting her from the wind storm.

Jacob cut those roots down with Durandal as he fell into them. As he removed the obstacles in his path, he revealed the other side, where Lust should have been.

Should have been, but was no longer there.

Where did she go?

Jacob didn't much time to search. Several dozen pillars burst from the ground, ascended high into the sky, curved around, and then tried to smash him.

Taking several massive back leaps, Jacob shouted as he spun around. A crescent erupted from Durandal. It cut through most of the pillars, though several still made it to him. Those he sliced apart the regular way. Finishing the pillars off, Jacob was about to begin his search for Lust—when a searing pain dug into his side.

He withheld a gasp and looked down. There was a spear of light jutting from the left side of his stomach. Jacob blinked. Somehow, the spear had pierced through his protective chi barrier.

H-how…?

"I bet you're wondering how I broke through your barrier," Lust said, appearing several yards to his left. She wore an exhilarated smile. "You see, a shield created by Linked Energy Manipulation is a lot like a really hard bubble. Sure, most things simply bounce off the bubble, but if you focus a really strong attack into a single point, well…" She gave a dainty shrug. "This was one of those weaknesses that I was talking about earlier. It looks like you haven't stamped most of them out, after all."

Jacob grabbed the light spear and, with an application of power, shattered it. He turned to face Lust, whose smile only grew wider.

"Are you sure you should still be fighting with that wound?"

"I'll be fine. I was in a lot worse shape when I fought against Alucard."

"Hmm…"

Swinging Durandal around with his left hand, Jacob generated a fierce wind that knocked Lust backwards. As she skidded along the ground, Jacob thrust his right hand forward, allowing a ball of blue energy to shoot from his knuckles like a bolt from a crossbow. It was blocked by the black shield that she favored. Jacob was already prepared for it to come up. He switched his grip on Durandal, drew his left arm back, and threw the weapon forward.

Durandal pierced straight through the shield. There was a shrill cry of agony from the other side. Cracks appeared along the shield before, without a single warning, it shattered, revealing Lust standing on the other side, Durandal impaling her left shoulder.

"It's over," Jacob said as he walked up to Lust, stopped in front of her, grabbed Durandal, and yanked it out of her chest.

The woman gasped as she fell to her knees. Blood sprayed from her shoulder and back like geysers shooting hot water. Looking down at the woman, Jacob felt only satisfaction at knowing that she was about to die.

"You're right," Lust rasped. "It is over."

The atmosphere shifted. Jacob had only a second to become aware of the danger. Lust looked up at him.

Her lips were curved in triumph.

"For you, that is."

Six monoliths rose around him, obsidian stones that had numerous archaic symbols drawn on them. They formed a circle around him. Jacob reached out to touch one, but he hissed when a barrier sprung up and stung his hand. He considered using Durandal to slice through it, but then something happened, and Jacob found himself unable to do much of anything.

He fell to his knees as something intangible pressed down on him. It felt like he was being crushed by some unidentifiable force. Electric arcs, like tendrils, skittered along the surface of the shield before they converged on Jacob without warning, inducing more pain than he could remember ever feeling.

Opening his mouth, Jacob tried to scream, but no sound came out. His back arched as pain flooded through him like a storm. He heard something crack, and he could've sworn it was his spine. As the pain heightened, his world suddenly went white, and then…

…everything went dark.

EPILOGUE – THE DEFEATED HERO

Lust breathed heavily through her nose as she struggled to remain upright. Her knees shook, her left arm was hideously swollen and reminded her of a bloody eel that had been skinned, and her head was pounding like Pride's Warhammer was banging around inside of her mind.

Several yards away, Jacob lay motionless on the ground. The battle had been a lot more fun than she'd anticipated. She could now see how Alucard had lost. That man might have been strong, but he lacked the tactics and experience that she had. There was no way he could have defeated someone like Jacob.

She walked up to Jacob, stopping a yard from his feet. His body was broken. Blood gushed from places where his skin had been burnt off. Several patches of flesh were boiling, his left eyelid had evaporated, leaving his eye exposed, and his limbs were bent at angles that human limbs shouldn't have been able to go.

"You were an excellent fight," she murmured. "I haven't fought anyone as powerful as you since I killed the first Pride. You should be quite proud of yourself."

Jacob's raspy breathing reached her ears. She was startled, having thought he was dead. So, even now, he still clung to life. That last attack would have killed even a member of the Dark Council. What admirable tenacity.

She grinned. "I think such a willingness to cling to life deserves a reward, don't you? Consider this my gift for amusing me so much."

Leaning down awkwardly, ignoring the way her body protested the action, she bent over and placed a kiss on the hero's lips. It wasn't just a mere kiss, though. As she pressed their lips together, she allowed a small amount of her life force to trickle into him. It would keep him alive long enough for someone to heal him. With luck, he would survive. If he didn't... well, then he didn't deserve to live anyway.

The other Dark Council members would be upset if they learned about what she was doing. They wouldn't approve of her saving the life of a hero, but their battle had left her exhilarated and intrigued. She wanted to see what this young man would do next.

Perhaps he'll be the one to end my boredom.

She leaned back up. Her body shook as jolts of pain traveled along her legs and arms. That boy really had taken her for a ride. How long had it been since she'd felt such a delicious sting of pain? Four hundred years? Five? She'd completely forgotten what pain felt like until now.

As she was about to stand, something strong and unyielding grabbed onto her forearm. She yelped and jerked back, stumbling to the ground. The thing grabbing her was a hand. It was Jacob's hand, to be precise. She stared at the hand, misshapen, the skin boiled raw, and then she looked at Jacob, who, even now, remained unconscious.

"Fu... ha... ha ha ha! Ha ha ha ha!" Grinning, she pried the boy's hand off her wrist and stood up. "I really am looking forward to seeing what you do next, hero. Make sure you entertain me."

Using what little of her magic remained, Lust teleported herself away. This day had been long, but fun, oh so much fun. It gave her hope for the future.

Wouldn't it be nice if every day was fun like this? The thought made her sigh in ecstasy. *One could only hope.*

-To Be Continued...

AFTERWORD

Hey, everyone! For those who have read my previous light novels, welcome back. For those who are new to my light novels, I am really happy you decided to pick up this story! I hope you enjoyed reading it.

Journey of a Betrayed Hero is a two volume series that I wrote after finally deciding it was time for me to try my hand at writing an isekai series, but I wanted to do something different for this story than other isekai stories. In most isekai light novels, the story begins when the main hero, or heroes, get summoned to this fantasy world and are asked to complete a task. This task can be anything from defeating the dark lord, fighting against hordes demons, or defending the world from extra-dimensional waves of monsters.

For this series, I wanted to do something a little different. That's why I decided to write a story about what happens after the hero has already completed the task he was given upon being summoned to another world. He has already fought against the dark lord and become the hero that saved the kingdom, but then he was betrayed by the people he saved and ended up leaving. He winds up becoming a barkeep and remains in obscurity for several years before Enyo shows up and asks for his help.

I've read numerous light novels in my time. Some of my favorite isekei series are *The Rising of the Shield Hero, How NOT To Summon a Demon Lord, RE:Zero – Staring Life in Another World –, Konosuba, Mushoku Tensei,* and *ARIFURETA: From Commonplace to World's Strongest.* All of them are fairly long series, spanning over one dozen volumes at the very least.

I feel the reason these series can afford to be so long is because the main plot isn't immediately apparent. Sure, some might have a "save us from the Demon Lord!" or the "save us from the Waves of Destruction!" plot, but even those don't become important until much later, and oftentimes the plot becomes far more complicated the further you get into the story, which leaves a lot of room to add plenty of filling in between the main story… like building your harem, grinding your characters, or killing your character over and over again after he was summoned to this other world for what seems like no real reason at first until new information about a certain Witch of Envy comes to light in.

This particular light novel series is very short because I didn't want to make a super long series that details volume upon volume of divergent subplots. I can't afford to like other series can because this story is hyper focused. The main plot is Jacob and Enyo's journey through Terrasole as they try to get to Jacob's original world. Anything that doesn't involve this was excluded because it simply wouldn't work with such a focused series. That's why this will only be a two-part series.

The next volume should come out within 3-4 months, if anyone is curious.

I may come back at some point and do a story on what happened when Jacob was first summoned to this world—like a prequel series or something. While this depends on how popular this series is, if it *does* happen, I can add all those delicious side quests that make isekai series so interesting.

Before I end this afterword, I would like to thank several people. First is my editor and proofreaders for helping me find and correct the grammar mistakes I missed. I really appreciate it. I also want to thank Aisoretto—my illustrator. This series has gone through three illustrators so far. My first artist bailed on me after I paid him upfront. Because I was $2,400 down the drain, I couldn't even think of hiring another artist for two whole years due to money issues. My second artist was much better. She apologized and refunded what I paid her upfront. Aisoretto is the third artist I hired to work with me on this series, and I'm very glad to have him. His artwork is really stellar!

The last people I want to thank are all of you. To the people who read this story, thank you so much! I hope you enjoyed it! To the people who wrote reviews for this story on Amazon, their blogs, and other places, you are awesome! You have no idea how much it means to me. Every time someone takes the time out of their day to leave a review, I'm overcome with emotion. To my readers who have decided to support me on my Patreon—from the bottom of my heart, thank you. Words alone can never express my gratitude. I could write a 500 page novel, and it still wouldn't be enough.

I'm still not a very good writer. I still have a lot to learn. I hope that I can continue improving and learning to be a better writer with your help.

Thank you again. I hope to see you all next volume!

~Brandon Varnell

WIDEREBURT: LEGEND OF THE REINCARNATED WARRIOR

Chapter 1: The Final Battle

The air burst all around me. Flames seared the hair off my arms and caused my skin to crack and burn. Blood seeped from my skin, looking almost like lava leaking from cracks in the earth's crust.

Though I quickly circulated my Spiritual Power, channeling the water element through my body to heal my wounds, I did not allow myself to sigh in relief. More explosions were detonating all around me, forcing me to swerve in every direction. What's more, by channeling the water element and using it to heal myself, I had been forced to split my attention two ways.

The lightning covering my body had grown weaker as a result of my split attention. In that moment, seven figures appeared above me. I glared up at the winged beasts flying over my head. They were naughty but shadows. However, those shadows were currently surrounded by intense Spiritual Auras that crashed into me like tidal waves rolling over a small village.

One of those great beasts released an avian cry before it swooped down, and the moment it did, the blazing heat surrounding my body grew even more fierce. Sweat broke out on my skin. It quickly dried up under this unfathomable heat. I could feel my skin getting singed once more, and I knew that I could no longer afford to run.

Since this creature was using fire, I decided to use water.

Dissipating the lightning in my body, I took a deep breath, and then circulated my Spiritual Power again. Instead of the sensation of static crawling across my skin, something soft and almost gel like covered my body. One step further. Grimacing as the heat from the creature closing in caused steam to rise from my body, I channeled more Spiritual Power into myself and transformed my entire body into water.

The great beast was finally upon me. What had appeared was an avian of such immense size that even the dragons living in the Misty Mountain Range could not compare to it. Wings of orange and red fire flapped, causing heat waves to distort the air. Colorful designs ran along its body. It was a mixture of red, orange, yellow, and blue. Its plumage was a brilliant white that burned like an illuminating flame. Red and yellow tails trailed behind it as though simulating the ends of a shooting star. Intense crimson eyes glared at me with a hatred that I knew was mutual.

Gnashing my teeth together, I turned around, tucked my fist into my torso, and put all of my Spiritual Power into my next attack.

The beast drew near. I waited until the last second. Then I quickly spun around, dodging the beast by a hair's breadth. It was so close that my body, currently composed entirely of water, was beginning to boil. However, I did not let myself get distracted. Thrusting out my fist, I channeled my Spiritual Power through it and created a massive spike of water that extended from my arm.

Even though the intense heat from the flames surrounding this creature was immense, I was no weakling myself. Water evaporated and created waves of billowing steam. Even so, the spear held firm, refusing to dissipate, and it soon penetrated the beast's chest. Rather than spewing blood, what emerged from the creature was a bright white flame.

As the beast cried in pain, I immediately retracted myself and prepared to attack again.

That was when one of the other beasts swooped down. I saw the shadow and sensed the intent to kill me and quickly moved away. Once I had reached what I deemed a safe distance from the firebird, I released my control over water and transformed into lightning again. Everything around me immediately sped up, allowing me to safely jump several dozen meters in less time than it took to blink.

The bird that had swooped past me was just as massive as the firebird, but instead of being coated in flames, this one had green and white feathers. Its soft feathers gave it a very gentle appearance. However, I knew from the thousands of razor sharp cuts I'd received during my earlier engagement that I couldn't underestimate its deceptively soft appearance. A long tail moved behind it like a tassel. If I looked closely, I could see the atmosphere around it being cut by thousands of wind blades.

A loud crash caused me to cast my gaze toward the ground. Flames spewed from the ground down below as the fire bird crashed into the forest. I felt a sense of grim satisfaction as the creature shrieked in agony. Brilliant white flames, the lifeblood of that great beast, were spewing from its chest like a fountain.

I did not have much time to admire my handiwork, for the green bird released a sharp cry before charging at me. Knowing that my element was weak against this creature that could control the wind, I used Flash Step Version 3: Lightning Step to move away as quickly as I could, but the beast remained stuck on my tail, creating a vacuum that cut through the atmosphere to increase its speed.

Frowning, I once more split my attention. I didn't do much this time. Channeling the light element into my finger, I took careful aim and sent a condensed beam of light at the wind bird. What I got in return was a satisfied shriek as my attack sheared through one of its wings. Greenish white blood spewed from the area where the limb had been severed. Without both wings, it was unable to maintain flight and fell to the ground below.

However, just like before, I was given no time to celebrate my success. Five other birds had just descended. Each one was just as big as the previous two. Each one possessed the ability to control a different element.

A powerful beam of light slammed into me without mercy, burning my back as it sent me sailing toward the ground. My scream was lost to the wind. My body felt like it was being thrown into the Sun. Everything hurt. However, I did my best to shunt aside the pain, increased the flow of lightning through my body, and rolled out from underneath the powerful beam of light.

The beam continued on. It struck the side of a mountain several kilometers below. An explosion so massive that the wind buffeted me despite its distance went up, sending plumes of smoke and rubble into the sky. When the attack died down, the mountain was gone. In its place was a crater so large I was sure it would be visible even if I moved beyond this planet's atmosphere.

"Damn..."

I looked at the result of that attack, and then turned back to glare at the beast who'd caused it. The massive bird flapped its wings as it glared back. This creature looked like it was made of pure light, a combination of white and yellow feathers that appeared both soft and translucent. Yellow eyes glowed with a power that seemed almost divine.

While the bird and I entered a glaring contest, an intense killing intent slammed into me, forcing me to swerve from the spot where I'd been floating.

Six spheres made of water flew past the spot where I'd been. They slammed into the ground far below. Each sphere created a crater that easily spanned ten or fifteen meters across.

I could not admire this attack, for the moment I dodged it, I was forced to move again. This time, seven blades of darkness cut through the air. They were nothing more than black ripples. I swerved over one of them, and then flew down to avoid another. Twisting my body, I managed to avoid two more, but the last one had been aimed at where I would be rather than where I was.

"HA!"

Channeling light into my palm, I slammed it into the blade of darkness, causing the air around me to crackle as arcs of light and dark Spiritual Power raced across the sky. Gritting my teeth as the dark blade pushed me back, I released a furious cry and poured even more Spiritual Power into my palm. The dark blade exploded as I finally tore through it.

The creature that had released this was a bird made from darkness so pure it was like a black hole. Sharp wings covered its body. The only part of it that wasn't black was its eyes, which were pure white and contained no pupil. Alongside it was a bird with blue feathers, one with yellow feathers, another with brown feathers, and the light bird that had attacked me earlier.

I took a heavy breath as sweat poured from my brow. However, I knew I couldn't stop. Without even trying to recover, I released the restraints on my Spiritual Power. My body became energized as though the last several hours had never happened. I could feel the Spiritual Power coursing through me like a tempest. Light mixed with water and lightning inside of me, some of which leaked out because my body simply couldn't withstand the power output.

"Dammit... I had been hoping to save this for your boss," I muttered in a bitter voice.

Whether or not the five elemental birds heard me, they certainly knew that my threat level had suddenly increased. All five of them screeched as they gathered their own Spiritual Power. It congealed around their mouths, forming spheres of condensed energy. Barely a second had passed before they launched their attacks. Five beams of water, lightning, light, darkness, and earth flew toward me.

I did not meet their attacks head on. I wasn't stupid.

Using the power of light, I immediately vanished from the spot where I'd been standing. Their attack went through my after image. I didn't give them a chance to be surprised. Reappearing several meters above the most troublesome of the five, I turned myself into a streak of light and descended before it realized what I was doing. I barely felt any resistance as my body blew a whole clean through the black bird.

Landing on the ground at almost the exact same instant I had moved from point A, I looked up to see that my attack had done what I intended. The black bird with powers over darkness now had a large hole in its chest. What's more, the edges were frayed and refused to heal. While darkness was the antithesis of light, the same was equally true.

"Kari, I still have no real grasp over your affinity, but it is only thanks to you that this was possible," I said to myself as I watched the massive bird slowly break into particles of darkness.

My attack enraged the four remaining birds, who quickly descended toward me. I didn't even need to use Spiritual Perception to feel their intent to kill me. Almost before I could even move, they had each launched their own attack. The four elements of water, light, lightning, and earth swirled around each other to create mixed beam of power so large it could engulf a small city.

But I was no longer there.

As their attacks slammed into the forest floor and caused even more damage to the environment, I was already in front of the water bird. I reached out with my hand and touched its head. The bird's eyes were crossed as it stared at me, but I just smiled at it. I'm sure my smile was quite cold.

The water bird lit up as I shoved as much lightning into it as I could. With a shriek so loud it was nearly inaudible, the bird lit up like fireworks during the Summer Solstice. Smoke soon rose from its body. However, it was too slow. This attack would kill it, but the other birds would get to me first.

Clicking my tongue, I raised my hand, which had turned into a five meter blade of lightning, and then I brought it down. My attack created a seam of light within the bird, a small line that appeared from its beak to its tail feathers. The bird peeled apart at the seam, the two halves almost gently falling away from each other before the elemental beast turned into water that rained upon the ground.

Barely a second had past before something sharp pierced my back. I couldn't even cry out in pain as the air was stolen from my lungs. The ground beneath and the sky above blurred past me in dull streaks. Gritting my teeth, I turned my head and found the enraged eyes of the light bird glaring at me. It had pierced my back with its beak.

"Don't think..." I struggled to raise my hand. "Don't think..." Light, lightning, and water swirled around my arm as I channeled all three elements. "Don't think this will be enough to do me in!!!"

With a roar of defiance, I crashed my fist into the light bird's beak. A loud cracking sound echoed from the beak as an incision line appeared. One incision became two, then two became three, four, eight, sixteen. It quickly multiplied before cracking underneath the power of my fist.

The bird immediately stopped flying as it thrashed and screeched in pain. However, the forward momentum it had generated was enough that I was not able to stop from flying until I generated enough force with my own Spiritual Power to stop myself.

Reaching behind my back after I had stopped moving, I pulled out what remained of the beak from my back and tossed it away. Warm blood spilled down my back. I ignored it as I eyed the three remaining elemental birds. The lightning bird, the wind bird, and the now injured light bird.

"Ha... ha... ha..."

My shoulders heaved as I glared at the birds. However, I didn't think my glare was very effective just then. The Spiritual Power flowing through me was fluctuating. The aura covering my body flickered in and out. I didn't reveal my thoughts, but I was swearing up a storm internally as my Spiritual Power started running dry.

This technique I was using wasn't complete yet. If I'd had time to finish it, then maybe I could have already ended this battle, but luck had not been on my side.

It looked like the birds were just about to renew their attack, and I myself was prepared to re-initiate hostilities, but all of us suddenly froze in place as an intense Spiritual Pressure filled the air. My breathing quickly grew heavier as sweat formed on my brow. It was a cold sweat. I tried to take in a breath, but the pressure was causing my lungs to struggle with the simple act of taking in oxygen. It felt like something was crushing them.

A figure had suddenly appeared in front of me. He was a luminous being more beautiful than the Sun, a creature of such incomparable beauty that even in my hatred, I could not deny there was not a single flaw to be found. Pure white robes covered his body. Long and silver hair flowed freely like a waterfall down his head all the way to his bare feet. His long, pointed ears were the clearest signs that he wasn't human.

He did not have a very muscular body. Indeed, I would have said his body was quite feminine. He was slender and willowy. However, I didn't let that fool me, and even if he had been a woman, I wouldn't have underestimated him like some people would have done.

Despite his beauty, there was something odd about this man. Every part of him seemed bright and divine—every part except his blood red eyes. They were a dark crimson that seemed tainted somehow. Furthermore, that dark aura surrounding him seemed to present a direct contradiction to his vibrant, almost divine appearance.

The man took a deep breath as he looked at the three birds. He surveyed them with a slight frown, and then quickly glanced at where I had killed the others. I wanted to move, to attack this man with everything I had, but some invisible force kept me in place.

Finally, he looked at me.

"**To think a half-blood like you was able to defeat four of my seven slaves,**" he murmured. "**You know I had enslaved these monsters specifically to kill you? Your powers are indeed great. Given enough time, you might even pose a threat to me. It seems trying to send enslaved Demon Beasts after you was a mistake. I should have just come myself.**"

"Great Overlord of the Seventh Plain…" My fists shook with barely restrained hatred as I stared at the being before me. "You took everything from me. My wife. My child. Everything. I have waited for this day, waited for the day I would finally face you again, for the day I would finally kill you."

The being before me, the one I called the Great Overlord of the Seventh Plain, chuckled as though I had said something amusing. It was a grating laugh, not at all like something I'd expect from such a feminine figure. His laugh caused the hair on my neck to prickle.

"**Had your wife not shielded you from me, she would not have died. She only has herself to blame.**" He paused, his head tilting as he stared impassively into my rage filled eyes. "**As for your daughter… I could not allow a human who possesses such divine blood to live. Had I not killed her, she would have become a threat.**"

"A threat?" I whispered. "We were just living peacefully when you attacked us unprovoked and without warning. We were no threat to you. You laid waste to our home, destroyed our civilization, and killed my family without even a hint of mercy or provocation."

The Great Overlord of the Seventh Plain snorted. "**You may not understand it now, but you are indeed a grave threat to me—**

no, you are perhaps the greatest threat to ever exist. What I did was necessary."

I didn't think the blood flowing through my veins could have run any colder than it already was, but I was wrong. It was like my blood had frozen over. Only a chilling coldness that seeped through my entire being remained.

"Necessary, you say?"

"Yes. Necessary."

"Necessary... for what?"

"To keep you from being able to interfere with my plans." The Great Overlord of the Seventh Plain spread his arms wide and chuckled again. **"Just look at what you have done. A half-blood who hasn't even learned to control even a tenth of his abilities has defeated four of my seven slaves, Divine-rank Demon Beasts capable of annihilating entire cities with a single attack, and you would have defeated all of them had I not intervened. I'd say this level of destruction warrants intervention."**

I had no idea what this monster was talking about, but I was done listening. He had attacked my family for a reason as dumb as protecting himself? From what? It was true that I had been the one who awakened him, but I had never harmed him nor had any intention to. Had he never appeared attacked my city, never attempted to kill me, never murdered my daughter, we would have left him alone.

My hatred surged, allowing me to overcome the intense pressure that had been pushing down on me. I compressed the last remaining Spiritual Power in my body. The aura that had been covering me vanished. To the average eye, it would have looked like my power had disappeared.

The Great Overlord of the Seventh Plain narrowed his eyes.

Then I vanished.

It happened in a flash. I appeared directly behind my foe, thrusting out my fist in a punch that caused the air to burst. However, without even looking behind him, the Great Overlord of the Seventh Plain placed his hand in the direction of my punch, catching it. A shockwave erupted from the contact.

I was already moving.

Appearing on his left in a manner that was almost like teleportation, I launched a powerful kick. This was also blocked. I was undeterred. I appeared again and again, moving all around him at speeds so fast I left multiple afterimages in my wake. One. Two. Four. Sixteen. Yet no matter how many punches and kicks I threw, no matter how fast I pushed myself, this monster blocked each and every one of them as though it was easier than breathing.

Meanwhile, I was running on empty.

With the last of my strength, I released a vicious scream and channeled all my energy into my fist. A bright glow erupted from it. The air around it distorted. Ripples spread through the sky as though the fabrics of reality itself were being torn apart.

The Great Overlord's eyes finally widened. With something resembling panic, he threw out his own punch, which glowed in the same manner as mine but with a dark energy that seemed vile. The air exploded between us as one fought to overpower the other. I gritted my teeth and pushed as hard as I could, wrecking my body. Blood exploded from my arms as my capillaries burst, my muscles tore apart like they were made of soggy parchment, and I could feel my very life being drained.

I didn't care. It didn't matter if I died so long as I killed this man.

Perhaps it was because I was so focused that I didn't see the attack coming at me until it was too late. However, when a fist appeared out of nowhere, all I could do was swear. The attack hit me. Pain overrode my ability to see, causing a white film to cover my eyes.

I think I must have passed out. When I came to, I was lying on my back, in the middle of a massive crater so large I couldn't even judge its size. The Great Overlord of the Seventh Plain was above me, a sword made of pure darkness grasped firmly within his right hand. He raised the sword and brought it down.

In a last ditch effort, I unleashed all of the Spiritual Power I had left, channeled it into my right hand, and met the blade with a punch. Our attacks struck each other. Light bent. Air warped. Lightning crackled. The area around our mutual attacks became distorted as strange cracks appeared in the atmosphere like the gaping maw to a bottomless abyss.

An explosion suddenly rent the air as the world around me was torn apart. The last thing I saw before darkness engulfed me was the Great Overlord's surprised crimson eyes.

To read more of WIEDERGEBURT: Legend of the Reincarnated Warrior, go to my Patreon and sign up at https://www.patreon.com/ BrandonVarnell

Hey, did you know?
Brandon Varnell has started a Patreon
You can get all kinds of awesome exclusives
Like:

1. The chance to read his stories before anyone else!
2. Free ebooks!
3. exclusive SFW and NSFW artwork!
4. Signed paperback copies!
5. His undying love!
Er... maybe we don't want that last one, but the rest is pretty cool, right?

To get this awesome exlusive conent go to:
https://www.patreon.com/BrandonVarnell
and sigh up today!

Have you been turned on to Brandon's Light Novels Yet?

Wait. That sounded kind of wrong.

Try out Brandon's first original English light novel series!

All Alex wanted was to become a hero...

Instead, he picked up a harem of beautiful women!

Follow Caspian's Journey to become a Sorceress's Knight in Arcadia's Ignoble Knight vol. 1-4!

He was their best Executioner

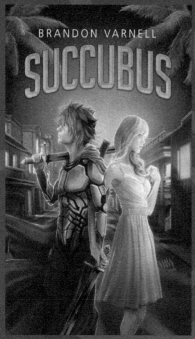

BRANDON VARNELL

SUCCUBUS

BRANDON VARNELL

ESCAPE

BRANDON VARNELL

ENCLAVE

BRANDON VARNELL

GRIGORI

Story by
Brandon Varnell

Illustrations by
Aisoretto

Summoned to another world...
...Betrayed by the kingdom he saved
Now he seeks a way to return home...
...By going on a Journeying with
The daughter of the dark lord he slaid...

Get Journey of a Betrayed Hero, volume 1 now!

Want to learn when a new book comes out!
Follow me on Social Media!

 @AmericanKitsune

 +BrandonVarnell

 @BrandonBVarnell

 http://bvarnell1101.tumblr.com/

 Brandon Varnell

 BrandonbVarnell

 https://www.patreon.com/
BrandonVarnell

CPSIA information can be obtained
at www.ICGtesting.com
Printed in the USA
BVHW072008190819
556223BV00014B/1116/P